# Competitive
# Structure
# of the
# International
# Banking
# Industry

# Competitive Structure of the International Banking Industry

Seung H. Kim
Stephen W. Miller
St. Louis University

**LexingtonBooks**
D.C. Heath and Company
Lexington, Massachusetts
Toronto

*Barnard*

*HG*
*2491*
*.K55*
*1983*

**Library of Congress Cataloging in Publication Data**

Kim, Seung Hee.
Competitive structure of the international banking industry.

Bibliography: p.
Includes index.
1. Banks and banking, Foreign—United States. 2. Banks and banking,
Foreign—Law and legislation—United States. 3. Banks and banking,
American. 4. Banks and banking, International. I. Miller, Stephen W.
II. Title.
HG2491.K55    1983        332.1'5'0973        81-47970
ISBN 0-669-05189-6

Published simultaneously in Canada

Second printing, April 1984

Printed in the United States of America on acid-free paper

International Standard Book Number: 0-669-05189-6

Library of Congress Catalog Card Number: 81-47970

*To our spouses, Kyung and Jane,*
*and our children, Jason, Lesley,*
*Christopher, and Andrew,*
*who bore the brunt*

# Contents

# Figure and Tables

# Foreword

As U.S. banks expanded their banking operations overseas in the 1960s to serve U.S. multinational firms, so did foreign banks follow a similar pattern in the 1970s by increasing their presence in the United States to accommodate their own national firms. This expansion of foreign-bank offices in the United States led to some concern on the part of both the U.S. banking community and the Congress. The U.S. banking community was disquieted by what it felt to be the absence of a level playing field for all banking competitors in the U.S. market. Lack of uniform federal legislation and inconsistent state standards dealing with foreign-bank supervision and regulation exacerbated the issue. Furthermore, U.S. banks considered the market environment created by foreign banks in their own backyard to be distinctly different from that in previous years and more difficult to manage profitably. Consequently, increasing pressures from the U.S. banking community and federal regulatory bodies led to congressional passage of the International Banking Act in 1978, basically establishing equal regulatory treatment for foreign and U.S. banks alike. Although this is a step in the right direction, it is expected that consideration and review of U.S. banking regulatory standards will continue as a result of the increasingly competitive environment in which U.S. banks are placed.

Although nationalistic and protectionist sentiments are on the rise in some sectors of the U.S. economy, as well as in other parts of the world, worldwide international banking should continue to grow as a financial intermediary, bringing together savers and providers of funds and borrowers and investors. This growth will improve the competitive environment in which international banking operations are provided in both the United States and overseas and will contribute to the efficient and effective flow of funds on a global scale. The United States will continue to serve a major role in this regard and lead in the financing of international trade.

This book should aid in the understanding of the international banking function in world trade and, in particular, the role that international banking competitors serve within the U.S. market. It provides a comprehensive and timely analysis of global banking and investment and the legal, financial, and market environments of the United States in which U.S. and foreign banks operate.

The examination of the impact of the U.S. legal environment on international banking competitors is thorough. Tracing U.S. banking legislation and regulatory standards from the Federal Reserve Act of 1913 to the present, it encompasses both direct and indirect legislation affecting banking operations in the U.S. market. Moreover, new legislation now being considered by Congress and future regulatory trends are analyzed. This book is unique in the manner in which it treats international asset and liability management. It develops a theoretical framework for asset and liability management on a global scale and presents recent empirical data as support. In addition, it examines the corresponding views of international banks, especially as affected by their perceptions of the volatility of international financial markets. Finally, the authors present an analysis of the competitive structure of the U.S. market environment in which U.S. and foreign banks offer their international financial products. It analyzes the differing marketing strategies currently employed by international banking rivals in the United States and reviews the future directions they may take in increasingly competitive environments.

This book is a fine addition to the field of international banking. Its comprehensive treatment of international banking operations with specific reference to the U.S. market is especially appealing. The authors' overall approach to this subject is singularly interesting through their attempt to operationalize the theoretical aspects of the macroenvironment through recommended micromanagerial corporate policy. Kim and Miller show both intellectual objectivity and candor, making this treatise recommended reading for practitioners, as well as students of international banking.

*Alfred F. Miossi*
Executive Vice-President
Continental Illinois National
Bank and Trust Co.

# Acknowledgments

During the course of our research and writing efforts over the past two years, there were many people who gave us assistance without which the completion of this book would not have been possible.

In particular, we would like to express our sincere appreciation to William "Bucky" Bush, president of Boatmen's National Bank of St. Louis. He gave us encouragement and facilitated our research efforts. Aside from spending innumerable hours with us, he graciously provided us with invaluable letters of introduction to the Bankers' Association for Foreign Trade and to numerous international banking executives across the United States. With his assistance, we were able to conduct personal interviews with both international bankers and corporate financial officers, a list of whom can be found in appendix A. We are also deeply grateful to these executive officers who gave us many hours of their time and whose comments became an important and integral part of our research.

We would like to thank Mary Condeelis, executive director, and the board members of the Bankers' Association for Foreign Trade who supported our efforts by encouraging their members to participate in our research. We are indebted to Robert Gemmill, associate director of the International Finance Division of the Federal Reserve Board, James Houpt of the Federal Reserve Board, Jack Herbert of the Federal Reserve Bank of Chicago, Diane Page of the U.S. Comptroller of the Currency, and Patrick Paradiso of Morgan Guaranty Trust Company, all of whom provided international banking data not readily available. We are grateful to several state banking commissioners who furnished us with generally difficult-to-obtain state banking regulations and opinions. We were able to gather this information with the help of Kenneth W. Littlefield, commissioner of finance of the state of Missouri, William C. Harris, commissioner of banks for the state of Illinois, Edward P. Eustace, deputy superintendent of banks for the state of New York, John R. Paulus, deputy director of the California State Banking Department, and Wilbert O. Bascom, chief of the Bureau of International Banking, the state of Florida.

Gratitude is also owed Rev. William Stauder, graduate dean and research administrator, St. Louis University, who funded a Beaumont Faculty Development Grant to underwrite part of our project. We are deeply appreciative of Dr. John P. Keithley, dean of our School of Business and Administration, who understood the problems of writing a book and gave us his moral support, facilitating our efforts whenever possible.

Our appreciation goes to our graduate assistants, Abdalla Eldarrat, Fritz Schwarz, and Susan Seymour, who assisted us many times. Special thanks are owed Cindy Maletich, who typed several versions of the manuscript and whose skills and patience were invaluable.

Finally, we would like to express our love and appreciation to our families, without whose continual support, sacrifice, and understanding the completion of this book would not have been possible.

Although all of these people provided us with a great deal of valued assistance, any errors or omissions that may be found within the book are our own.

# Introduction

The 1970s saw a sharp escalation in foreign-bank presence in the United States. Federal and state regulatory agencies expressed heightened levels of concern with regard to increases in the size and number of foreign banks locating within the United States. Joined with allegations by U.S. banking competitors that foreign banks enjoyed competitive advantages within the U.S. legal environment, mounting pressure finally resulted in congressional passage in 1978 of the International Banking Act. This attempt to place both foreign and U.S. banks on an equal regulatory footing was both praised and criticized. Yet as the need for international banking services escalated in the United States and overseas, U.S. banks found that they were competing not only with foreign banks but among themselves for increasing shares of this lucrative business. Domestic banks discovered that they could expand their financial offerings and improve their profitability by satisfying the ever-increasing international trading needs of both U.S. and foreign customers. Still though, an increased foreign-bank presence in the United States placed substantial competitive pressures on U.S. banks seeking these opportunities.

The result today is a strongly competitive situation in which both U.S. and foreign banks increasingly vie with each other for crucial market position in often-overlapping customer segments. Pressure for well-defined corporate strategic plans is immense, as profitability for these banking competitors is severely conditioned by accurate and efficient asset and liability management and marketing strategy.

The time is ripe for a thorough examination of both the intricacies of this industry and the future trends and consequences inherent in the international financial offerings of major U.S. and foreign banking competitors in the U.S. market. Prior studies of international banking competition have concentrated on overseas or on only segments of the industry within the U.S. market. Often dated, these efforts have taken an aggregate macroeconomic approach without due regard to the microbusiness decision-making variables of successful international banking strategy. Therefore, this book is designed to provide both a timely analysis and a comprehensive examination of the competitive structure of the international banking industry in the United States.

This book is aimed at a comparison of the financial and market characteristics of major U.S. and foreign-banking competitors offering international banking services in the United States. A comprehensive examination is made with regard to the legal, financial, and market environments of U.S. money-center and regional banks, Edge Act corporations, and foreign-bank branches, agencies, and subsidiaries. To achieve

1

this objective, the book encompasses both macroenvironmental factors and micromanagerial decision-making variables.

An understanding of the interrelationship of these two sets of variables is crucial for the operational aspects of international banking. Bank management as well as students of international business can gain from astute observance of these interactions. Microlevel decision making of individual banking competitors in the areas of asset and liability management and marketing strategy are heavily affected by the macroenvironmental factors of legal, financial, economic, and market considerations. Thus, changing interest rates in international financial markets affect bank-management strategy in financing methods and loan-portfolio composition. Moreover, competitive market conditions significantly affect the types of international financial products offered by different banking competitors. Figure I-1 summarizes this interrelationship and sets the stage for the organizational content of the subsequent chapters.

Chapter 1 describes the historical growth pattern of U.S. international banking in conjunction with the overall development of international business. It analyzes the structure and direction of U.S. trade, U.S. foreign direction investment, foreign direct investment in the United States, and the Eurodollar market.

Chapter 2 deals with the expansion of the foreign-bank presence in the United States and discusses the legal and financial advantages of various organizational forms of foreign banks. It also assesses the geographical distribution of foreign banks in the United States.

Chapter 3 reviews and analyzes the historical development of federal and state regulatory standards dealing with banking operations in the United States. Beginning with the Federal Reserve Act of 1913, eleven different pieces of federal legislation and regulation are covered, including the 1978 International Banking Act and the Federal Reserve Board authority for international banking facilities. Some unique aspects of state banking legislation are reviewed with regard to New York, California, Illinois, Florida, and Missouri.

Chapter 4 explains the basic functions of international banking organizations and presents a conceptual framework for effective asset and liability management. Chapter 5 then compares and contrasts the asset and liability structure of large U.S. banks and foreign banks. In particular, it highlights the empirical results of asset-liability gap analysis and capital-adequacy tests based on recent data.

Chapter 6 analyzes the competitive market structure in the United States in which banking competitors offer their international financial products and fee services. The market interpretation is based on a statistical test of survey-questionnaire results from international banking competitors throughout the United States, personal interviews with selected international

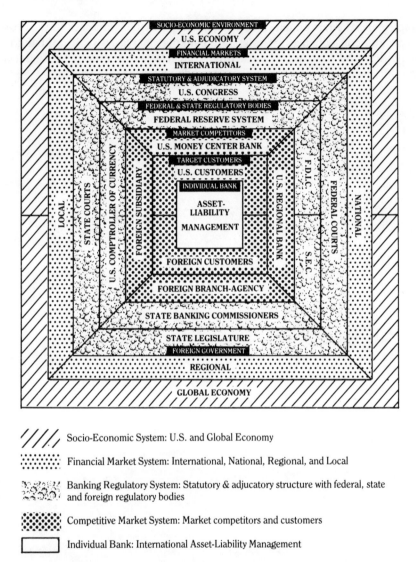

**Figure I-1.** The Environment for U.S. and Foreign Competitors Offering International Banking Services

banking officers and corporate financial officers of several major multinational corporations, and a review of the current literature in international banking and marketing.

Finally, future trends in international banking are discussed in chapter 7. The changing nature of the U.S. legal environment, market structure, and financial environment is analyzed with particular reference to the prospects and consequences of interstate banking, increased U.S. nonbanking activities, and innovative marketing strategies and international financial product development. Appendixes provide reference information.

# 1

# Historical Background

As the United States became the political and economic leader of the world after World War II, the U.S. dollar became the international currency. New York City, where most international banking took place, became the financial center of the world. As a result, U.S. bankers became involved in financing the Marshall Plan, other foreign aid, and the import-export transactions of international business customers.

At the close of World War II, the United States was the only major country whose industrial facilities had not been destroyed by conflict. Production facilities in many countries—England, Germany, France, and Japan—were nearly devastated. The United States became the sole supplier of capital equipment, food, and many consumer goods during the reconstruction period. U.S. multinational firms invested heavily and participated eagerly in Europe's reconstruction efforts in the 1950s. In the 1960s they also increased their investment in less-developed countries. During this period, the United States experienced balance-of-trade surpluses and served as the world's banker by borrowing short and lending long. Foreign countries kept their international reserves in short-term U.S. assets while the United States invested abroad in long-term fixed assets and bank loans.

Until the early 1960s, the United States was able to finance foreign direct investment with its trade surplus funds. As Western Europe and Japan recovered from the war, however, they began to export abroad and to compete with the United States in world markets. Consequently U.S. net foreign direct investment grew larger than its trade surplus. Then in 1971, for the first time in recent U.S. history, the United States incurred a trade deficit. European countries, Germany in particular, and Japan experienced trade surpluses. As fluctuating exchange rates took hold in 1973, their currencies became stronger vis-à-vis the U.S. dollar. Consequently foreign direct investment moved into the United States in the 1970s. Since the United States was still considered a politically safe nation, a majority of Eurodollars were kept in U.S. banking institutions in Europe.

Historically international banking has followed its international business customers. Initially in the 1960s, U.S. money-center banks in New York City, Chicago, and San Francisco dominated international banking activities in the United States in order to finance the international trade and investment of their large customers. As the volume of international trade and investment increased over the years and as the number of international business firms increased from just the Fortune 500 companies to medium-sized firms throughout the country, both U.S. regional banks and Edge corporations began to penetrate in other areas in the United States.

### Growth of International Business

The volume of U.S. trade has increased significantly since 1950 in both absolute and relative values (table 1-1). U.S. exports increased from the relatively small amount of $10.2 billion in 1950 to $221.8 billion in 1980. In relative terms, U.S. exports as a percentage of Gross National Product (GNP) increased from 3.6 percent in 1950 to 8.5 percent in 1980. U.S. imports also jumped from a negligible amount of $9.1 billion and 3.2 percent of GNP in 1950 to $249.1 billion and 9.5 percent of GNP in 1980.

The volume of trade, both exports and imports combined, was only 6.7 percent of GNP in 1950 but increased to 18 percent in 1980. As table 1-1 shows, the United States exhibited trade surpluses throughout the 1950-1970 period. In 1971, however, it experienced a trade deficit, and the magnitude of the deficit accelerated throughout the 1970s. In other words, foreign countries, particularly Western and less-developed nations, have been exporting more of their goods to the United States in recent years.

Several factors contributed to the U.S. trade deficits. Major industrial countries such as West Germany and Japan have become more competitive,

**Table 1-1**
**U.S. Exports, Imports, and Trade Balance**

| Year | Gross National Product (GNP) | Exports | Imports | Balance | Ratio of Exports to GNP | Ratio of Imports to GNP |
|------|------|------|------|------|------|------|
| 1950 | 286.2 | 10.2 | − 9.1 | 1.1 | 3.56 | 3.18 |
| 1955 | 399.3 | 14.4 | − 11.5 | 2.9 | 3.61 | 2.88 |
| 1960 | 506.0 | 19.7 | − 14.8 | 4.9 | 3.89 | 2.93 |
| 1965 | 688.1 | 26.5 | − 21.5 | 5.0 | 3.85 | 3.13 |
| 1970 | 982.4 | 42.5 | − 39.9 | 2.6 | 4.33 | 4.06 |
| 1971 | 1,063.4 | 43.3 | − 45.6 | − 2.3 | 4.07 | 4.29 |
| 1972 | 1,171.1 | 49.4 | − 55.8 | − 6.4 | 4.22 | 4.76 |
| 1973 | 1,306.6 | 71.4 | − 70.5 | 0.9 | 5.47 | 5.40 |
| 1974 | 1,412.9 | 98.3 | − 103.7 | − 5.4 | 6.96 | 7.34 |
| 1975 | 1,528.8 | 107.1 | − 98.0 | 9.1 | 7.01 | 6.41 |
| 1976 | 1,700.1 | 114.7 | − 124.0 | − 9.3 | 6.75 | 7.29 |
| 1977 | 1,887.2 | 120.8 | − 151.7 | − 30.9 | 6.40 | 8.04 |
| 1978 | 2,156.1 | 142.1 | − 175.8 | − 33.7 | 6.59 | 8.15 |
| 1979 | 2,419.9 | 182.1 | − 211.5 | − 29.4 | 7.53 | 8.74 |
| 1980 | 2,626.1 | 221.8 | − 249.1 | − 27.3 | 8.45 | 9.49 |

Source: Various issues of *Survey of Current Business,* U.S. Department of Commerce, and *Federal Reserve Bulletin,* Federal Reserve Board, Washington, D.C.

and their labor productivity has been increasing at a greater rate than that of the United States. Although the high capital endowment of the United States played an important role in the 1960s, a decrease in its technological lead has been considered one of the most-important factors behind the U.S. trade deficits. For instance, new capital investment, and research and development have been slipping in the major U.S. industries—steel, automobiles, textile, and electronics. Furthermore, in recent years, U.S. imports from developing countries have increased substantially. Once it was thought that wages in developing countries were cheaper. However, labor-cost or productivity comparisons, rather than money wage comparisons alone, are the meaningful indicators of competitiveness in the world market. Output per man-hour measures the combined productivity of labor and capital, as well as managerial factors. In other words, production costs can be high for reasons other than just wages. Higher costs for capital and management can drive up overall costs. According to recent statistical analysis, labor-productivity differentials between the United States and developing countries are much greater than wage differentials. Theoretically, high labor productivity is reflected in lower prices and better-quality goods and services. That is why developing countries have been successful in selling their products, especially semimanufactured goods such as textiles and electric appliances.

The U.S. trade situation has worsened since 1973 when the Organization of Petroleum Exporting Countries (OPEC) imposed oil embargoes and increased oil prices. This is a good example of how international cartels can unilaterally impose higher prices on their trading partners. Yet the United States, like many other countries, continues to be vulnerable and still depends on a large percentage of its oil requirements from Arab countries.

It has been argued that foreign countries offer greater subsidies to their exporters and impose more-restrictive import policies than does the United States. However, to the extent that most U.S. trading partners reduced tariffs, allowing U.S. products in their markets under the guidelines of the General Agreement for Tariffs and Trade (GATT) and to the extent that the United States is able to acquire new technologies in the future, U.S. chances of regaining competitiveness in world markets are enhanced.

**Direction of U.S. Trade**

Europe used to be the major trading partner of the United States (table 1-2). Asia, however, has replaced Europe in recent years. The U.S. exported $14.8 billion to and imported $11.4 billion from Europe in 1970, while U.S. exports to Asia totaled $10 billion and imports $9.6 billion in the same year. But in 1980, the position changed, with the total volume of trade with Europe

**Table 1-2**
**Geographical Distribution of U.S. Exports and Imports**
*(billions of dollars)*

| | 1965 | | | | 1970 | | | | 1975 | | | | 1980 | | | |
|---|---|---|---|---|---|---|---|---|---|---|---|---|---|---|---|---|
| | Exports | | Imports | | Exports | | Imports | | Exports | | Imports | | Exports | | Imports | |
| | ($) | (%) | ($) | (%) | ($) | (%) | ($) | (%) | ($) | (%) | ($) | (%) | ($) | (%) | ($) | (%) |
| **Selected regions** | | | | | | | | | | | | | | | | |
| Africa | 1.2 | 6.3 | .9 | 5.7 | 1.6 | 4.8 | 1.1 | 4.0 | 5.0 | 5.8 | 8.3 | 11.3 | 9.0 | 4.9 | 32.3 | 15.7 |
| Asia | 4.5 | 23.4 | 4.5 | 28.5 | 10.0 | 30.1 | 9.6 | 35.2 | 28.2 | 32.4 | 27.3 | 37.0 | 60.2 | 32.6 | 79.1 | 38.5 |
| Europe | 8.9 | 46.3 | 6.3 | 39.9 | 14.8 | 44.6 | 11.4 | 41.8 | 29.9 | 34.4 | 20.9 | 28.4 | 67.5 | 36.6 | 46.8 | 22.8 |
| Latin America | 3.8 | 19.8 | 3.7 | 23.4 | 5.7 | 17.2 | 4.8 | 17.6 | 15.6 | 17.9 | 11.8 | 16.0 | 36.0 | 19.5 | 29.9 | 14.6 |
| Middle East | .8 | 4.2 | .4 | 2.5 | 1.1 | 3.3 | .4 | 1.4 | 8.3 | 9.5 | 5.4 | 7.3 | 11.9 | 6.4 | 17.3 | 8.4 |
| Total | 19.2 | 100.0 | 15.8 | 100.0 | 33.2 | 100.0 | 27.3 | 100.0 | 87.0 | 100.0 | 73.7 | 100.0 | 184.6 | 100.0 | 205.4 | 100.0 |
| **Selected countries** | | | | | | | | | | | | | | | | |
| Japan | 2.1 | 18.0 | 2.4 | 22.9 | 4.7 | 22.9 | 5.9 | 25.4 | 9.6 | 21.6 | 11.3 | 25.2 | 20.8 | 23.8 | 30.9 | 31.3 |
| France | .9 | 7.7 | .6 | 5.7 | 1.5 | 7.3 | .9 | 3.9 | 3.0 | 6.8 | 2.2 | 4.9 | 7.5 | 8.6 | 5.3 | 5.4 |
| West Germany | 1.5 | 12.8 | 1.3 | 12.4 | 2.7 | 13.2 | 3.1 | 13.4 | 5.2 | 11.7 | 5.4 | 12.1 | 11.0 | 12.6 | 11.8 | 11.9 |
| United Kingdom | 1.6 | 13.7 | 1.4 | 13.3 | 2.5 | 12.2 | 2.2 | 9.5 | 4.9 | 11.0 | 3.7 | 8.3 | 12.7 | 14.5 | 9.8 | 9.9 |
| Canada | 5.6 | 47.8 | 4.8 | 45.7 | 9.1 | 44.4 | 11.1 | 47.8 | 21.7 | 48.9 | 22.2 | 49.5 | 35.4 | 40.5 | 41.0 | 41.5 |
| Total | 11.7 | 100.0 | 10.5 | 100.0 | 20.5 | 100.0 | 23.2 | 100.0 | 44.4 | 100.0 | 44.8 | 100.0 | 87.4 | 100.0 | 98.8 | 100.0 |

Source: U.S. Department of Commerce, *Highlights of U.S. Exports and Imports*, December 1979 and 1980.

amounting to $114.3 billion and with Asia to $139.3 billion. Moreover, it is clear that the third largest trading partner for the U.S. remains Latin America.

All of the major trading partners of the United States remain advanced countries—Japan, France, West Germany, England, and Canada—mainly because these countries enjoy a relatively high level of income and produce similar complementary and substitute goods demanded in both markets. Furthermore, these advanced countries possess the types of financial institutions necessary to accommodate the trade-finance needs of their customers. In recent years, however, U.S. trade with the developing countries of Asia and the Middle East has increased as these areas continue to raise their level of income and reduce restrictive tariffs and trade barriers.

**U.S. Direct Investment Abroad**

U.S. direct investment abroad in 1950 was evenly distributed between developed and developing countries, amounting to $5.7 billion each (table 1-3). Then U.S. investment in developed countries, particularly Canadian and European, accelerated and reached $157.1 billion in 1980, accounting for 74 percent of total U.S. foreign direct investment. On the other hand, U.S. direct investment in developing countries amounted to only $52.7 billion in 1980. Of the total, Latin America shared 73 percent. As expected, such U.S. direct investment has been predominantly in manufacturing, followed by trade, petroleum, and banking, and insurance.

The motives for the U.S. investment movement into advanced countries were both macro-oriented and micro-oriented. First, because developed countries were politically and socially stable, the business risk was low. Second, advanced countries had higher per-capita income and possessed the ability to purchase manufactured goods produced by U.S. investors. Third, the market size of the advanced countries was vast and attractive to U.S. investors, especially since tariffs for manufactured goods were lowered in European countries after the establishment of the Common Market. Fourth, it was relatively easy for U.S. investors to invest in advanced countries because they were culturally similar and possessed adequate social and financial infrastructures.

U.S. direct investment has continued to increase in developing countries in the last two decades, primarily because the level of income has improved substantially in countries such as South Korea, Taiwan, Brazil, Mexico, and those of the Middle East. Furthermore, according to the product-life-cycle theory, after new-product innovation in the United States and production in advanced countries during the product-maturity stage, multinational firms shift their investment to low-cost locations in developing countries.[1] From

**Table 1-3**
**U.S. Foreign Direct Investment, by Geographical Areas and Industry**
*(billions of dollars)*

| Areas | 1950 ($) | 1950 (%) | 1953 ($) | 1953 (%) | 1960 ($) | 1960 (%) | 1965 ($) | 1965 (%) | 1970 ($) | 1970 (%) | 1975 ($) | 1975 (%) | 1980 ($) | 1980 (%) |
|---|---|---|---|---|---|---|---|---|---|---|---|---|---|---|
| Developed countries | 5.7 | 48 | 10.8 | 55 | 19.3 | 61 | 32.2 | 65 | 51.8 | 69 | 90.6 | 73 | 157.1 | 74 |
| Petroleum | 1.0 | 9 | 2.5 | 13 | 4.9 | 15 | 7.7 | 16 | 11.2 | 15 | 20.1 | 16 | 34.2 | 16 |
| Manufacturing | 3.0 | 25 | 5.2 | 27 | 9.3 | 29 | 15.9 | 32 | 25.6 | 34 | 45.4 | 37 | 71.4 | 33 |
| Other | 1.7 | 14 | 3.1 | 15 | 5.1 | 17 | 8.7 | 17 | 15.0 | 20 | 25.1 | 20 | 51.5 | 26 |
| Canada | 3.5 | 30 | 6.8 | 35 | 12.2 | 38 | 15.4 | 31 | 21.0 | 28 | 31.0 | 25 | 44.6 | 21 |
| Petroleum | .4 | 3 | 1.4 | 7 | 2.7 | 9 | 3.4 | 9 | 4.3 | 6 | 6.2 | 5 | 10.6 | 5 |
| Manufacturing | 1.9 | 16 | 3.1 | 16 | 4.8 | 15 | 6.9 | 14 | 9.0 | 12 | 14.7 | 12 | 18.8 | 8 |
| Other | 1.3 | 11 | 2.3 | 11 | 3.7 | 12 | 5.1 | 10 | 7.7 | 10 | 10.1 | 8 | 15.3 | 7 |
| Europe | 1.7 | 14 | 3.1 | 16 | 6.7 | 21 | 14.0 | 28 | 25.3 | 34 | 49.2 | 40 | 95.7 | 45 |
| Petroleum | .4 | 3 | .8 | 4 | 1.8 | 6 | 3.4 | 7 | 5.5 | 7 | 11.1 | 9 | 19.9 | 9 |
| Manufacturing | .9 | 8 | 1.7 | 9 | 3.8 | 12 | 7.6 | 15 | 13.8 | 18 | 26.0 | 21 | 45.4 | 21 |
| Other | .4 | 3 | .6 | 3 | 1.1 | 3 | 3.0 | 6 | 6.0 | 8 | 12.1 | 10 | 30.3 | 14 |
| Other areas | .4 | 3 | .9 | 5 | 1.5 | 5 | 3.0 | 6 | 5.6 | 7 | 10.4 | 8 | 16.8 | 8 |
| Developing countries | 5.7 | 48 | 8.0 | 41 | 11.1 | 35 | 15.2 | 31 | 19.2 | 25 | 26.3 | 21 | 52.7 | 25 |
| Petroleum | 2.2 | 19 | 2.9 | 15 | 5.0 | 16 | 6.5 | 13 | 6.6 | 9 | 2.5 | 2 | 10.3 | 5 |
| Manufacturing | .8 | 7 | 1.5 | 8 | 1.7 | 5 | 3.4 | 7 | 5.5 | 7 | 10.5 | 9 | 17.7 | 8 |
| Other | 2.7 | 22 | 3.6 | 18 | 4.4 | 14 | 5.3 | 11 | 7.1 | 9 | 13.3 | 10 | 24.7 | 11 |
| Latin America | 4.6 | 39 | 6.3 | 32 | 8.3 | 26 | 10.9 | 22 | 12.9 | 17 | 22.0 | 18 | 38.3 | 18 |
| Petroleum | 1.3 | 11 | 1.6 | 8 | 3.1 | 10 | 3.6 | 7 | 2.7 | 4 | 3.3 | 3 | 4.3 | 2 |
| Manufacturing | .8 | 7 | 1.4 | 7 | 1.5 | 5 | 2.9 | 6 | 4.5 | 6 | 8.6 | 7 | 14.5 | 7 |
| Other | 2.5 | 21 | 3.3 | 17 | 3.7 | 11 | 4.4 | 8 | 5.7 | 7 | 10.1 | 8 | 19.5 | 9 |
| Other areas | 1.2 | 10 | 1.8 | 9 | 2.8 | 9 | 4.3 | 9 | 6.2 | 8 | 4.1 | 3 | 14.4 | 7 |
| Unallocated | .4 | 3 | .7 | 4 | 1.4 | 4 | 2.0 | 4 | 4.5 | 6 | 7.1 | 6 | 3.7 | 2 |
| All areas | 11.8 | | 19.5 | | 31.8 | | 49.5 | | 75.5 | | 124.0 | | 213.5 | |

Source: U.S. Department of Commerce, *Survey of Current Business* (February 1981).
Note: Because of rounding, total amounts based on industry and areas may not be equal.

there, the product may be reexported to the home country, as well as to other third markets. Moreover, in order to boost economic development, developing countries have encouraged foreign investors to establish joint ventures by offering tax incentives. At the same time, they have discouraged imports through higher tariffs and nationalistic purchasing policies.

**Foreign Direct Investment in the United States**

In contrast to the relative obscurity of early foreign investment in the United States, today such investment has become significantly more visible and constroversial.[2] Foreign direct investment is defined as the book value of the foreign direct investors' equity in and net outstanding loans to their U.S. affiliates. A U.S. affiliate is a U.S. business firm in which a foreign investor owns 10 percent or more of the voting securities. From a visibility standpoint, the reported growth rate in the book value of foreign direct investment in the United States rose from an average annual rate of 5.6 percent in the period 1961-1970 to 14.7 percent in the period 1971-1980. The U.S. Department of Commerce reported that by year-end 1980, foreign direct investment in the United States amounted to over $65 billion (table 1-4). The foreign direct-investment position in 1980 represents a substantial growth of 73 percent over the approximately $34 billion in 1973. Geographically, the advanced countries of Europe, Canada, and Japan contributed $57.5 billion, which accounted for 88 percent of the total foreign direct investment in the United States. Of the total amount, the Netherlands shared 25 percent, the United Kingdom 17 percent, and Canada 15 percent. The percentage ownership by Germany, the Netherlands Antilles, Japan, and Switzerland ranged from 6 to 8 percent, while France had a relatively low 4 percent. Interestingly, the OPEC members, which together had less than 1 percent of the total, were unchanged from 1979. Of course, their investment has been primarily in real estate and trade.[8]

As is the case for U.S. direct investment abroad, foreign direct investment in the United States is concentrated heavily in manufacturing—about 40 percent of the total. Of the total investment in manufacturing, chemical, machinery, and food products shared the greatest percentage. The petroleum and trade industries had about 20 percent each, while the insurance and finance industries held about 8 percent each of the total foreign direct investment.

Although foreign investors have varied reasons for investing in the United States, a few critical factors stand out as basic motivating influences during the recent upward trend. First, foreign multinational firms have increased in size and number through ordinary growth and merger movement

## Table 1-4
## Foreign Direct Investment Position in the United States at Year-End, 1980
*(millions of dollars)*

| | All Industries | Petroleum | Manufacturing | | | | | | Trade | Finance | Insurance | Real Estate | Other |
|---|---|---|---|---|---|---|---|---|---|---|---|---|---|
| | | | Total | Food Products | Chemicals and Allied Products | Primary and Fabricated Metals | Machinery | Other Manufacturing | | | | | |
| All countries | 65,483 | 12,253 | 24,134 | 4,092 | 7,859 | 3,572 | 4,007 | 4,603 | 13,772 | 4,829 | 5,060 | 2,429 | 3,006 |
| Canada | 9,810 | 1,137 | 5,148 | 2,186 | 139 | 839 | 1,288 | 696 | 1,148 | 354 | 444 | 542 | 1,036 |
| Europe | 43,467 | 9,884 | 15,036 | 1,747 | 5,798 | 2,068 | 2,461 | 2,962 | 8,908 | 3,031 | 4,152 | 871 | 1,586 |
| European Communities (9) | 37,850 | 9,687 | 12,022 | 1,430 | 4,550 | 1,720 | 1,781 | 2,541 | 7,542 | 2,815 | 3,533 | 855 | 1,396 |
| Belgium and Luxembourg | 1,873 | 1,224 | 221 | 24 | 122 | 61 | -48 | 62 | 158 | 160 | 7 | 28 | 75 |
| France | 2,672 | 240 | 1,393 | 38 | 312 | 522 | 91 | 430 | 583 | 333 | 44 | -1 | 80 |
| Germany | 5,290 | 48 | 2,137 | 27 | 1,789 | 165 | 382 | -226 | 1,759 | 162 | 696 | 120 | 368 |
| Italy | 334 | a | 7 | 10 | -14 | 3 | -3 | 11 | 200 | 95 | 17 | 13 | 1 |
| Netherlands | 16,159 | 8,319 | 3,931 | 879 | 910 | 91 | 881 | 1,170 | 1,113 | 1,099 | 632 | 504 | 562 |
| Denmark and Ireland | 180 | 3 | 56 | -1 | 13 | a | 14 | 29 | 96 | 5 | a | 0 | 19 |
| United Kingdom | 11,342 | -147 | 4,277 | 453 | 1,419 | 878 | 464 | 1,064 | 3,633 | 961 | 2,136 | 191 | 290 |
| Other Europe | 5,618 | 197 | 3,013 | 317 | 1,247 | 348 | 680 | 421 | 1,366 | 216 | 619 | 16 | 190 |
| Sweden | 1,345 | 128 | 620 | 1 | 51 | 71 | 461 | 37 | 577 | -85 | 103 | 2 | 1 |
| Switzerland | 3,682 | 25 | 2,308 | 299 | 1,198 | 255 | 202 | 354 | 559 | 203 | 498 | 2 | 88 |
| Other | 591 | 44 | 86 | 17 | -1 | 22 | 17 | 31 | 231 | 98 | 19 | 11 | 102 |
| Japan | 4,219 | 52 | 834 | 25 | 227 | 238 | 176 | 169 | 2,251 | 754 | 85 | 109 | 134 |
| Australia, New Zealand, and South Africa | 257 | -3 | 86 | 1 | 6 | 50 | -10 | 39 | 134 | -69 | 16 | 41 | 52 |
| Latin America | 6,702 | 1,140 | 2,994 | 143 | 1,686 | 334 | 93 | 737 | 948 | 440 | 361 | 587 | 233 |
| Latin American Republics | 931 | 21 | 121 | 45 | 50 | a | -5 | 30 | 120 | 229 | 331 | 98 | 11 |
| Panama | 695 | 13 | 136 | 42 | 58 | 6 | 16 | 15 | 81 | 59 | 329 | 68 | 8 |
| Other | 236 | 8 | -15 | 3 | -7 | -6 | -21 | 16 | 39 | 170 | 2 | 30 | 3 |
| Other Western Hemisphere | 5,771 | 1,119 | 2,873 | 98 | 1,635 | 334 | 98 | 707 | 828 | 211 | 30 | 489 | 221 |
| Middle East | 740 | 4 | 48 | a | 3 | 44 | 1 | a | 174 | 290 | a | 265 | -42 |
| Israel | 213 | 0 | 3 | a | 3 | 0 | 0 | 0 | 16 | 215 | 0 | a | -20 |
| Other | 527 | 4 | 45 | 0 | a | 44 | 1 | a | 159 | 75 | a | 265 | -22 |
| Other Africa, Asia, and Pacific | 288 | 38 | -12 | -10 | 1 | -1 | -1 | -1 | 208 | 30 | 2 | 14 | 8 |
| Memorandum | | | | | | | | | | | | | |
| OPEC | 576 | 20 | 57 | 3 | -1 | 44 | -7 | 18 | b | 84 | 1 | 280 | b |

Source: *Survey of Current Business* (August 1981).
aLess than $500,000 (±).
bSuppressed to avoid disclosure of data of individual companies.

abroad, while simultaneously attracted to the vast consumer market in the United States. Second, as a result of increasingly protectionist sentiments and legislation in the United States, foreign firms have felt serious threats to their U.S. markets unless they established manufacturing operations there. Third, because the U.S. stock market has been depressed since the early 1970s, foreign investors have found it easier to acquire U.S. firms with their trade surplus dollar holdings. Fourth, foreign banks in the United States have assisted and accelerated the process of foreign direct investment in the United States. Fifth, the recent growth and internationalization of Euro-dollar markets have made it much easier for foreign investors to invest in the United States, not only from Europe but from Asia and Latin America as well.

**Eurodollar Markets**

In order to finance an increasing volume of international trade and invest-ment, one's international liquidity position must increase concurrently. In this connection, the Eurocurrency market has played an important role in international money and capital markets. In fact, the Eurodollar market became a significant phenomenon in international financial markets because it accounted for more than 70 percent of the total of Eurocurrency markets. The concept of Eurocurrency is similar to that of the Eurodollar, except that the former includes both U.S. dollars and other key currencies such as the German mark, British pound, Swiss franc, and French franc. Since the world does not have a separate currency of its own, the U.S. dollar still serves as the medium of exchange for international transactions.

Eurodollars are U.S. dollar deposited in foreign banks. These deposits, denominated in U.S. dollars, include deposits in foreign branches of U.S. banks. The major Eurodollar market is located in London but has spread to major financial centers in Europe and Asia. Eurodollar deposits arise when the owner of a demand deposit at a U.S. bank transfers ownership of that deposit to a foreign bank in exchange for a dollar-denominated deposit claim against the foreign banks, usually for higher interest earnings. Eurodollar deposits may be made by individuals, corporations, or other nonbanking institutions. The dollar deposited may have been acquired through a current trade or capital transaction already denominated in dollars or through the purchase of dollars in the foreign-exchange market.[4] Although Eurodollars are created at a European bank, the European bank must have dollar deposits with U.S. commercial banks in order to make the dollar balance useful. In other words, the original dollar deposits at U.S. commercial banks never leave the country. What has happened during the creation of Eurodollars is simply the transfer of ownership from a U.S. resi-

dent to a foreign resident—in this case a European bank. Eurodollar transactions have to be ultimately cleared through the U.S. commercial banking
system. The creation of Eurodollars does not increase or decrease the U.S.
money supply, which is controlled by the federal reserve system.

What became a startling phenomenon in the 1970s was the ever-
increasing size of Eurodollar markets. Although the Eurodollar market existed before World War II, its size became more meaningful in the early
1960s when the U.S. balance of payments experienced deficits, especially in
capital accounts. It accelerated in the 1970s when the United States experienced trade deficits, and the oil embargo brought about a huge ac-
cumulation of petrodollars. Both gross and net amounts in the Eurodollar
currency market increased from the relatively negligible amounts of $20
billion gross and $14 billion net in 1964 to $1,365 billion gross and $705
billion net in 1980 (table 1-5). These figures are based on Morgan Guaranty
Trust Company statistics, which include Eurocurrency holdings at banks in
various countries throughout the world and foreign-currency claims on
domestic as well as foreign residents. According to the Bank for Interna-

**Table 1-5**
**Eurocurrency Market**
*(billions of dollars)*

| Year | Gross Liabilities[b] | Net Liabilities[a] | Eurodollar as Percentage of Gross Market |
|------|-----------|-----------|------------------|
| 1964 | 20 | 14 | 83 |
| 1965 | 24 | 17 | 84 |
| 1966 | 29 | 21 | 83 |
| 1967 | 36 | 25 | 84 |
| 1968 | 50 | 34 | 82 |
| 1969 | 90 | 50 | 84 |
| 1970 | 115 | 65 | 81 |
| 1971 | 150 | 85 | 76 |
| 1972 | 205 | 110 | 78 |
| 1973 | 310 | 160 | 73 |
| 1974 | 390 | 215 | 77 |
| 1975 | 480 | 250 | 78 |
| 1976 | 590 | 310 | 79 |
| 1977 | 725 | 380 | 76 |
| 1978 | 925 | 485 | 74 |
| 1979 | 1,185 | 600 | 72 |
| 1980 | 1,365 | 705 | 73 |

Source: Morgan Guaranty Trust Co., *World Financial Markets* (New York, 1970-1981).

[a]Figures exclude interbank deposits.

[b]These gross figures are larger than those published by the Bank for International Settlements,
which includes many offshore centers such as Bahrain, Singapore, and Hong Kong. BIS reports
eight inside-area banks in Belgium-Luxembourg, France, Germany, Italy, the Netherlands,
Sweden, Switzerland, and the United Kingdom.

tional Settlements, the size of gross and net Eurocurrency markets is somewhat smaller, with $750 billion and $515 billion, respectively, in 1980.[5] The Bank for International Settlements includes only foreign-currency claims of banks in eight major European countries against nonresidents, excluding residents' claims.[6] In either case, however, the Eurocurrency market, the amount of Eurodollars held at banks outside of the United States, was far greater than the U.S. money supply during the peak period of November 1980, when the money supply (MIA) reached $393 billion.[7]

The multiple expansion of Eurodollar credit has been possible mainly because most European countries have no reserve requirements, or at least very negligible ones on Eurodollar deposits when compared to the higher reserve requirements against deposits in the United States. The velocity of Eurodollars is therefore greater, with larger loanable funds circulating in greater numbers throughout the European banking system.

The major participant in the Eurodollar market in terms of both sources and uses of the fund has been London, which handled more than 30 percent of the total business. Other major centers for Eurodollar market trading are Belgium, Luxembourg, France, the Netherlands, Japan, Singapore, Bahamas, and the Caymans. It is argued, however, that the size of the Eurodollar markets in the U.S. offshore centers of the Caribbean islands may diminish as international banking facilities (IBFs) become fully effective after December 3, 1981. U.S. banks then will shift their Eurodollar operations from these islands back to the United States. It is also contended that the IBF will move some of Eurodollar business from London to New York.[8]

According to recent statistics in *World Financial Markets*, published by Morgan Guaranty Trust Company of New York, the gross and net amounts of Eurocurrency markets were $1,655 billion and $855 billion, respectively, as of September 1981. Of the total, deposits by nonbank private businesses were $395 billion, or 24 percent of the gross figure. The remaining 76 percent of the gross Eurocurrency deposits is held by international banks. It is significant that since 1972, both Eurocurrency deposits made by and Eurocurrency loans made to nonbank private businesses have increased immensely, proving that private corporations and individuals are now important participants in Eurocurrency markets.

The major factors affecting the recent growth of the Eurodollar market can be summarized:

1.  As a result of the U.S. balance-of-payment deficits, both advanced and developing foreign countries accumulated dollar earnings. In particular, OPEC countries deposited their petrodollars at Eurobanks.
2.  A large number of U.S. multinational firms needed dollar-denominated working capital abroad and transferred dollar holdings from U.S. parent companies.

**Table 1-6**
**Eurocurrency Markets in Major Countries**
*(billions of U.S. dollars)*

|  |  | 1975 | 1976 | 1977 | 1978 | 1979 | March 1980[a] | June 1980[a] |
|---|---|---|---|---|---|---|---|---|
| **Europe-based market** | | | | | | | | |
| A. | Gross | 351 | 411 | 517 | 663 | 847 | 864 | 933 |
|  | Austria | n.a. | n.a. | 8 | 11 | 15 | 15 | 16 |
|  | Belgium | 19 | 23 | 30 | 41 | 52 | 55 | 64 |
|  | Luxembourg | 30 | 39 | 54 | 72 | 96 | 95 | 107 |
|  | Denmark | n.a. | n.a. | 2 | 3 | 4 | 4 | 3 |
|  | France | 52 | 62 | 80 | 104 | 127 | 124 | 133 |
|  | Germany | 12 | 15 | 19 | 23 | 24 | 22 | 24 |
|  | Ireland | n.a. | n.a. | 2 | 2 | 3 | 2 | 3 |
|  | Italy | 18 | 19 | 26 | 34 | 44 | 38 | 41 |
|  | Netherlands | 19 | 24 | 30 | 40 | 49 | 50 | 54 |
|  | Spain | 3 | 4 | 5 | 7 | 11 | 11 | 11 |
|  | Sweden | 3 | 3 | 3 | 3 | 9 | 9 | 11 |
|  | Switzerland | 18 | 21 | 26 | 37 | 38 | 37 | 37 |
|  | United Kingdom | 178 | 202 | 231 | 287 | 377 | 402 | 429 |
| B. | Net | 205 | 247 | 300 | 377 | 475 | 491 | 540 |
| **Non-European market** | | | | | | | | |
| C. | Gross | 132 | 184 | 222 | 282 | 349 | 370 | 388 |
|  | Bahamas and Caymans | 62 | 91 | 106 | 124 | 139 | 145 | 147 |
|  | Bahrain | 2 | 6 | 16 | 23 | 28 | 29 | 33 |
|  | Canada | 14 | 17 | 18 | 22 | 26 | 29 | 31 |
|  | Hong Kong | 9 | 13 | 17 | 20 | 25 | 27 | 30 |
|  | Japan | 20 | 22 | 22 | 34 | 45 | 50 | 51 |
|  | Kuwait | 2 | 2 | 3 | 4 | 5 | 6 | 6 |
|  | Netherlands Antilles | 0 | 1 | 2 | 3 | 5 | 5 | 6 |
|  | Panama | 8 | 10 | 10 | 19 | 32 | 31 | 32 |
|  | Philippines | 1 | 1 | 1 | 2 | 2 | 2 | 2 |
|  | Singapore | 13 | 17 | 21 | 27 | 38 | 43 | 47 |
|  | United Arab Emirates | 2 | 3 | 2 | 3 | 4 | 4 | 4 |
| D. | Net | 54 | 74 | 87 | 110 | 136 | 145 | 152 |
| **Total worldwide Eurocurrency market** | | | | | | | | |
| E. | Gross (A + C) | 483 | 594 | 739 | 945 | 1,196 | 1,234 | 1,322 |
| F. | Net (B + D) | 259 | 321 | 387 | 487 | 611 | 636 | 692 |

Source: Grindlays Bank, London, 1981.
Note: Totals may not add, due to rounding.
[a]Provisional.

3.  Because of stringent government regulations in the United States—higher reserve requirements, regulation Q, and lending limits—U.S. banks incurred higher costs of funding. It became much more difficult to place loans at home, so they moved to banking abroad.

4.  The Eurodollar market, free from government intervention, is flexible
    and able to meet the maturity needs of borrowers and lenders, ranging
    from overnight to several years.

A significant stimulus to the growth of the Eurodollar market is directly
attributable to the ever-increasing volume of petrodollars. According to International Monetary Fund (IMF) statistics, during the 1974-1976 period,
OPEC countries had total export earnings of $250 billion and balance-of-
payments surpluses of $143 billion on current account.[9] Furthermore, a
U.S. Treasury estimate showed that OPEC countries invested the bulk of
the trade surplus funds in Eurodollars and certificates of deposits of U.S.
and European countries. The main reason why OPEC countries could not
utilize the surplus funds, investing in short-term financial assets abroad, is
that they do not have the absorptive capacity to invest and import. Both
U.S. and European banks, in turn, loaned these Eurodollars to non-oil-
producing countries, which experience tremendous trade deficits due to increased oil prices.

In summary, the Eurodollar market had three major effects on international banking in the 1970s. First, Eurodollars affected the monetary-policy
objectives of the United States and European countries, often in opposite
ways. What was frustrating for the United States during the tight-money
policy of 1979 and 1980 was that dollar credits were available through
Eurodollar borrowings. The high interest rate credit policy of the federal
reserve did not deter borrowings by U.S. banks and business firms because
loanable funds were available in Eurodollar markets at lower costs. On the
other hand, during the 1974-1976 recession, the federal reserve's easy-
money policy did not help much because U.S. investors shifted their
deposits to European banks that paid higher interest rates. This shift of
loanable funds from the United States to European banks did not help
reduce interest rates at home. Similarly, Eurodollar-receiving countries,
particularly Germany, complained that the inflow of Eurodollars was infla-
tionary. In Germany, Eurodollars were converted by German banks to Ger-
man marks, and the German central bank had no choice but to provide Ger-
man marks to German commercial banks.

The second most important effect of the Eurodollar market on the international scene is its financial intermediation function. Surplus funds
from savers are transferred to investors through international banks on a
worldwide scale. This is particularly true when the U.S. economy is ex-
periencing a recession: the domestic market growth potential is saturated,
the demand for loanable funds is low, and surplus funds cannot find proper
investors. U.S. international banks place these surplus funds abroad where
investment opportunities are greater for more-profitable projects. U.S.

banks serve as international financial intermediaries by pooling together financial resources that were not profitably utilized at home and making loans to foreign investors in greater need of investment funds. Eurodollar loans are made to foreign governments and foreign-government corporations whose creditworthiness is often excellent. Eurodollar intermediation has financed many foreign investments and has contributed to a great extent to the overall increase in international trade and investment.

The last and perhaps the most-significant effect that the Eurodollar market has had is that it has created an efficient international market. Before the emergence of the Eurodollar market, international financing was handled by each separate national financial market. There was no linkage between domestic national markets and third-party international markets. It is generally agreed that the introduction of Eurodollars brought foreign competition into the domestic financial market and lowered the interest rates that domestic banks used to charge. This was true in the early 1960s when British banks nearly monopolized international financing in London, charging monopoly interest rates. However, the newly created Eurodollar loans competed with British banks and lowered British bank interest rates on international financing. This was also true in recent years when U.S. banks abandoned prime-rate charges but used the London interbank offer rates (LIBOR) as the base point for international risk premiums. Because Eurodollars are free from government control and do not require reserve requirements and compensating balances, Eurobanks are capable of offering higher deposit rates and lower loan rates than their U.S. counterpart banks. In addition to a lower cost of capital, Eurodollar markets can afford a narrower interest-risk spread between the deposit and lending rate because Eurodollar loans carry lower overhead and personnel costs. Additionally Eurobanks can operate on a smaller margin between loan revenues and deposit expenses by taking advantage of the economies of scale of Eurodollar transactions, as the Eurodollar market is essentially a wholesale market. Interest-rate comparisons between U.S. and Eurodollar markets are shown in table 1-7.

It is difficult, if not impossible, to compare U.S. domestic and Eurodollar interest rates on an effective basis, mainly because the nominal interest rates do not reflect such hidden costs as compensating balance requirements on U.S. loans and management fees and commission charges on Eurodollar loans. It is reasonable, however, to stipulate that the nominal interest-rate differentials between Eurodollar and U.S. money-market rates have reflected the risks involved in the two markets. The Eurodollar loan rate is based on the LIBOR plus a risk premium of the borrower. Both Eurodollar deposits and loan rates take into account the risk premium of the market. However, the interest-rate differential between U.S. and Eurodollar markets has narrowed in recent years because the latter's risk of

**Table 1-7**
**U.S. and Eurodollar Interest Rates**

| Date | U.S. Prime Rate[a] | Three-month Certificate of Deposit Rate[b] | Eurodollar Deposit Rate[c] | LIBOR[d] |
|---|---|---|---|---|
| January 1975 | 9.50% | 6.50% | 7.44% | 7.57% |
| July 1975 | 7.50 | 6.75 | 6.94 | 7.07 |
| January 1976 | 6.75 | 5.00 | 5.25 | 5.38 |
| July 1976 | 7.00 | 5.38 | 5.63 | 5.76 |
| January 1977 | 6.25 | 4.95 | 5.25 | 5.38 |
| July 1977 | 6.50 | 5.75 | 6.25 | 6.38 |
| January 1978 | 7.99 | 6.95 | 7.25 | 7.38 |
| July 1978 | 9.00 | 7.99 | 8.50 | 8.63 |
| January 1979 | 11.75 | 10.25 | 10.31 | 10.44 |
| July 1979 | 11.75 | 10.30 | 11.31 | 11.44 |
| January 1980 | 15.25 | 13.35 | 14.39 | 14.49 |
| July 1980 | 11.00 | 8.90 | 9.81 | 9.93 |
| January 1981 | 20.00 | 16.00 | 17.50 | 17.63 |
| July 1981 | 20.50 | 17.75 | 18.68 | 18.81 |
| November 1981 | 16.00 | 11.35 | 12.00 | 12.13 |

Source: Morgan Guaranty Trust Co., *World Financial Markets* (New York, 1982).
Notes: All rates are end-of-month figures.
[a]Prime rates charged by Morgan Guaranty Trust Co.
[b]Three-month dealer placed certificate-of-deposit rates by Morgan Guaranty Trust Co.
[c]Three-month Eurodollar time deposit rates.
[d]LIBOR plus 0.125 to adjust for risk premium for prime borrowers.

illiquidity has been gradually eliminated as the size of the Eurodollar market has increased. At present, the interest-rate differential exists mainly because of more-stringent U.S. government regulation. Furthermore, the risk of government controls and intervention still exists in the Eurodollar market. This is illustrated by the fact that the Eurodollar rate has deviated from the bounding effect range whenever the U.S. or British government has imposed controls on the flow of capital on an international scale.[10] In spite of such market distortion and imperfections, however, it is reasonable to conclude that, in relative terms, the Eurodollar market is probably the most free market available in today's world of international banking.

**Movement of U.S. Banks Abroad**

The growth of foreign branches of U.S. banks abroad began in 1958 and accelerated in the 1960s and the 1970s. Aside from accommodating the financial needs of U.S. multinational firms in foreign countries, the complex and unfavorable legal restrictions of the United States often forced banks to move abroad to nations where government regulations were less burden-some. For instance, the U.S. interest-equalization tax, the foreign-credit restraint program, and the monetary capital-control program were all intended to restrict the outflow of U.S. capital abroad. Executive order 7387, dated January 1, 1968, restricted domestically funded foreign loans but did not restrict foreign loans funded overseas.[11] Consequently U.S. banks set up branches abroad to participate in European money and capital markets and to make Eurodollar loans.

Another contributing factor to the growth of U.S. banks abroad is related to the fact that earnings from international banking have been much greater than those from domestic banking operations. According to a study by Salomon Brothers of New York, total earnings of the thirteen largest U.S. banks increased from $177 million in 1970 to $836 million in 1975.[12] Meanwhile domestic earnings of these banks declined in the same period. In terms of growth rates, the earnings of these banks from their foreign operations were over 34 percent per year from 1970 to 1975, while the growth of domestic earnings was only 0.7 percent.

Another consideration in the establishment of foreign branches by U.S. banks is the ability to serve foreign business firms in local markets. Initially U.S. bank branches abroad facilitated the financing needs of U.S. multinational firms. Wherever banking services were established, however, U.S. bank branches penetrated the local banking market. In many instances, local foreign banks lacked the complete range of banking services and modern banking facilities. Foreign branches of U.S. banks with large financial and personnel resources from the parent bank could provide financial and marketing information for local business firms doing business with the United States. Furthermore the foreign branches of U.S. banks increased the efficiency of funding through the global network of the parent bank.

The real accelerated growth in foreign branches of U.S. banks took place in the late 1960s (table 1-8). The number of foreign branches of U.S. banks increased from 181 in 1964 to 375 in 1968 and 789 in 1979. Total assets of these branches also followed a similar pattern of growth, showing $6.9 billion, $23.0 billion, and $313 billion in 1964, 1968, and 1979, respectively.

England has the largest share of total assets and deposits of all U.S. branches overseas. London has long been the focal point for Eurodollar operations of both U.S. and other foreign banks actively engaged in international banking. London is still a major financial center in Western Europe, and major foreign banks there provide short-term money-market outlets and investment banking for institutions throughout Europe. Furthermore international banks clear their international deposit balances in London.

Until 1978, continental Europe was the second most important region for U.S. banks to establish their branches. In 1979, however, the size of U.S. branch assets in the Far East exceeded those in continental Europe

**Table 1-8**
**Overseas Branches of Member Banks of the Federal Reserve System**

| Year | | England | Continental Europe | Latin America | Far East | Other | Total |
|------|---|---------|-----------|-----------|-----|-------|-------|
| 1964 | Number of branches | 17 | 15 | 78 | 40 | 31 | 181 |
|      | Assets | 2,690 | 1,097 | 810 | 1,543 | 798 | 6,938 |
| 1965 | Number of branches | 21 | 21 | 88 | 50 | 31 | 211 |
|      | Assets | 4,257 | 1,354 | 878 | 1,700 | 913 | 9,102 |
| 1966 | Number of branches | 22 | 26 | 102 | 57 | 37 | 244 |
|      | Assets | 6,445 | 2,022 | 1,052 | 1,808 | 1,057 | 12,384 |
| 1967 | Number of branches | 25 | 34 | 133 | 63 | 40 | 295 |
|      | Assets | 8,178 | 2,721 | 1,270 | 2,267 | 1,222 | 15,658 |
| 1968 | Number of branches | 35 | 46 | 178 | 72 | 44 | 375 |
|      | Assets | 13,177 | 4,121 | 1,736 | 2,663 | 1,321 | 23,018 |
| 1969 | Number of branches | 40 | 64 | 203 | 76 | 76 | 459 |
|      | Assets | 24,753 | 6,464 | 1,584 | 3,257 | 5,062 | 41,120 |
| 1970 | Number of branches | 44 | 72 | 223 | 79 | 118 | 536 |
|      | Assets | 29,668 | 9,496 | 2,055 | 4,423 | 6,969 | 52,611 |
| 1971 | Number of branches | 48 | 80 | 229 | 83 | 137 | 577 |
|      | Assets | 35,143 | 12,913 | 2,519 | 6,221 | 10,258 | 67,054 |
| 1972 | Number of branches | 53 | 89 | 227 | 97 | 161 | 627 |
|      | Assets | 40,914 | 13,033 | 2,602 | 7,119 | 13,769 | 77,437 |
| 1973 | Number of branches | 56 | 100 | 236 | 110 | 192 | 694 |
|      | Assets | 58,490 | 19,897 | 4,870 | 11,092 | 23,700 | 118,049 |
| 1974 | Number of branches | 58 | 108 | 241 | 125 | 200 | 732 |
|      | Assets | 65,230 | 24,385 | 5,983 | 18,036 | 26,902 | 140,536 |
| 1975 | Number of branches | 59 | 115 | 244 | 129 | 215 | 762 |
|      | Assets | 67,871 | 24,176 | 7,551 | 21,001 | 42,081 | 162,680 |
| 1976 | Number of branches | 62 | 111 | 202 | 131 | 225 | 731 |
|      | Assets | 72,840 | 27,289 | 7,320 | 24,703 | 61,698 | 193,850 |
| 1977 | Number of branches | 61 | 110 | 199 | 138 | 222 | 730 |
|      | Assets | 82,726 | 32,475 | 8,705 | 29,126 | 74,837 | 227,868 |
| 1978 | Number of branches | 62 | 113 | 199 | 146 | 241 | 761 |
|      | Assets | 93,812 | 34,969 | 11,316 | 32,163 | 85,319 | 257,580 |
| 1979 | Number of branches | 64 | 108 | 212 | 154 | 251 | 789 |
|      | Assets | 118,256 | 37,701 | 15,111 | 38,151 | 103,706 | 312,925 |

Source: Federal Reserve Board, Washington, D.C., 1981.
Note: Assets data are in millions of dollars.

in 1979. As in London, the entry of U.S. banks into continental Europe brought about intensive competition in international banking. In the Far East except for Japan, increased international trade and investment activity with middle-income countries such as Korea, Taiwan, Hong Kong, Malaysia, and the Philippines increased the asset share of U.S. branches in this region. Branch assets rose to $38.2 billion in 1979, which accounted for 12 percent of the total assets of U.S. branches abroad. In recent years, the assets of U.S. branches in other areas have increased visibly, mainly due to the tax- and regulation-free Caribbean islands of the Bahamas and the

Caymans. For instance, these island nations held assets of U.S. branches of $88.3 billion, which accounted for 28 percent of the total. Furthermore, they had 150 branches of U.S. banks, which accounted for 19 percent of total number of U.S. branches abroad.

### Growth of Edge Act Corporations

In the 1970s, U.S. banks were obliged to serve not only large multinational corporations in money centers but also middle American firms doing international business in other regions of the country. This is why the number of Edge Act corporations has increased in recent years.

The Edge Act corporation is a federally chartered subsidiary of a bank organized under the Federal Reserve Act for the purpose of engaging in international banking or financial operations. Edge Act corporations may accept deposits, make loans, and provide other banking and financial services as long as a business transaction is directly or indirectly related to international trade and finance.

Edge Act corporations possess two major privileges that domestic commercial banks do not. First, Edge Act corporations can take advantage of interstate banking. Under the guidelines stipulated in the International Banking Act of 1978, regulation K was amended on July 14, 1979, by the Federal Reserve Board to allow Edge corporations to establish branches rather than separate subsidiaries across state lines. Under the new provision, an Edge Act corporation can make a loan to an individual customer of up to 10 percent of the total consolidated capital and surplus of all the bank's branch Edges in different states rather than that of just one Edge branch in one state. The use of a consolidated Edge Act corporation instead of separately formed corporations also provides for a larger lending limit. This is, of course, a major benefit to banks.[13]

Second, Edge Act corporations can hold stock in nonbanking companies and can provide a variety of financial services, including long-term financing, through either debt or equity, in foreign countries. Section 25 of the Federal Reserve Act permits domestic banks to acquire stocks in foreign-banking institutions but not in nonbanking companies; however, Edge Act corporations may underwrite, distribute, and deal in debt and equity securities outside the United States. This privilege is not allowed to U.S. domestic banks.

Initially Edge corporations were formed in large urban cities, such as New York City and San Francisco, to perform nonbanking business. Then Edges penetrated other regions to provide banking services outside the state where the parent bank was located. In 1955, there were only six Edge corporations, but these have grown to 38 in 1964 and 85 in 1980.

**Table 1-9**
**Total Assets of U.S. Banking Edge Corporations**
*(billions of U.S. Dollars)*

|  | 1972 | 1973 | 1974 | 1975 | 1976 | 1977 | 1978 | 1979 | 1980 | 1981 |
|---|---|---|---|---|---|---|---|---|---|---|
| **New York** | | | | | | | | | | |
| Amount of assets | $4.0 | $4.2 | $7.3 | $5.1 | $6.8 | $7.6 | $10.3 | $10.4 | $9.6 | $9.6 |
| Number of Edges | 21 | 23 | 23 | 23 | 23 | 23 | 25 | 25 | 26 | 27 |
| **Chicago** | | | | | | | | | | |
| Amount of assets | | .1 | .1 | .2 | .2 | .2 | .2 | .4 | .4 | .7 |
| Number of Edges | 2 | 3 | 6 | 6 | 6 | 6 | 6 | 6 | 8 | 15 |
| **California** | | | | | | | | | | |
| Amount of assets | .3 | .7 | .9 | .8 | .9 | 1.0 | .9 | 1.2 | 2.0 | 2.3 |
| Number of Edges | 6 | 9 | 12 | 13 | 13 | 13 | 13 | 14 | 15 | 23 |
| **Houston and other U.S. cities** | | | | | | | | | | |
| Amount of assets | | .1 | .1 | .2 | .2 | .3 | .4 | .6 | .5 | .6 |
| Number of Edges | 3 | 3 | 6 | 7 | 7 | 7 | 9 | 10 | 14 | 13 |
| **Miami** | | | | | | | | | | |
| Amount of assets | .1 | .2 | .3 | .5 | .6 | .8 | 1.0 | 1.4 | 2.0 | 2.4 |
| Number of Edges | 7 | 7 | 9 | 9 | 9 | 10 | 10 | 15 | 22 | 24 |
| **Total** | | | | | | | | | | |
| Amount of assets | 4.4 | 5.3 | 8.8 | 6.8 | 8.7 | 9.9 | 12.8 | 14.0 | 14.6 | 16.3 |
| Number of Edges | 39 | 45 | 56 | 58 | 58 | 59 | 63 | 70 | 85 | 119 |

Source: Board of Governors of the Federal Reserve System.
Note: The table includes banking Edges only, excluding nonbanking Edges. Total value include other cities. For instance, the number of Edge officies in other cities was seventeen in 1981, which is a substantial increase from earlier years.

New York City has the largest number of Edges—twenty-six—in the United States (table 1-9). Both money-center and regional bank Edges are represented in New York City. In 1981, banking Edges there had assets of $9.6 billion, which was 60 percent of all banking Edge assets in the United States. New York City is an excellent base for Edge operations because most international banks are represented there, as well as the headquarter offices of large U.S. and foreign multinational corporations. Because of New York City's central position in international finance, many banks from other parts of the country established Edge offices there to settle international clearing balances and to maintain close personal ties to their international customers.[14]

Edge branches have spread to other money centers and regional cities. Miami has the second largest number of Edges after New York because Miami looks to Latin America. California, particularly San Francisco and Los Angeles, has special ties with Japan and other Asian countries. Most Houston Edges deal with the oil-rich OPEC countries and the major grain customers of the world through their port facilities and shipping operations. During the past several years, Edge offices have also mushroomed in other regional cities—St. Louis, Atlanta, Seattle, Cleveland, Dallas, and Minneapolis.

## Notes

1. Raymond Vernon, "International Investment and International Trade in the Product Cycle," *Quarterly Journal of Economics* (May 1966): 190-207.

2. J. Arpan and D. Ricks, "Foreign Direct Investments for the U.S. and Some Attendant Research Problems," *Journal of International Business Studies* (Spring 1974):1-7.

3. U.S. Department of Commerce, *Survey of Current Business* (Washington, D.C., August 1981).

4. Walter Woodworth, *The Money Market and Monetary Management* (New York: Harper & Row, 1972), p. 163.

5. Nicholas Carlozzi, "Regulating the Eurocurrency Market," *Business Review*, Federal Reserve Bank of Philadelphia (March-April 1981): 15-23.

6. Steven Davis, *The Management Function in International Banking* (New York: John Wiley, 1979), p. 20.

7. Demand deposits held at all commercial banks in the United States.

8. David Ashley, "Will the Eurodollar Market Go Back Home?" *Banker* (February 1981):93-97.

9. A. Angelini, M. Eng, and F. Lees *International Lending, Risk, and the Euromarkets* (New York: John Wiley, 1979), pp. 24-25.

10. G. Dufey and I. Giddy, *The International Money Market* (Englewood Cliffs, N.J.: Prentice-Hall, 1978), pp. 50-53.

11. Comptroller General of the U.S., U.S. General Accounting Office, *Considerable Increase in Foreign Banking in the U.S.* (Washington, D.C., August 1979), pp. 1-7.

12. Salomon Brothers, *United States Multinational Banking* (New York: Salomon Brothers & Co., 1976), pp. 5-20.

13. Gerald Anderson, "Current Developments in the Regulation of International Banking," *Economic Review*, Federal Reserve Bank of Cleveland (January 1980):1-15.

14. James V. Houpt, "Performance and Characteristics of Edge Corporations," *Staff Studies*, Federal Reserve Board (Washington, D.C., January 1981), pp. 2-13.

# 2 Foreign Banks in the United States

During the 1970s, the expansion of foreign banking in the United States was dramatic. Foreign banks grew in terms of both total assets and number of offices. Concern was manifest in both the U.S. Congress and U.S. banking institutions. Foreign-bank size, competition, and equity were the prime issues. It is appropriate, therefore, to analyze the growth of these foreign banks from three viewpoints: by country of origin, by geographical location in the United States, and by organizational type: agency, branch, subsidiary, and investment company.

## Growth of Foreign-Bank Assets and Offices

The real expansion of foreign banking in the United States occurred in the 1970s. The historical origin of foreign banks in the United States, however, goes back to the 1870s when British, Canadian, and Japanese banks set up operations in New York, California, Oregon, and Washington. Early British banks to open offices in the United States were the Hong Kong and Shanghai Banking Corporation, Lloyds Bank, Barclays, and Westminster Bank. These banks came to the United States to finance trade, transfer funds, and participate in the New York bond and stock markets.

Foreign banking in the United States dwindled during World War I and the Great Depression of the 1930s. Its resurgence in the United States began after World War II when the U.S. dollar became the international medium of exchange. The real stimulus to foreign banking came on January 1, 1961, when New York State allowed foreign banks to open branches in New York. The new law was promulgated at the urging of not only foreign banks but also U.S. banks.[1]

Just as U.S. banks had followed the international operations of U.S. multinational corporations, so did foreign banks repeat the pattern with their pursuit of home-country subsidiaries, which had moved into the United States during the 1970s.[2] After an initial period of rapid growth for foreign banks from 1972 to 1974, the rate slowed somewhat between 1975 and 1977 (table 2-1). Then the foreign-banking boom reaffirmed itself from 1978 to 1979, primarily due to fears of further restrictions on entry to the United States.[3]

**Table 2-1**
**Total Assets of U.S. Banking Institutions Owned by Foreign Banks**
*(millions of U.S. dollars)*

| Year | Total | | | Agencies | | | Branches | | | Subsidiary Banks | | | Investment Companies | | |
|---|---|---|---|---|---|---|---|---|---|---|---|---|---|---|---|
| | Number[a] | Assets | % | Number[a] | Assets | % | Number[a] | Assets | % | Number[a] | Assets | % | Number[a] | Assets | % |
| 1972 | 105 | $ 26,105 | 100 | 53 | $14,421 | 55.3 | 24 | $ 5,676 | 21.7 | 25 | $ 4,646 | 17.8 | 3 | $1,362 | 5.2 |
| 1973 | 119 | 36,612 | 100 | 62 | 21,752 | 59.4 | 27 | 7,081 | 19.3 | 27 | 5,922 | 16.2 | 3 | 1,858 | 5.1 |
| 1974 | 160 | 55,395 | 100 | 75 | 28,790 | 52.0 | 52 | 12,330 | 22.3 | 30 | 11,955 | 21.6 | 3 | 2,320 | 4.1 |
| 1975 | 179 | 63,689 | 100 | 82 | 27,875 | 43.8 | 60 | 19,675 | 30.9 | 33 | 13,386 | 21.0 | 4 | 2,753 | 4.3 |
| 1976 | 196 | 74,845 | 100 | 91 | 30,086 | 40.2 | 67 | 26,892 | 35.9 | 33 | 15,544 | 20.8 | 5 | 2,323 | 3.1 |
| 1977 | 247 | 92,695 | 100 | 115 | 28,999 | 31.3 | 93 | 43,190 | 46.6 | 34 | 18,291 | 19.7 | 5 | 2,216 | 2.4 |
| 1978 | 295 | 127,585 | 100 | 140 | 39,751 | 31.1 | 110 | 62,546 | 49.0 | 39 | 22,779 | 17.9 | 6 | 2,510 | 2.0 |
| 1979 | 334 | 168,388 | 100 | 164 | 54,102 | 32.1 | 125 | 84,928 | 50.4 | 39 | 26,375 | 15.7 | 6 | 2,983 | 1.8 |
| 1980 (May) | 339 | 171,553 | 100 | 168 | 58,620 | 34.1 | 128 | 84,575 | 49.3 | 37 | 25,600 | 15.0 | 6 | 2,759 | 1.6 |

Source: Board of Governors of the Federal Reserve System.

Note: Does not include offices located in territories or possessions of the United States.

[a]Number of offices. The number indicates the number of banks making reports to the Federal Reserve Bank on a consolidated basis. Some banks have more than one office in the same state.

As table 2-1 shows, total assets of foreign-banking institutions grew from $26.1 billion in 1972 to $171.5 billion in 1980, a 650 percent increase. The total number of foreign banking offices increased from 105 in 1972 to 339 in 1980.

Total assets of foreign banks are broken down in table 2-1 by organizational type: agencies, branches, subsidiaries, and investment companies. In 1972, assets of foreign-bank agencies amounted to $14.4 billion, which accounted for 55.2 percent of total assets of foreign banking institutions. Foreign branches and subsidiaries banks attained $5.7 billion and $4.6 billion respectively in the same year, which accounted for 21.7 percent and 17.8 percent of total assets. By 1980, the relative share of these institutions changed. Assets of foreign branches increased to $84.6 billion in 1980 or 49.3 percent of total assets, while the relative share of foreign-bank agencies decreased to 34.1 percent. Assets of foreign-bank subsidiaries experienced a slow but steady growth in the 1972-1980 period, while assets of foreign investment companies remained negligible, with less than 1 percent of total foreign-bank assets in the United States.

Although the growth rate of foreign banking assets is much greater than that of U.S. institutions involved in international banking, the absolute-dollar amount of foreign-bank assets is still small in comparison to that of U.S. competitors. The total combined assets of U.S. Edge Act corporations, large U.S. commercial banks, and foreign branches of U.S. banks increased 250 percent during the 1972-1980 period, whereas foreign-bank assets grew more than six times during the same period (table 2-2). Nevertheless, the total assets of all foreign-banking institutions in the United States in 1980 account for no more than 23 percent of the assets of the large commercial banks that conduct the bulk of U.S. international banking business. Furthermore, total assets of foreign banks accounted for only 13 percent of the combined assets of all institutions, as shown in table 2-2. Another interesting comparison is that the assets of U.S. bank branches overseas are more than twice as large as assets of foreign banking institutions in the United States. It is also estimated that U.S. banks carry on approximately $450 billion worth of international banking business, an amount 2.5 times the total assets of all foreign banking institutions in the United States. In summary, the statistics indicate that it is reasonable to refute the argument that the assets of foreign banks in the United States are growing dangerously large and controlling a significant amount of the U.S. banking industry.[4]

It is reasonable to infer that the recent growth in foreign banks in the United States was directly attributable to the American open and national treatment policy. This policy is based on a principle of nondiscrimination that fosters competitive equality for both foreign and U.S. banks. This principle was clearly inscribed in the International Banking Act of 1978. In

**Table 2-2**
**Total Assets of Foreign Banks, Banking Edge Corporations, and Large U.S. Commercial Banks**
(*millions of U.S. dollars*)

| Year | Foreign Banks | Edge Corporations[a] | Large U.S. Commercial Banks[b] | Foreign Branches of U.S. Banks | Total |
|------|---------------|----------------------|--------------------------------|--------------------------------|-------|
| 1972 | $ 26,105 (5.7) | $ 5,100 (1.1) | $350,941 (76.4) | $ 77,437 (16.8) | $ 459,583 (100) |
| 1973 | 36,612 (6.6) | 6,000 (1.1) | 392,014 (70.9) | 118,049 (21.4) | 552,675 (100) |
| 1974 | 55,395 (8.5) | 9,100 (1.4) | 449,821 (68.7) | 140,536 (21.4) | 654,852 (100) |
| 1975 | 63,689 (9.2) | 7,900 (1.2) | 456,974 (66.1) | 162,680 (23.5) | 691,243 (100) |
| 1976 | 74,845 (9.9) | 10,100 (1.3) | 476,487 (63.1) | 193,850 (25.7) | 755,282 (100) |
| 1977 | 92,695 (10.8) | 11,300 (1.3) | 524,773 (61.3) | 227,868 (26.6) | 856,636 (100) |
| 1978 | 127,585 (12.8) | 14,600 (1.5) | 595,921 (59.9) | 257,580 (25.8) | 995,686 (100) |
| 1979 | 168,388 (14.9) | 16,200 (1.4) | 633,644 (56.0) | 312,925 (27.7) | 1,131,157 (100) |
| 1980 | 171,553 (13.5) | 18,118 (1.4) | 735,728 (57.7) | 350,131 (27.4) | 1,275,530 (100) |

Sources: James V. Houpt, *Performance and Characteristics of Edge Corporations*, Board of Governors of the Federal Reserve System (January 1981), and the Federal Reserve Board, Washington, D.C.

Note: Figures in parentheses are percentages of total figures.

[a]Amounts shown include assets of foreign branches but not of foreign subsidiaries. Data do not eliminate intrafamily transactions; in other words, they do not reflect consolidated statements.

[b]Those with total assets of more than $1 billion.

fact, prior to the 1978 act, foreign banks seemingly possessed competitive advantages over U.S. banks in regard to the establishment and operations of their banking business in the United States.

Contrary to the U.S. open policy, many foreign countries, both advanced and developing, still practice discriminatory policies toward foreign banks coming into their home markets. This restrictive policy is clearly evidenced by the fact that many countries do not allow at all or limit the acquisition of their domestic banks by foreign entities. According to a study made by the U.S. Department of Treasury, 44 countries among 141 surveyed prohibit any foreign ownership of domestic banks (table 2-3).[5] Thirty-four countries limit foreign-bank acquisitions to less than a controlling interest in domestic banks. Such advanced countries as the United Kingdom, Japan, Canada, and Australia do not allow majority ownership by foreign banks. Although there were growing sentiments in the U.S. Congress to consider reciprocity, the U.S. government has not implemented such measures.[6] It is our judgment that the national treatment policy is a positive approach, which aids the free flow of international capital and investment. Reciprocity is a passive approach, following the discriminatory policies of other countries. Table 2-4 lists those countries that impose no apparent limit on foreign control of local banks.

Although it is evident that foreign-bank agencies played a dominant role in the U.S. market in the early 1970s, branches became the major force in later years, an indication that foreign banks have succeeded in penetrating U.S. domestic deposit markets. Most foreign banks initially set up agencies to serve their home-country customers doing business in the United States. Once their banking operations were firmly established, however, they slowly moved into broader U.S. domestic competition by accepting deposits through branch-bank offices. Indeed these deposits are still considered a relatively cheap source of funds.

In other words, in recent years foreign banks have established banking offices in U.S. money-center locations in order to increase dollar funding sources. According to interviews with international banking officers, many foreign banks also moved to the United States to be close to the foreign-exchange markets. Since the establishment of fluctuating exchange rates in 1973, both U.S. and foreign banks have actively participated in foreign-exchange markets. The impact of fluctuating exchange rates often has been enormous in terms of the earnings per share of large multinationals, the clients of international bankers. In addition, multinational bankers themselves have been pressured into realistic analyses of the strength and weaknesses of major trading currencies: the U.S. dollar, the German mark, the Canadian dollar, the British pound sterling, the Swiss franc, and the Japanese yen. Many multinational banks have reported losses due to exchange-rate changes in foreign-currency loans and in foreign-exchange

**Table 2-3**
**Countries Prohibiting or Limiting Foreign-Bank Ownership**

Countries prohibiting all forms of bank presence
By law

| Afghanistan | Czechoslovakia | Iraq | Madagascar |
|---|---|---|---|
| Bulgaria | Ethiopia | Laos | Somalia |
| Cuba | Guinea | Libya | Nepal |

By current policy or administrative practice

| Benin | Kuwait | | Surinam | United Arab Emirates |
|---|---|---|---|---|
| Guyana | Netherlands | Antilles | Tanzania | |

Countries permitting foreign-bank presence only by representative offices
By law

| Algeria | Portugal | Sweden | Soviet Union |
|---|---|---|---|
| Burma | Venezuela | Syria | Yugoslavia |
| Colombia | | | |

By policy or administrative practice

| People's Republic of China | Poland |
|---|---|
| El Salvador | Saudi Arabia |
| German Democratic Republic | Trinidad and Tobago |
| Guatemala | Turkey |
| India | Mexico |
| Indonesia | New Zealand |
| Norway | |

Other countries[a] probibiting foreign banks from purchasing any interest in indigenous banks[b]

| Bangladesh | Papua New Guinea |
|---|---|
| Pakistan | |

Specific maximum foreign participation allowed by law (%)

| Australia | 10 | The Gambia | 20 |
|---|---|---|---|
| Bermuda | 40 | Japan | 5 |
| Canada | 10[c] | Nigeria | 40 |
| The Congo | 49 | Philippines | 30[e] |
| Denmark | 30[d] | Republic of Korea | 10 |
| Ecuador | 20 | Upper Volta | 49 |
| Finland | 20 | | |

Specific maximum foreign participation allowed in practice (%)

| Bahrain | 49 | Oman | 49 |
|---|---|---|---|
| Dominican Republic | 30 | Qatar | 49 |
| Greece | 49 | Singapore | 20 |
| Iceland | 49 | South Africa | 50 |
| Morocco | 50 | United Kingdom | 15[f] |

No majority control; no specific maximum

| Central African Empire | Ireland | Netherlands | Trinidad and Tobago |
|---|---|---|---|
| Cyprus | Malaysia | Oman | Tunisia |
| Egypt | Malta | Qatar | |

Source: Steven Weiss, "National Policies on Foreign Acquisitions of Banks," *Bankers Magazine* (January-February 1981):27-28.

[a]In addition to those listed in the previous two sections of this table.

[b]These countries permit foreign-bank branches; many of the countries appearing in subsequent tables also permit foreign branches.

[c]Canada permits an individual foreign party to own up to 10 percent of a bank, and up to 25 percent of any bank may be foreign owned.

[d]Denmark requires a merger if any part, foreign or domestic, acquires 30 percent or more of a bank.

[e]40 percent with presidential approval

[f]Limit applies only to non-EEC acquisitions of interests in major existing banks.

**Table 2-4**
**Countries Imposing No Limit on Foreign Control of Local Banks**

| | | |
|---|---|---|
| Argentina | France | Mozambique |
| Austria | Gabon | Niger |
| Bahamas | W. Germany | Panama |
| Barbados | Ghana[c] | Paraguay |
| Belgium | Honduras | Rwanda |
| Belize | Hong Kong | Senegal |
| Botswana | Israel | Seychelles |
| Bolivia | Italy | Sierra Leone |
| Burundi | Ivory Coast | Spain |
| Cameroon[a] | Jamaica | Sri Lanka |
| Rep. of Cape Verde[b] | Kenya | Sudan |
| Cayman Islands | Lebanon | Switzerland |
| Chile | Luxembourg | Uruguay |
| Costa Rica | Mali | Zaire |
| Djibouti | Mauritania | Zambia |
| Fiji | Mauritius | |

Source: Steven Weiss, "National Policies on Foreign Acquisitions of Banks," *Bankers Magazine*, (January-February 1981):27-28.
[a]Maximum two-thirds foreign equity participation in any domestic bank.
[b]No laws pertaining to foreign bank entry.
[c]Maximum foreign ownership is 60 percent.

dealings. The cases in point are the failure of the Herstatt Bank in West Germany and Franklin National Bank of the United States.[7]

**Country Origin of Foreign Banks**

The growth of European and Japanese banks has been principally responsible for the tremendous increase in foreign banking assets in the United States (table 2-5). Together their banking offices shared 79 percent of the total assets of all foreign banks in the United States in 1980. The fact that European and Japanese banks shared such a large percentage of foreign-bank assets is easily understood when it is realized that their home countries are the principal trading partners of the United States. Data in table 2-5 also indicate that Canadian banks rank third in asset size because Canada continues to remain one of the major investment partners of the United States. Bank assets in the "others" category also increased in recent years, contributing 5.7 percent to the total assets of foreign banks in 1972 and 10.8 percent in 1980. This is partly due to the fact that banks from developing countries in Asia, Latin America, and the Middle East established offices in the United States as their level of income and dollar export earnings increased.

Nevertheless differences remain in the banking strategies of foreign countries. An indication of the aggressiveness with which Europeans approached the U.S. market in the 1970s is illustrated by their preference for

**Table 2-5**
**Total Assets of U.S. Banking Institutions Owned by Foreign Banks, by Country**
*(millions of U.S. dollars)*

| Year | Japan | Canada | Europe | Others | Total |
|---|---|---|---|---|---|
| 1972 | 11,313 (43.3) | 5,305 (20.3) | 8,003 (30.7) | 1,483 (5.7) | 26,105 (100) |
| 1973 | 18,011 (49.2) | 6,418 (17.5) | 9,857 (26.9) | 2,326 (6.4) | 36,612 (100) |
| 1974 | 23,707 (42.8) | 8,490 (15.3) | 20,362 (36.8) | 2,837 (5.1) | 55,395 (100) |
| 1975 | 25,225 (39.6) | 7,023 (11.0) | 27,254 (42.8) | 4,187 (6.6) | 63,689 (100) |
| 1976 | 27,747 (37.1) | 7,532 (10.1) | 33,755 (45.1) | 5,811 (7.7) | 74,845 (100) |
| 1977 | 28,869 (31.1) | 10,387 (11.2) | 43,619 (47.1) | 9,819 (10.6) | 92,695 (100) |
| 1978 | 42,436 (33.3) | 12,154 (9.5) | 59,374 (46.5) | 13,622 (10.7) | 127,585 (100) |
| 1979 | 57,495 (34.1) | 18,411 (10.9) | 73,364 (43.6) | 19,118 (11.4) | 168,388 (100) |
| 1980 (May) | 65,255 (38.0) | 17,359 (10.1) | 70,544 (41.1) | 18,395 (10.8) | 171,553 (100) |

Source: Board of Governors of the Federal Reserve System.

Notes: Does not include offices located in territories or possessions of the United States.

Figures in parentheses are percentages of the total.

the branch form of organization. Japanese banks converted many of their agencies to branches in later years because branches allowed them to manage better their dollar position and funding sources and to develop a retail banking business. Yet most Japanese banks continue to work closely with their own trading companies, while European banks concentrate more heavily on money-market activities and direct competition with U.S. banks. In particular, European banks were able to undercut U.S. competitors due to the expertise they were able to provide in foreign monetary transactions.[8] Moreover, the appreciation of both major European and Japanese currencies in the 1970s served to influence the growth rate of their respective banking operations in the United States. At one time, Canadian bank agencies had the number one foreign banking position in the United States, but this was before European and Japanese bank branches became the dominant force in the late 1970s. Canadian banks have been limited to the agency form of operation in New York State because New York State law requires reciprocity for its state banks as a condition for establishment of a foreign-bank branch in New York. Canadian law has not yet allowed New York banks to establish branches in Canada.

Foreign banks from developing countries are now following the footsteps of their European and Japanese predecessors by limiting their services to their respective government and home-country customers. But foreign banks in general tend to specialize in such wholesale banking operations. Indeed it is much more difficult for them to enter retail banking due to the cost involved and a less than prestigious reputation.

**Distribution of Foreign Banks in Different States**

Table 2-6 shows the geographical locations of foreign banks in the United States by states. In 1980, New York held the largest amount of foreign banking assets: $121.4 billion or 71 percent of the total. Assets of foreign banks in New York, California, and Illinois together accounted for 97 percent of the total assets of foreign banks in the United States. States in the "others" category include Massachusetts, Virginia, Florida, Texas, Michigan, Oregon, and Washington and account for the remaining assets as classified in table 2-7 (also see appendix C).

Foreign banks doing business in the United States were licensed and supervised under state law until the enactment of the International Banking Act in 1978. The first state to allow foreign banks to enter was Massachusetts in 1906, followed by Oregon in 1907, California in 1909, and New York in 1911. The state of New York did not allow foreign banks to establish branches until 1961, although it allowed the operation of foreign-bank agencies, representative offices, and subsidiary offices. Today New

**Table 2-6**
**Total Assets of U.S. Banking Institutions Owned by Foreign Banks, by States**
(*millions of U.S. dollars*)

| Year | New York Assets | New York Number | California Assets | California Number | Illinois Assets | Illinois Number | Other States Assets | Other States Number | Total Assets | Total Number |
|---|---|---|---|---|---|---|---|---|---|---|
| 1972 | $ 20,190 | 65 | $ 5,431 | 34 | $ 34 | 1 | $ 449 | 5 | $ 26,105 | 105 |
| 1973 | 25,530 | 70 | 10,116 | 41 | 112 | 2 | 854 | 6 | 36,612 | 119 |
| 1974 | 38,507 | 81 | 14,860 | 53 | 686 | 18 | 1,342 | 8 | 55,395 | 160 |
| 1975 | 43,598 | 88 | 16,799 | 58 | 1,555 | 24 | 1,737 | 9 | 63,689 | 179 |
| 1976 | 50,278 | 100 | 19,629 | 61 | 2,459 | 24 | 2,479 | 11 | 74,845 | 196 |
| 1977 | 67,728 | 123 | 20,418 | 77 | 3,320 | 30 | 1,229 | 17 | 92,695 | 247 |
| 1978 | 92,780 | 144 | 28,448 | 90 | 3,916 | 31 | 2,441 | 30 | 127,585 | 295 |
| 1979 | 123,365 | 159 | 35,492 | 97 | 5,394 | 34 | 4,137 | 44 | 168,388 | 334 |
| 1980 (May) | 121,444 | 163 | 38,428 | 97 | 6,060 | 34 | 5,622 | 45 | 171,553 | 339 |

Source: Board of Governors of the Federal Reserve System.
Notes: Does not include offices located in territories or possessions of the United States.
Number designates number of foreign banks.

**Table 2-7**
**Assets of Foreign Banks in the United States, June 30, 1980**
(*millions of dollars*)

| State | Agencies | Branches | Subsidiary Banks |
|---|---|---|---|
| New York | $20,670 (63) | $64,984 (104) | $31,565 (29) |
| California | 25,758 (85) | 24 (1) | 21,905 (30) |
| Illinois | — | 5,943 (31) | 1,767 (5) |
| Florida | 224 (14) | | 1,996 (21) |
| Oregon | | 2,219 (7) | |
| Washington | | 1,405 (8) | |
| Virginia | | | 3,016 (7) |
| Michigan | | | 1,054 (1) |
| Georgia | 1,090 (9) | | |
| Washington, D.C. | | | 676 (3) |
| Texas | | | 373 (4) |
| Others | 18 (2) | 193 (9) | 2,844 (16) |
| Total | $47,760 (173) | $74,768 (159) | $65,196 (116) |

Source: Federal Reserve Board, Washington, D.C., 1981.
Figures in parentheses are the number of bank offices that are not consolidated on a state basis.

York has all types of foreign banking operations, almost equally distributed among agencies, branches, subsidiaries, and representative offices. California shows a heavy concentration of subsidiary banks and foreign-bank agencies but only a handful of foreign-bank branches. This is because California did not permit foreign banks to accept deposits unless they secured Federal Deposit Insurance Corporation (FDIC) insurance, which was not available to foreign banks until 1978. Although Illinois holds the third position in foreign banking assets, it did not allow foreign banks to establish branches in the state until 1973, and only in 1980 did Illinois approve the Bank Holding Company Act to allow commercial banks to acquire subsidiary banks in different parts of the state. Because of restrictive policies on foreign branching, most states, with the exception of New York, still do not have many branches under their jurisdiction.

In 1961, New York became the pioneer state in allowing foreign banks to establish branches. The reasons for passing such a law were both financial and political. First, many New York banks were involved in international banking and had branches abroad. Unless foreign banks were allowed to establish branches in the state, New York banks feared that foreign countries might retaliate against their branches abroad. Second, New York banks argued that such a law would benefit the state of New York by increasing international banking-related employment and trade financing and bringing foreign capital into the state. Finally, they believed that such a law would increase New York's prestige as an international financial center. Initially Chase Manhattan and Citibank worked closely with the New York State banking commissioner in drafting a bill that would be acceptable to both banks and the supervisory authorities. A compromise draft bill was accepted by the Association of New York Clearinghouse Banks and finally approved and passed by the New York State legislature. It became effective on January 1, 1961.[9]

Foreign banks tend to concentrate in large urban port cities—New York, Chicago, San Francisco, Miami, and Houston—where major trade activities take place. Most foreign banks, particularly branches, devote more than 50 percent of their loans to trade financing. Foreign banks often serve as a trade financing link between the United States and their home countries and also assist trade transactions between the United States and third-party nations. This linkage has increased the flow of trade-financing activities between the United States and the rest of the world.

Many foreign banks act as important depositories for U.S. dollars from foreign governments and business firms located in large cities, particularly New York City, where different ethnic groups have sizable populations. Moreover, foreign banks are very active and successful in making loans and soliciting deposits from these ethnic business groups and individuals. This is certainly true for Israeli, Italian, Greek, and Puerto Rican banks. For instance, most Puerto Rican banks in New York hired Spanish-speaking officers to serve the Puerto Rican community. In California, where the Asian community is large, Japanese and Korean banks cater to ethnically oriented firms and individuals. In the case of Japanese banks, there are also ties with Japanese trading companies in New York and California.

## Organizational Forms of Foreign Banking

The selection of a particular organizational form for its U.S. operations reflects the type of business in which a foreign bank is engaged, in addition to petinent legal and regulatory differences. Basically there are five types of organizational forms: representative offices, agencies, branches, subsidiary banks, and investment companies.

*Representative Offices*

The representative office is typically established to do the preliminary work before a formal banking office is opened. This groundwork includes serving as a liaison between the parent bank and the local banking supervisory agency and providing research on the new banking market. Representative offices are not authorized to perform banking functions, however, they facilitate banking transactions through correspondent banks by promoting the parent bank's interest. They disseminate information regarding the parent bank and cultivate customer-parent bank relations. Since representative offices are not directly engaged in banking functions, they are exempt from state supervisory purview and tax payments.

*Agencies*

Agencies can make commercial and industrial loans and finance international transactions. They cannot accept deposits, sell certificates of deposits, or perform trust functions. One exception to this general rule is that they can accept credit balances, accounts to which the proceeds of loans or collection can be credited. Because they do not accept regular deposits, they are not subject to legal fractional reserve requirements and regulations Q. Furthermore, agencies are not limited to 10 percent of the capital and surplus account of the parent bank for making individual customer loans. The absence of this maximum-loan limit on agencies enables them to make larger loans. The maximum-loan limit of 10 percent does, however, apply to foreign-bank branches and subsidiaries.[9]

Many foreign-bank agencies serve as fiscal agents for their home-country governments. In general, most agencies play a prominent role in financing trade for their home-office customers. They also participate in U.S. money-market activities as a part of their portfolio management activities. For example, Canadian agencies in New York hold three basic types of credit balances: from the Canadian government, their parent bank, and their corporate customers. Since they are not subject to the U.S. fractional reserve requirements and regulation Q, they are able to offer attractive interest rates on loans to U.S. customers, particularly straight loans to brokers and dealers. Furthermore, the Canadian agencies are more adept at handling the Canadian side of transactions for U.S. customers than are U.S. banks.[10]

Table 2-8 shows the twenty-five largest agencies of foreign banks in the United States. The average asset size of these agencies is over $1 billion. Of the total of twenty-five agencies, fifteen are stationed in California and ten are in New York. The majority of the twenty-five agencies belong to Japan,

**Table 2-8**

**Twenty-Five Largest U.S. Agencies of Foreign Banks, June 30, 1980**

| Entity Name | Location of Bank | Total Assets of U.S. Office[a] | Country Origin |
|---|---|---|---|
| Bank of Tokyo Ltd. Agency | New York | $4,380 | Japan |
| Bank of Tokyo Ltd. Agency | California | 2,715 | Japan |
| Fuji Bank Ltd. Agency | New York | 2,549 | Japan |
| Fuji Bank Ltd. Agency | California | 1,827 | Japan |
| Bank of Montreal Agency | New York | 1,723 | Canada |
| Mitsubishi Bank Ltd. Agency | California | 1,567 | Japan |
| Tokai Bank Ltd. Agency | California | 1,449 | Japan |
| Ind. Bank of Japan Ltd. Agency | New York | 1,379 | Japan |
| Sanwa Bank Ltd. Agency | California | 1,227 | Japan |
| Dai-Ichi Kangyo Agency | California | 1,146 | Japan |
| Indus. Bank of Japan Agency | California | 1,108 | Japan |
| Toronto Dominion Agency | New York | 1,096 | Canada |
| Canada Impl. Bank of Comm. Agency | New York | 1,093 | Canada |
| Sumitomo Bank Ltd. Agency | California | 877 | Japan |
| Bank of Montreal Agency | California | 875 | Canada |
| Bank of Nova Scotia Agency | New York | 824 | Canada |
| Royal Bank of Canada Agency | New York | 785 | Canada |
| Taiyo Kobe Bank Ltd Agency | California | 681 | Japan |
| Banco Do Brazil Agency | California | 679 | Brazil |
| Banca Comm Italiana Agency | California | 671 | Italy |
| Banco Do Brazil Agency | California | 655 | Brazil |
| Bancomer Sa | New York | 595 | Mexico |
| Bank of Tokyo Ltd. Agency | California | 588 | Japan |
| Daiwa Bank Ltd. Agency | New York | 537 | Japan |
| Mitsui Bank Ltd. Agency | California | 507 | Japan |

Source: Federal Reserve Board, Washington, D.C., December 30, 1980.
[a]Millions of dollars.

with fifteen. The Bank of Tokyo agency alone had total assets of $4.4 billion in 1980. Among the twenty-five agencies, Canada had six, and the remaining belong to Brazil, Italy, or Mexico.

According to our interviews, the Japanese banks chose to open agencies in both California and New York to accommodate the financing needs of large Japanese trading companies. These needs are unique because the companies are an integrated conglomerate, which handles not only international trade but also manufacturing, wholesaling, and retail business. In view of the extensive borrowing requirements of the trading companies, the Japanese agencies are able to make larger loans, unrestricted by the 10 percent of capital rule that applies to foreign-bank branches and subsidiary banks. Because of the special trade and investment relationship between the United States and Canada, Canadian bank agencies have been somewhat unique in managing their dollar holdings. Customarily Canadian agencies have held trade balances as well as dollar proceeds from securities issued by the Canadian government and corporations. Canadian agencies have been extremely active in foreign-exchange markets and take much greater risks than do the U.S. commercial banks. Furthermore they are not subject to the U.S. reserve requirement and regulation Q. Also, Canadian bank agencies have been successful in placing dollar loans in the Eurodollar market at attractive interest rates.

Overall foreign-bank agencies operate with low overhead cost because they do not require extensive office facilities with expensive computer facilities and staff personnel. Another cost advantage of the agency is the absence of FDIC assessments because agencies do not hold regular deposits.[11] Also, the regulatory bank examination of agencies is somewhat less cumbersome and costly.

Generally U.S. domestic banks have not resented the presence of foreign-bank agencies primarily because they are not direct competitors in deposit and loan markets. Furthermore the agencies do maintain working and correspondent balances with U.S. domestic banks. Foreign-bank branches, on the other hand, often do compete with U.S. domestic banks.

*Branches*

A definite advantage of foreign-bank branches over agencies can be found in the former's full banking privileges. Branches, however, are subject to a number of restrictions similar to those that apply to U.S. domestic banks. The maximum loan a branch can make to any one customer is subject to regulatory limits based on the parent bank's capital and surplus. Although foreign-bank branches are restricted by the 10 percent rule, the average loan size of foreign-bank branches is much greater than the average U.S. bank loan because the average asset size of U.S. banks is extremely small (about $50 million) in comparison to the foreign bank's parent company.[12]

The International Banking Act of 1978 made it possible for branches, like agencies, to obtain national charters from the comptroller of the currency. Foreign-bank branches were allowed in New York State in 1961 and in Illinois in 1973, but until recently, foreign branches were not eligible for FDIC insurance in California, which was a part of the requirement to establish branches in that state.

Most foreign banks have indicated that they prefer to establish branches rather than subsidiaries. The main reason is that the parent bank can control the operations of the branch without setting up a separate board of directors. In the case of subsidiary banks, they are required to form a separate board consisting of a majority of U.S. citizens. Sometimes it is difficult to find suitable local board members who fit into the overall objectives of the parent bank. Furthermore, the branch requires less capitalization because the capital calculation includes the parent capital. According to recent interviews, because foreign-bank branches still specialize in wholesale banking like their agency brethren, they also do not have to rent, equip, staff, and maintain a modern banking office as do retail banks.

On the other hand, foreign-bank branches are subject to more-stringent state legislation than are subsidiary banks. For instance, in New York where the bulk of foreign-bank branches are located, foreign branches must maintain extra assets equivalent to 108 percent of liabilities and maintain a guarantee deposit composed of cash and government securities equivalent to 5 percent of liabilities with a New York bank.

All of the twenty-five largest branches of foreign banks are located in New York (table 2-9). All of them have assets of $1 billion or more, far greater than the average asset size of U.S. commercial banks. Such differences in average asset size between foreign-bank branches and U.S. banks are directly related to the fact that foreign banks generally have nationwide branch-banking systems in their home countries, whereas the United States has a unit-banking system with about 14,000 individual banks. For instance, the Swiss Bank Corporation branch in New York has total assets of $4.8 billion, which makes it the largest branch in the United States. The second and third largest branches belong to Japanese banks: Dai-Ichi Kangyo with $3 billion and Mitsubishi Bank with $2.8 billion, respectively. The ownership of the largest twenty-five branches is split between the following countries: Japan, nine, Switzerland, three, Germany, three, France, three, United Kingdom, three, Italy, three, and Netherlands, one. The major activities of the foreign branches are trade financing, the investment of dollar resources, foreign-exchange dealings, and transfer of funds abroad. Although they have depended heavily on funding sources from their parent and home-country corporate customers in the past, now because of the high interest rates and the tight money situation in the United States, foreign branches participate in the U.S. money market to raise funds by issuing certificates of deposit and bankers' acceptances. Most of the branches are heavily involved in international financing and wholesale banking and generally have not competed with U.S. domestic banks for retail business to any large extent. On the other hand, foreign subsidiary banks have promoted and solicited domestic retail deposits and compete directly with U.S. domestic banks.

## Subsidiary

Foreign banks generally open a new (de novo) bank or acquire an existing bank with anticipation that they will be able to attract a significant volume of retail business, both deposits and loans. Most subsidiary banks solicit

**Table 2-9**
**Twenty-Five Largest U.S. Branches of Foreign Banks, June 30, 1980**

| Entity Name | Location of Bank | Total Assets of U.S. Office[a] | Country of Origin |
|---|---|---|---|
| Swiss Bank Corporation | New York | 4,821 | Switzerland |
| Dai-Ichi Kangyo Bank Ltd. | New York | 3,004 | Japan |
| Mitsubishi Bank Ltd. | New York | 2,840 | Japan |
| Crédit Lyonnais | New York | 2,590 | France |
| Union Bank of Switzerland | New York | 2,465 | Switzerland |
| National Westminster Bank | New York | 2,162 | United Kingdom |
| Sanwa Bank Ltd. | New York | 2,028 | Japan |
| Barclays Bank International | New York | 1,975 | United Kingdom |
| Sumitomo Bank Ltd. | New York | 1,966 | Japan |
| Algemene Bank Nederland | New York | 1,952 | Netherlands |
| Tokai Bank Limited | New York | 1,859 | Japan |
| Banco Di Roma | New York | 1,705 | Italy |
| Commerzbank Akt. | New York | 1,527 | Germany |
| Credito Italiano | New York | 1,514 | Italy |
| Mitsui Bank Ltd. | New York | 1,450 | Japan |
| Société Générale | New York | 1,380 | France |
| Taiyo Kobe Bank Ltd. | New York | 1,361 | Japan |
| Lloyds Bank International Ltd. | New York | 1,335 | United Kingdom |
| Mitsui Trust and Banking Co. Ltd. | New York | 1,310 | Japan |
| Crédit Industriel et Commerciel | New York | 1,301 | France |
| Long-Term Credit Bank of Japan | New York | 1,222 | Japan |
| Swiss Credit Bank | New York | 1,185 | Switzerland |
| Deutsche Bank AG | New York | 1,146 | Germany |
| Westdeutsche Landesbank | New York | 1,116 | Germany |
| Banca Commerciale Italiana | New York | 1,045 | Italy |

Source: Federal Reserve Board, Washington, D.C., December 30, 1980.
[a]Millions of dollars.

the bulk of their deposits domestically and make loans to local businesses and individuals. Until 1978, when California did not allow foreign-bank branches because of FDIC restrictions, the only alternative available for Japanese banks was to establish subsidiaries, which were most successful in attracting deposits through ethnic appeal. Until that time, it was also true in New York that Canadian banks could not establish branches there because of the reciprocity agreement. Therefore, Canadian subsidiary banks were established mainly to complement the activities of agencies.

A subsidiary bank is legally separate from the parent bank and can be either federally or state chartered. The subsidiary bank has a full range of banking powers and is subject to the same restrictions as U.S. domestic banks. The degree of control by the parent bank over the subsidiary depends on the degree of ownership. The maximum loan a subsidiary bank may make to any one customer is based on the subsidiary bank's own capital, separate from the parent bank.

Subsidiary banks are choice organizational forms for developing middle American and retail banking markets; foreign branches and agencies are better suited for trade financing and multinational corporate lending. Foreign banks consider the ownership of a U.S. subsidiary bank a good investment. They can obtain technically advanced banking services and diversify their equity holdings in the politically and economically safe U.S. economy.[13] In some instances, subsidiaries serve the needs of a particular ethnic group associated with the home country of the parent bank.[14]

The increase of foreign-bank subsidiaries in the United States has been a recent phenomenon. More than half of the existing 116 foreign-bank subsidiaries, both de novo and acquired banks, were established in the late 1970s. The major owners of the subsidiary banks came from major industrialized countries. Public attention to foreign ownership of U.S. banks arose in 1972-1973 when two large U.S. banks—Franklin National Bank and the Bank of California—were purchased by foreign interests. The public alarm at foreign-bank ownership in the U.S. was intensified in 1978 when three major foreign acquisition proposals were made for Marine Midland Bank, National Bank of North America, and Union Bank. All three of these banks were among the top fifty largest banks in the United States. Although the U.S. Congress was startled by the increasing number of foreign banks in the United States, it should be remembered that total assets of foreign-bank subsidiaries are still less than 5 percent of total commercial banking assets in the United States.[15]

Table 2-10 list the twenty-five largest subsidiaries owned by foreign banks in the United States.[16] All twenty-five rank within the top three hundred U.S. banks. For instance, Marine Midland Bank, with total assets of $11 billion, was the twelfth largest bank in the United States in 1980. Of the twenty-five largest subsidiary banks, twenty were located in New York and California, where laws did not favor the establishment of branches until 1978. Following the general pattern, a majority of these twenty-five subsidiary banks are owned by banks based in major industrialized countries: the United Kingdom, Japan, France, Spain, and the Netherlands.

*Investment Company*

New York is the only state that allows the establishment of investment companies that handle both commercial and investment banking business. However, the International Banking Act of 1978 seriously hampered the creation of investment companies by requiring foreign banks entering the United States to choose between investment banking and commercial banking.[17] The banking functions of the investment company are limited to short- and medium-term loans, the issuance of acceptances, remittance of

**Table 2-10**
**Twenty-Five Largest Foreign Subsidiary Banks in the United States, June 30, 1980**

| Type[a] | Entity Name | Location of Bank | Total Assets of U.S. Office[b] | Country of Origin |
|---|---|---|---|---|
| ACQ | Marine Midland Bank N.A. | New York | 10,961 | Hong Kong |
| ACQ | Union Bank | California | 5,789 | United Kingdom |
| ACQ | National Bank of North America | New York | 4,072 | United Kingdom |
| De novo | Republic National Bank of New York | New York | 3,946 | Brazil |
| De novo | European-American Bank and Trust | New York | 3,913 | Other Western Europe |
| De novo | California First Bank | California | 3,231 | Japan |
| ACQ | Bank of California N.A. | California | 3,220 | France |
| De novo | Bank of Tokyo Trust Co. | New York | 2,590 | Japan |
| ACQ | Lloyds Bank California | California | 2,552 | United Kingdom |
| ACQ | Bank of Virginia | Virginia | 1,990 | Spain |
| De novo | Sumitomo Bank of California | California | 1,723 | Japan |
| ACQ | La Salle National Bank | Illinois | 1,124 | Netherlands |
| ACQ | Bank of the Commonwealth | Michigan | 1,054 | Saudi Arabia |
| De novo | Bank Leumi Trust Co. of New York | New York | 964 | Israel |
| De novo | Henry Schroder Bank and Trust Co. | New York | 879 | United Kingdom |
| ACQ | First American Bank of Virginia | Virginia | 819 | More than one country |
| ACQ | Bank of the West | California | 749 | France |
| De novo | Barclays Bank of California | California | 710 | United Kingdom |
| De novo | Golden State Sanwa Bank | California | 706 | Japan |
| De novo | Fuji Bank and Trust Company | New York | 667 | Japan |
| De novo | California Canadian Bank | California | 666 | Canada |
| ACQ | First American Bank N.A. | Washington, D.C. | 642 | More than one country |
| De novo | Barclays Bank of New York | New York | 540 | United Kingdom |
| De novo | Industrial Bank of Japan Trust Co. | New York | 522 | Japan |
| De novo | Daiwa Bank Trust Co. | New York | 521 | Japan |

Source: Federal Reserve Board, Washington, D.C., December 30, 1980.
[a]ACQ = acquired bank; de novo = newly established bank.
[b]Millions of dollars.

funds, foreign-exchange transactions, and related activities. They may not accept deposits but may hold credit balances.

Some of the large investment companies are Belgian-American Banking Corporation, J. Henry Schroeder Banking Corporation, French American Banking Corporation, and the American Swiss Credit Company. Basically these companies finance high-risk trade and participate in venture-capital business, especially in Latin America. The high-risk nature of their operations results in a client list of numerous small firms without an established reputation. Furthermore, they promote importing and exporting, offering financial and marketing advice to their customers. They also maintain expertise in particular areas of the world where most domestic and foreign banks are unwilling to do business.

**Notes**

1. S. Khoury, *Dynamics of International Banking* (New York: Praeger Publishers, 1980), pp. 86-87.

2. J.R. Woolridge and K.D. Wiegel, "Foreign Banking Growth in the United States," *Bankers Magazine* (January-February 1981):30-38.

3. Ronan L. Gaynor, "Trends in U.S. Regulation of Foreign Banks," *Banker* (February 1981):99-104.

4. Office of Controller General of the U.S., Controller General of the United States, *Considerable Increase in Foreign Banking in the United States since 1972* (Washington, D.C., August 1, 1979), pp. 5-17.

5. U.S. Department of the Treasury, *Report to Congress on Foreign Government Treatment of U.S. Commercial Banking Organizations* (Washington, D.C., 1979), pp. 5-31.

6. Steven Weiss, "National Policies on Foreign Acquisitions of Banks," *Bankers Magazine* (January-February 1981):25-27.

7. A. Angelini, M. Eng, and F. Lees,*International Lending Risks and the Eurodollars* (New York: John Wiley, 1979), pp. 20-23.

8. Gaynor, "Trends in U.S. Regulation," pp. 99-104.

9. Z. Zwick, *Foreign Banking in the U.S.,* Joint Economic Committee of the U.S. Congress, 1966, pp. 2-4.

10. Ibid., pp. 14-15.

11. Gerald H. Anderson, "Current Developments in the Regulation of International Banking," *Economic Review*, Federal Reserve Bank of Cleveland (January 1980):1-15.

12. "Large Canadian Banks Rile Many U.S. Rivals," *Wall Street Journal*, July 10, 1981.

13. Judith Walter, "Foreign Acquisitions of U.S. Banks," Staff Papers, U.S. Controller of the Currency (Washington, D.C., June 1980), pp. 3-14.

14. "Recent Growth in Activities of U.S. Offices of Foreign Banks," *Federal Reserve Bulletin* (October 1976):815-823.

15. Walter, "Foreign Acquisitions," pp. 1-5.

16. The list of foreign ownership includes a single institution or person that owns 10 percent or more of registered securities of the bank. C.W. Longbrake, M. Quinn, and J. Walter, "Foreign Acquisitions of U.S. Banks: Facts and Patterns," Staff Papers, U.S. Controller of the Currency (June 1980), pp. 6-7.

17. Khoury, *Dynamics of International Banking*, p. 110.

# 3

# U.S. Legislative Environment for International Banking Activities

The legal environment in which major banking competitors offer international banking services within the domestic United States appears as a complex and rapidly changing structure. While essentially unchanged for nearly half a century, U.S. banking law has begun a metamorphosis that is certain to have lasting effects on the competitive structure of the international banking industry in the United States. For banking in general, the 1980s will be witness to substantial competitive and regulatory changes, leading to a nationwide expansion and more-aggressive marketing of all financial product offerings. This challenge to the U.S. financial structure will significantly affect banking strategy; all facets of the banking industry are likely to be affected. It is especially significant to note that a number of factors—increasing technological innovation, worldwide politicoeconomic and monetary uncertainties, and a spreading internationalization of the marketplace—will most certainly affect the competitive environment for the international financial products offered within the United States by both domestic and foreign banks.

To understand fully the competitive milieu in which U.S. and foreign banks offer international banking services requires an awareness of both the present U.S. legal structure as it affects the banking industry and a historical review of banking legislation and a sensitivity toward the future direction that such regulations may take.

## Overview of the Legal Environment

Prior to 1978, foreign-bank entry to the U.S. market was controlled exclusively by state banking law. Foreign banks came under federal law only if they became members of the federal reserve system, were nationally chartered, or controlled a subsidiary bank, in which case the Bank Holding Company Act applied.[1] Without federal regulation, supervision, or examination and with inconsistent state regulation, foreign banks seemed to enjoy several competitive advantages.[2]

First, the absence of federal reserve requirements and, in the case of branches, FDIC insurance premium assessments, and lower state-controlled capital requirements provided the foreign competitors with a cost advantage. Second, foreign banks, with the exception of foreign-owned subsidiaries,

47

were subject neither to the McFadden nor the Bank Holding Company acts.[3] Thus, by state invitation they could cross state boundaries at will, a market advantage substantially denied to U.S. banks. Finally, foreign banks seemed to possess considerable advantage in the financial market-place in their ability to hold equity in U.S. securities firms and to pursue nonbanking activities forbidden to domestic banks by the Glass-Steagall provisions of the 1933 Banking Act and the 1970 amendments to the Bank Holding Company Act.[4]

Without question, the primary weakness in this regulatory environment centered around the absence of federal control. A national policy of equitable treatment for all banks was impossible without the ability of either the Federal Reserve Board, the comptroller of the currency, or the FDIC to control the operations of foreign banks. Even though states could regulate and supervise the activities of a foreign banking office within their jurisdiction, coordination and consistency of supervision and examination of foreign multistate banking organizations were still unattainable.

Early attempts to facilitate the operations of U.S. banks in the international trading arena were made at both the federal and state levels. Beginning with the passage of the Federal Reserve Act of 1913, the authority of U.S. banks to conduct international bank business was greatly expanded.[5] Amending legislation authorizing Agreement Corporations in 1916 and Edge Act legislation, initially passed in 1919 and further revised in 1957 and 1963, enabled domestic U.S. banks to cross state lines with subsidiaries to engage in an array of international banking and financing activities.[6] Furthermore, the 1970 amended version of the Bank Holding Company Act sought to allow U.S. banks to move across state boundaries within the operational areas considered reasonable and related to normal bank activities. Ultimately state regulatory authorities tried to restrict foreign ownership of banking institutions, limiting foreign access to state credit markets and, thus, they hoped, improving the market position of U.S.-owned banks. However, not until 1978 and the passage of the International Banking Act did it appear that the issue of competitive advantage to foreign banks was directly confronted.[7]

Seemingly a legislative genesis aimed at international banking activities was created with the International Banking Act (IBA). It was the most-comprehensive treatment of foreign-bank competition in the United States ever attempted. Its primary purpose was to establish a policy of equitable national treatment for all banks in the United States, both foreign and domestically owned. It brought state-licensed institutions controlled by foreign banks under the residual authority of the Federal Reserve Board and allowed federal charter of foreign banking operations. Equity in competition was facilitated by a series of dual-sided regulations. Foreign banks could have access to the services of the central bank and establish Edge Act corporations; however, foreign branching was severely limited, relegating such branch operations to basically Edge Act status. Further, foreign banks could no longer escape the Federal Reserve Board's capital and reserve requirements, the FDIC's deposit insurance regulations, and the basic restrictions of the Bank Holding Company Act.

The IBA of 1978 was not flawless, nor was it the last legislative word on the subject of international banking services. Branch-banking restrictions and numerous nonbanking activities of foreign banks were, in fact, excluded by a grandfather clause from the act's provisions if permission for operations was granted or actual operations were begun before the law took effect. In addition, the issue of Eurocurrency markets was not directly addressed.

This latter issue was left to the provisions of the Depository Institutions Deregulation and Monetary Control Act of 1980. Under Title I of this legislation, specifically referred to as the Monetary Control Act, the Federal Reserve Board was empowered to impose reserve requirements on Eurodollar holdings of foreign branches in the United States and U.S. branches abroad.[8] Prior to enactment, it was contended that foreign parent banks with operations in the United States and U.S. bank branches overseas possessed a cost of funding advantage over U.S. domestic banks due to the absence of these reserve requirements. However, it was soon realized that enforcement of Eurodollar reserves for U.S. bank branches overseas would make them less competitive in world financial markets and for foreign Eurobanking offices would be impossible or, at best, impractical in the face of national resistance to encroachments upon home-country sovereignty.[9] As a consequence, efforts began either to eliminate or at least lower the proposed reserve requirements on Eurodollar holdings of all banks operating in the United States. Nonetheless, it was not until the board of governors of the federal reserve authorized the establishment of international banking facilities (IBFs) on December 3, 1981, that these Eurodollar reserve requirements were effectively removed.[10] Thus, domestic U.S. banks along with foreign-controlled banking operations in the United States could now realistically deal in Eurodollar markets at home. Even though these operations were limited to foreign-related assets and liabilities, were subject to federal taxation, and were required to book deposits for a minimum of two days, they still possessed a considerable competitive advantage. Such cost advantages as state and local exemption from taxation, lack of reserve requirements and deposit interest-rate ceilings, general freedom from U.S. investment regulations, along with less political risk and overall transaction time convenience led to an even more equitable competitive atmosphere for U.S. banks offering international banking services.

Moreover, in the 1980s, states have once again entered into the fray, at least those significantly involved in international business. In general, state regulatory environments have been amended to correspond to the provisions of the IBA and Federal Reserve Board rules for IBFs. However, although Illinois, New York, Florida, California, and Missouri have encouraged foreign-bank operation, they have zealously guarded their right to require foreign banks to adhere to state banking law. States have yearned for the additional economic activity that would be generated by foreign banks, especially added investment, but at the same time they have mirrored the concerns of their home-state banking industry regarding the necessity for a "level playing-field" for all competitors. Pursuant to this issue of competitive equity and reciprocity, in 1981 the Conference of State Bank Supervisors brought suit against the comptroller of the currency, challenging his authority under the IBA to charter and supervise foreign-bank offices exclusively under his own regulations. The states asserted that the comptroller could approve foreign-bank offices only with regard to rules imposed by states on foreign banks with state charters. Although the decision is subject to appeal, a federal district court ruled in favor of the comptroller, contending that only if a state refused to charter all foreign banks could it deny entry to a federally chartered foreign-bank office. The court added that to find in favor of the states would effectively deny the federal option now allowed.[11]

This is where the regulatory environment now stands with respect to the international banking industry in the United States. Its importance to the understanding of the competitive structure of the industry is immutable. However, the full weight of this legal issue may not be fully understood without noting some of the intricacies of specific pieces of legislation that have brought the industry to its present state.

**Legislative Intricacies**

*Federal Reserve Act (Public Law No. 43, 63rd Congress,*
*Approved December 23, 1913)*

The Federal Reserve Act of 1913 is generally credited with strengthening the national banking system through creation of an autonomous central bank consisting of twelve geographical districts, each with its own federal reserve bank, and a coordinating board of governors in Washington, D.C. Section 25 of the act addressed the issue of U.S. national banking involvement in international transactions. Although state-chartered banks and private unincorporated banks were free to engage in international banking, U.S. national banks were not.[12] National banks were not permitted to own foreign banks and prior to enactment of this legislation had access to foreign markets only through foreign correspondent banks. Thus, the first real impetus to spur national banking involvement in international financial transactions comes from this section, which reads, in part:

> Any national banking association possessing a capital and surplus of $1,000,000 or more may file application with the Federal Reserve Board, upon such conditions and under such regulations as may be prescribed by the said board, for the purposes of securing authority to establish branches in foreign countries or dependencies of the United States for the *furtherance of the foreign commerce of the United States*, and to act, if required to do so, as fiscal agents of the United States. . . . the Federal Reserve Board shall have the power to approve or reject such application if, in its judgment, the amount of capital proposed to be set aside for the conduct of foreign business is inadequate, or if for other reasons the granting of such application is deemed inexpedient.

> Every national banking association which shall receive authority to establish foreign branches shall be required at all times to furnish information concerning the condition of such branches to the Comptroller of the Currency upon demand, and the Federal Reserve Board may order special examinations of the said branches at such time or times as it may deem best. Every such national banking association shall conduct the accounts of each foreign branch independently of the accounts of other foreign branches.[13]

It is clear that national banks, those that were federally chartered, could now establish foreign branches. They needed only to demonstrate at least $1 million in capital and surplus and to receive approval of the newly created Federal Reserve Board with regard to branch capitalization. National banks were also required to segregate the accounts of foreign branches from each other and to submit to review by both the Federal Reserve and the comptroller of the currency. An integral facet of this enabling legislation was the authorization of bankers' acceptances, empowering national banks to accept bills of exchange arising from international transactions.

*Amendment to the Federal Reserve Act:*
*Agreement Corporations (Public Law No. 270,*
*64th Congress, Approved September 7, 1916)*

After the passage of the Federal Reserve Act of 1913, there was neither the significant increase in volume of bankers' acceptances that had been expected nor was there a rush to take advantage of the new authority to establish national bank branches abroad. In fact, from 1913 to 1916 only one national bank expanded overseas.[14] To spur further expansion in the area of international finance, Congress found it necessary to amend the Federal Reserve Act, creating what has come to be known as agreement corporations. National banks with capital and surplus of at least $1 million could, individually or together with other banks, invest up to 10 percent of their capital and surplus in state-chartered corporations for the purpose of conducting international banking business. Such authority required that the state-chartered institution enter into an agreement with the Federal Reserve Board to observe any restrictions on the type and manner of activities that might be imposed. Thus, section 25 of the Federal Reserve Act was amended to read, in part:

> Any national banking association possessing a capital and surplus of $1,000,000 or more may file application with the Federal Reserve Board for permission to exercise, upon such conditions and under such regulations as may be prescribed by the said board, either or both of the following powers:

> First. To establish branches in foreign countries or dependencies of insular possessions of the United States for the furtherance of the foreign commerce of the United States, and to act if required to do so as fiscal agents of the United States.

> Second. To invest an amount not exceeding in the aggregate ten per centum of its paid-in capital stock and surplus in the stock of one or more banks or corporations chartered or incorporated under the laws of the United States or of any state thereof, and principally engaged in international or foreign banking, or banking in a dependency or insular possession of the United States either directly or through the agency ownership, or control of local institutions in foreign countries, or in such dependencies or insular possessions.

> . . . The Federal Reserve Board shall have the power to approve or reject such application in whole or in part if for any reason the granting of such application is deemed inexpedient, and shall also have the power . . . to increase or decrease the number of places where such banking operations may be carried on.

> Every national banking association operating foreign branches shall be required to furnish information concerning the condition of such branches to the Comptroller of the Currency upon demand, and every member bank investing in the capital stock of banks or corporations . . . shall be required to furnish information concerning the condition of such banks or corporations to the Federal Reserve Board upon demand, and the Federal Reserve Board may order special examinations of the said branches, banks, or corporations at such time or times as it may deem best.

> Before any national bank shall be permitted to purchase stock in any such corporation the *said corporation shall enter into an agreement or undertaking, with the Federal Reserve Board* to restrict its operations or conduct its business in such a manner or under such limitations and restrictions as the said board may prescribe. . . . If at any time the Federal Reserve Board shall ascertain that the regulations . . . are not being complied with . . . such national banks may be required to dispose of stock holdings in the said corporation upon reasonable notice.

> Every such national banking association shall conduct the accounts of each foreign branch independently of the accounts of other foreign branches established by it. . . .

Any director or other officer, agent, or employee of any member bank may, with approval of the Federal Reserve Board, be a director or other officer, agent, or employee of any such bank or corporation above mentioned in the capital stock of which such member bank shall have invested.[15]

Now, national banks could not only branch overseas but could conduct international banking business from a domestic or foreign base under much more liberal terms of state charters. Despite the fact that no capitalization minimums were required and there were no restrictions on the nationalities of the owners or directors of the agreement corporations, only three such corporations were chartered over the next two years.[16] Eventually the functions of this corporate entity would be integrated into yet another attempt by the U.S. Congress to expand U.S. banking involvement in international transactions.

*Amendment to the Federal Reserve Act:*
*Edge Act Corporations (Public Law No. 106,*
*66th Congress, Approved December 24, 1919)*

Congress again felt that a further effort was needed to increase the international activities of U.S. banks, for only three agreement corporations were chartered from 1916 to 1919. Thus, the Federal Reserve Act of 1913 was again amended, in 1919, to allow the Federal Reserve Board to charter corporations to engage in international banking and financing operations. The amendment was generally referred to as the Edge Act, after its sponsor, Senator Walter Edge of New Jersey, and those corporations chartered under the act became known as Edge Act corporations.

Under section 25(a) of this legislation, it was provided that, subject to approval and authorization of the Federal Reserve Board, banking corporations were:

to be organized for the purpose of engaging in international or foreign banking or other international or foreign financial operations, or in banking or other financial operations in a dependency or insular possession of the United States, either directly or through the agency, ownership, or control of local institutions in foreign countries, or in such dependencies or insular possessions. . . .

. . . to elect or appoint directors, all of whom shall be citizens of the United States. . . .

[to have] a majority of the shares of the capital stock of any such corporation . . . at all times . . . held and owned by citizens of the United States, by corporations the controlling interest in which is owned by citizens of the United States, chartered under the laws of the United States or of a state . . . , or by firms or companies, the controlling interest in which is owned by citizens of the United States. . . .

[empowered to] . . . purchase, sell, discount, and negotiate . . . notes, drafts, checks, bills of exchange, acceptances, . . . cable transfers, and other evidences of indebtedness; to purchase and sell . . . securities, including the obligations of the United States or of any state thereof but not including shares of stock in any corporation except as herein provided; to accept bills or drafts drawn upon it . . . to issue letters of credit; to purchase and sell coin, bullion, and exchange; to borrow and to lend money; to issue debentures, bonds, and promissory notes . . . , but in no event having liabilities outstanding . . . exceeding ten times its capital stock and surplus; to receive deposits outside of the United States and to receive only such deposits within the United States as may be incidental to or for the purpose of carrying out transactions in foreign countries or dependencies or insular possessions of the United States. . . . Whenever a corporation . . . receives deposits in the United States . . . it shall carry reserves in no event less than 10 per centum of its deposits.

[empowered to] . . . purchase and hold stock or other certificates of ownership in any other corporation organized under the provisions of this section, or under the laws of any foreign country or a colony or dependency thereof, or under the laws of any state, dependency, or insular possession of the United States but not engaged in the general business of buying or selling goods, wares, merchandise or commodities in the United States, and not transacting any business in the United States except such as in the judgement of the Federal Reserve Board may be incidental to its international or foreign business: Provided, however, that . . . no corporation organized hereunder shall invest in any one corporation an amount in excess of 10 per cent of its own capital and surplus, except in a corporation engaged in the business of banking, when 15 per centum of its capital and surplus may be so invested: Provided further, that no corporation organized hereunder shall purchase, own, or hold stock or certificates of ownership in any other corporation organized hereunder or under the laws of any state which is in substantial competition therewith, or which holds stock or certificates of ownership in corporations which are in substantial competition with the purchasing corporation. . . . [or] shall carry on any part of its business in the United States except such as . . . shall be incidental to its international or foreign business.

[to have] no corporation . . . organized under the provisions of this section with a capital stock of less than $2,000,000. . . . but the aggregate amount of stock held in all corporations engaged in business in this section and in Section 25 of the Federal Reserve Act as amended shall not exceed 10 per centum of the subscribing bank's capital and surplus.[17]

There were a number of important distinctions between allowances for Edge and agreement corporations. First, Edge corporations were federally chartered and thus not subject to state law as generally were agreement corporations. Second, although there were no nationality restrictions regarding stock ownership and corporate directors of agreement corporations, the majority of Edge shareholders and all Edge corporate directors had to be U.S. citizens. Third, Edge corporations were obliged to have a minimum capitalization of $2 million, as compared to agreement corporations, which required no minimums. Fourth, authority to invest in Edges was given by statute; equivalent authority for agreement corporations was subject to Federal Reserve Board approval. Fifth, Edge corporations could not only engage in international banking, as could Agreement corporations, but were specifically authorized to operate in long-term financing and could invest in nonbanking firms that carry on international or foreign business. Finally, Edge legislation was very explicit with regard to a 10 percent reserve requirement on all deposits and restrictions on issuance of bonds and debentures, whereas the 1916 amendment to the Federal Reserve Act omitted any reference to these issues.

Although section 25(a) of the Federal Reserve Act would not be further amended until passage of the 1978 IBA, regulation K, the operating regulation of the board of governors of the federal reserve system relating to foreign banking and financing corporations, was revised in 1957 and again in 1963. These revisions significantly affected the evolution of Edge operations.

The 1957 revision brought agreement corporations within the scope of regulation K.[18] Previously, the agreements between corporations and the Federal Reserve had entailed a magnitude of variability; however, now such signed agreements would be confirmed to, first, regulation K and second, state law. As a consequence, agreement corporations began to look very much like Edge banking corporations. In addition, the 1957 revision provided for two specific types of Edge Act corporations: banking and financial. Both types could buy and sell foreign exchange; receive checks, drafts, bills, acceptances, notes, bonds, and other securities for foreign collection; and buy and sell securities for customer accounts abroad. Banking corporations could also accept deposits by foreigners, create bankers' acceptances, and hold stock in banking or bank-related corporations, although they were prohibited from issuing bonds and debentures. In contrast, the financing corporations were barred from accepting deposits and holding equity in banking corporations but could invest in nonbanking corporations involved in international business and provide long-term financing in either debt or equity form. In 1963, however, a second revision of regulation K served to remove the designation of two separate types of Edge corporations.[19] Financial and banking corporations were allowed to merge all functions into one corporation. The strict distinction between deposits as the source of funds for banking corporations and debenture-type liabilities for financing corporations was eliminated, as were distinctions regarding the types of credit provided by banking and financing corporations. Still, certain distinctions aimed at banking and investment operations were maintained. An Edge corporation with aggregate demand deposits and acceptance liabilities exceeding its capital and surplus was considered to be involved in banking and thus severely restricted in securities underwriting and subject to a lending limit of 10 percent of its capital and surplus to any one borrower. Otherwise a corporation was considered an investment Edge and could lend up to 50 percent of its capital and surplus to a single borrower.

Regulation K was further revised in 1979, but this time as an attendant condition of a major revision in U.S. banking law: the IBA of 1978.[20] One major purpose of the IBA and accompanying revisions of regulation K was to permit the Edge corporation to compete effectively with various foreign-bank types in the United States and abroad in an increasingly worldwide competitive environment. Thus, beginning June 14, 1979, Edge corporations no longer were required to be separately incorporated in each state of operation. The new revision allows Edges to incorporate in one state and then establish branches across state lines. In this way, increased efficiency and lower costs of operation are obtained. Further, such consolidation permits capital merger of all offices, resulting in larger legal limits for single customers. The new regulations also make Edge deposits subject to regulation D, as is the case for member banks of the federal reserve system. This eliminates the previous 10 percent mininum reserve requirements. Moreover, required capital and surplus for Edges were reduced from the previous 10 percent maximum of aggregate liabilities to 7 percent of risk assets, thereby increasing permitted leverage. Domestic lending activities of Edge corporations were liberalized by permitting the financing of domestic production of goods and services for which export orders exist or which are identifiable as being export. Previously Edges could finance only shipment and storage of goods for export. Also, the requirement that the directors of Edge corporations be U.S. citizens is eliminated, and foreign banks are now allowed to own a majority equity interest in Edges. Finally, under the authority of the IBA, the board of governors of the federal reserve system is empowered to study and make further recommendations to Congress as to even broader powers for Edge corporations. Thus, consideration is now being given to Edge membership in the federal reserve system and to permitting these corporations to provide a full range of banking and depository services to any customer that has more than two-thirds of its purchases or sales in international commerce.

It is expected that this most recent revision to regulation K will lead to a more-equitable competitive field for all banking competitors offering international banking services in the United States. In fact, present industry observation does show that U.S. banks have been able to expand their international banking business on a national scale through Edge corporation branches and that smaller regional banks increasingly have been able to participate in this movement. Furthermore, discriminatory effects of the former regulatory environment, prohibiting foreign-bank branches and agencies from entering some states, have been removed by these new regulations. Thus, foreign banks can now make use of Edge corporations to further their international banking business.

*Acts and Amendments Affecting Foreign Banks in
the United States Since 1978*

Prior to 1978 and the passage of the IBA, foreign banks in the United States were generally beyond federal control and subject to neither the McFadden Act, the Glass-Steagall provisions of the Banking Act, nor the Bank Holding Company Act and its amendments. Thus, in retrospect, it becomes necessary to examine the regulatory constraints associated with this legislative group in order to comprehend the advantageous position previously held by foreign banks and the consequent treatment afforded these organizations after 1978.

**McFadden Act of 1927.** The historical issue of branch banking in the United States was initially addressed by the McFadden Act of 1927. Prior to that time, federally chartered banks had no power to branch. The purpose of McFadden was to give national banks the comparable power to branch that state banks enjoyed at that time, but the result was to bar national banks from branching across state lines. The conditions under which a national bank could retain, establish, or operate its branches are set down in sections 7, 8, and 9 of the legislation. They are, in part, the following:

> A national banking association may retain and operate such branch or branches as it may have in lawful operation at the date of the approval of this Act, and any national banking association which has continuously maintained and operated not more than one branch for a period of twenty-five years immediately preceding the approval of this Act may continue to maintain and operate such branch.

> If a state bank is hereafter converted into or consolidated with a national banking association, or if two or more national banking associations are consolidated, such . . . association may, with respect to any of such banks, retain and operate any of their branches which may have been in lawful operation by any bank at the date of approval of the Act.

> A national banking association may, after the date of the approval of this Act, establish and operate new branches within the limits of any city, town, or village of which the population by the last decennial census was less than twenty-five thousand. No more than one such branch may be thus established where the population . . . does not exceed fifty thousand; and not more than two such branches where the population does not exceed one hundred thousand. In any such municipal unit where the population exceeds one hundred thousand the determination of the number of branches shall be within the discretion of the Comptroller of the Currency.

> No branch of any national banking association shall be established or moved from one location to another without first obtaining the consent and approval of the Comptroller of the Currency. . . .

This section shall not be construed to amend or repeal Section 25 of the Federal Reserve Act, as amended, authorizing the establishment by national banking associations of branches in foreign countries, or dependencies, or insular possessions of the United States. . . .

Any such state bank which, at the date of approval of this Act, has established and is operating a branch or branches in conformity with the state law, may retain and operate the same while remaining or upon becoming a stockholder of such Federal Reserve bank; but no such state bank may retain or acquire stock in a Federal Reserve bank except upon relinquishment of any branch or branches established after the date of the approval of this Act beyond the limits of the city, town, or village in which the parent bank is situated.[21]

The result was to authorize national banks to establish full-service branches in their head-office municipalities within a state. This was later modified by section 23, paragraph (c), of the Banking Act of 1933, whereby national banks could branch outside of the head-office municipality if allowed by state law.

The whole issue of branch banking, both intrastate and interstate, is still volatile. As of July 1979 twelve states still prohibited any type of full-service intrastate branching, sixteen permitted limited branching (geographical limitations), and only twenty-two allowed unlimited branching within their boundaries.[22] This evolving situation has led to the growth of bank-holding companies and subsequent passage of appropriate legislation. In fact, regardless of the form the banking organization takes, at the time of this writing only the states of South Dakota and Delaware have enacted even limited legislation allowing out-of-state banks into their state regions.[23]

Concerning the question of foreign banks, it is clear that McFadden exempts the formation of foreign branches by U.S. national banks from its provisions, but it does not address the U.S. operations of bank branches of foreign parents. The latter banking organizations were left to state regulatory authority and did not really come under federal rules until 1978.

As a consequence of federal and state restrictions on branching, greater impetus was given to the formation of bank-holding companies in which one or more commercial banks were controlled by a corporate entity. Since this type of organization was beyond the bounds of the McFadden Act, it could operate virtually in a manner tantamount to branching. In 1933, however, the Banking Act was passed, and for the first time the issue of holding companies was addressed.

**Banking Act of 1933: Glass-Steagall Provisions.** The Banking Act of 1933 was a response to the bank failures and financial panic of the depression era. It circumscribed limits regarding a number of past banking practices deemed to be abusive and risky. Through the years, this legislation has also been called the Glass-Steagall Act. Technically, though, *Glass-Steagall* refers to four sections of the Banking Act, those dealing with securities; hence, the phrase *Glass-Steagall provisions.*

Primarily the Banking Act seeks to separate commercial and investment banking functions for national and state member banks and bank-holding companies. Under sections 16, 20, 21, and 32, the so-called Glass-Steagall provisions, such banks and affiliates were subject to the following:

> The business of dealing in investment securities by the national banking association shall be limited to purchasing and selling such securities without recourse, solely upon the order, and for the account of, customers, and in no case for its own account, and the association shall not underwrite any issue of securities: Provided, that the association may purchase for its own account investment securities under such limitations and restrictions as the Comptroller of the Currency may by regulation prescribe, but in no event shall the total amount of any issue of investment securities of any one obligor or maker purchased . . . and held by the association or its own account exceed at any time 10 per centum of the total amount of such issue outstanding, but of limitation shall not apply to any such issue the total amount of which does not exceed $100,000 and does not exceed 50 per centum of the capital and the association, nor (2) shall the total amount of the investment securities of any obligor or maker purchased . . . and held by the association for its own account exceed at any time 15 per centum of the amount of the capital stock of the association actually paid in and unimpaired and 25 per centum of its unimpaired surplus fund . . . investment securities shall mean marketable obligations evidencing indebtedness of any person, copartnership, association, or corporation in the form of bonds, notes and/or debentures. . . . Except as hereinafter provided or otherwise permitted by law, nothing herein contained shall authorize the purchase by the association of any shares of stock of any corporation. The limitations and restrictions herein contained as to dealing in, underwriting and purchasing for its own account, investment securities shall not apply to obligations of the United States, or general obligations of any state or of any political subdivision thereof, or obligations issued under authority of the Federal Farm Loan Act, . . . or issued by the Federal Home Loan Banks or the Homeowners' Loan Corporation: Provided, that . . . the association shall not invest in the capital stock of a corporation organized under the law of any state to conduct a safe-deposit business in an amount in excess of 15 per centum of the capital stock of the association actually paid in and unimpaired and 15 per centum of its unimpaired surplus.

> . . . no member bank shall be affiliated in any manner . . . hereof with any corporation, association, business trust, or other similar organization engaged principally in the issue, flotation, underwriting, public sale, or distribution at wholesale or retail or through syndicate participation of stocks, bonds, debentures, notes or other securities. . . .

> . . . it shall be unlawful—

> (1) For any person, firm, corporation, association, business trust, or other similar organization, engaged in the business of issuing, underwriting, selling, or distributing, at wholesale or retail, or through syn-

dicate participation, stocks, bonds, debentures, notes, or other securities, to engage at the same time to any extent whatever in the business of receiving deposits subject to check or to repayment upon presentation of a passbook, certificate of deposit, or other evidence of debt, or upon request of the depositor; or

(2) For any [of same] . . . , other than a financial institution or private banker subject to examination and regulation under State or Federal law, to engage . . . in the business of receiving deposits subject to check or to repayment upon presentation of a passbook certificate of deposit, or other evidence of debt, or upon request of the depositor, unless such person, firm, corporation, association, business trust, or other similar organization shall submit to periodic examination by the Comptroller of the Currency or by the Federal Reserve Bank of the district. . . .

. . . no officer or director of any member bank shall be an officer, director, or manager of any corporation, partnership, or unincorporated association engaged primarily in the business of purchasing, selling, or negotiating securities, and no member bank shall perform the functions of a correspondent bank on behalf of any such individual [or organization] . . . and no such individual [or organization] . . . shall perform the functions of a correspondent for any member bank or hold on deposit any funds on behalf of any member bank, unless . . . there is a permit . . . issued by the Federal Reserve Board; . . . if in its judgment it is not incompatible with the public interest, and to revoke any such permit whenever it finds . . . that the public interest required such revocation.[24]

Still in effect, Glass-Steagall has substantially affected the operations of the commercial banking industry in the United States. Moreover, the act addressed the issue of holding-company affiliates for the first time in U.S. legislative history. Banks and bank-holding companies, with minor exceptions, were required to limit their investments to securities that could be described as marketable debt instruments. They were prohibited from investing in riskier equity such as common stocks and revenue bonds. Thus, equity investment, inclusive of dealing for a bank organization's own account or underwriting such, was denied, and divestment of all affiliates involved in like operations was required.

At present, the comptroller of the currency has prescribed the following regulations and exceptions regarding investment and underwriting activities of national and state member banks:

Type I security: A bank may deal in, underwrite, and buy and sell for its own account, without limitation, securities issued by the U.S. Treasury, most federal agencies, and the general obligations of states and their political subdivisions.

Type II security: A bank may deal in, underwrite, and buy and sell for its own account, subject to a 10 percent limit of its capital and surplus to any one issuer, securities issued by such agencies as the International Bank for Reconstruction and Development, the Inter-American Development Bank, the Asian Development Bank, and the Tennessee Valley Authority, and those issued by any state or its political subdivisions for housing, university or dormitory purposes.

Type III security: A bank may buy and sell, subject to a 10 percent limit of its capital and surplus to any one issuer, but neither deal in nor underwrite for its own account such securities as corporate debt instruments, foreign corporate or government bonds, and assessment and revenue bonds of states and political subdivisions issued for purposes other than housing or university dormitories.[25]

Some notable exceptions to these guidelines concern the safe-deposit business, ownership of buildings housing banking operations, certain federal mortgage and loan associations, agricultural credit corporations, temporary possession of defaulted equity collateral, and limited investment in a foreign banking corporation. It is this last allowance, coupled with type III security limitations on foreign corporate bonds, that is of some competitive concern to the U.S. banking industry. While U.S. banks are premitted equity in foreign banks or corporations up to 10 percent of their capital and surplus, foreign banks, even though now subject to the Bank Holding Company Act under the provisions of the IBA, may hold substantially more equity in a foreign company that is principally engaged in business outside the United States.[26] As a consequence, foreign banking organizations, like U.S. nonbanking concerns, have been able to participate more fully in equity investment, whereas U.S. banks and bank-holding companies have not. The only exception has been through the operations of U.S. investment Edges, which do not possess the full strength of the parent bank's capitalization.

Although the 1933 Banking Act forced bank-holding companies to divest themselves of any equity securities business and to submit to examination by the Federal Reserve, which could deny it permission to vote its own shares in a member bank, it did little else to restrict holding-company expansion. Thus, bank-holding companies continued to grow by acquiring additional banks, regardless of the competitive effects on the market, and those holding companies, consisting of only state-chartered nonmember banks, remained beyond even the sparse limitations set up by the Federal Reserve.

**Bank Holding Company Act of 1956.** Although there were numerous attempts to regulate bank-holding companies further, it was not until 1956 and the passage of the Bank Holding Company Act that success was achieved.[27] The legislative purpose was to regulate the process by which a bank-holding company could expand and acquire additional banks and by which it could engage in nonbanking activities. Therefore, to define further a bank-holding company, to prevent undue concentration of banks, and to preserve and reaffirm the historical separation between banking and commerce, the act provides:

> "Bank Holding Company" means any company (1) which directly or indirectly own, controls, or holds with power to vote, *25 per centum or more of the voting shares of each of two or more banks or of a company* which is or becomes a bank holding by virture of this Act, or (2) which controls in any manner the election of a majority of the directors of each of two or more banks, or (3) for the benefit of those shareholders or members 25 per centum or more of the voting shares of each of two or more banks or a bank holding company is held by trustees. . . .

> It shall be unlawful except with the prior approval of the [Federal Reserve] Board (1) for any action to be taken which results in a company becoming a bank holding company . . . (2) for any bank holding company to acquire direct or indirect ownership or control of any voting shares of any bank if, after such acquisition, such company will directly or indirectly own or control more than 5 per centum of the voting shares of such banks; (3) for any bank holding company or subsidiary thereof, other than a bank, to acquire all or substantially all of the assets of a bank; or (4) for any bank holding company to merge or consolidate with any other bank holding company. . . .

> In determining whether or not to approve any acquisition or merger or consolidation . . . the [Federal Reserve] Board shall take into consideration the following factors: (1) the financial history and condition of the company or companies and the banks concerned; (2) their prospects; (3) the character of their management; (4) the convenience, needs, and welfare of the communities and the area concerned; (5) whether or not the effect . . . would be to expand the size or extent of the bank holding company system involved beyond limits consistent with adequate and sound banking, the public interest, and the preservation of competition in the field of banking.

> . . . no application shall be approved . . . which shall permit any bank holding company or any subsidiary thereof to acquire, directly or indirectly, any voting shares of interest in, or all or substantially all of the assets of any additional bank located outside of the State in which such bank holding company, maintains its principal office and place of business or in which it conducts its principal operations unless the acquisition of such shares or assets of a State bank by an out-of-state bank holding company is specifically authorized by the statute laws of the state in which such bank is located, by language to that effect and not merely by implication.

> Except as otherwise provided in this Act, no bank holding company shall—

> (1)  . . . acquire direct or indirect ownership or control of any voting shares of any company which is not a bank, or

(2)  . . . retain direct or indirect ownership or control of any voting shares of any company which is not a bank or a bank holding company or engage in any business other than that of banking or of managing or controlling banks or of furnishing services to or performing services for any bank of which it owns or controls 25 per centum or more of the voting shares.

[possess any] . . . certificate evidencing share of any bank holding company [bearing] . . . any statement purporting to represent shares of any other company except a bank or a bank holding company, nor shall the ownership, sale or transfer of shares of any bank holding company be conditioned in any manner, whatsoever upon the owernship, sale, or transfer of shares of any other company except a bank or a bank holding company.

The prohibitions . . . shall not apply—

(1)  to shares owned or acquired by a bank holding company in any company engaged solely in holding or operating properties used wholly or substantially by any bank with respect to which it is a bank holding company in its operations or acquired for such future use or engaged solely in conducting a safe deposit business, or solely in the business of furnishing services to or performing services for such holding company and banks with respect to which it is a bank holding company, or in liquidating assets acquired from such bank holding company and such banks;

(2)  to shares acquired by a bank holding company which is a bank, or by any banking subsidiary of a bank holding company, in satisfaction of a debt previously contracted in good faith, but such bank holding company or such subsidiaries shall dispose of such shares within a period of two years . . .

(3)  to shares acquired by a bank holding company from any of its subsidiaries which subsidiary has been requested to dispose of such shares by any Federal or State authority having statutory power to examine such subsidiary . . . within a period of two years . . .

(4)  to shares which are held or acquired by a bank holding company which is a bank or by any banking subsidiary of a bank holding company, in good faith in a fiduciary capacity, except where such shares are held for the benefit of the shareholders of such bank holding company or any of its subsidiaries, or to shares which are of the kinds and amounts eligible for investment by National banking associations . . . or to shares lawfully acquired and owned prior to the date of enactment of this Act . . .

(5)  to shares of any company which are held or acquired by a bank holding company which do not include more than 5 per centum of the outstanding voting securities of such company, and do not have a value greater than 5 per centum of the value of the total assets of the bank holding company, or to the ownership by a bank holding company of shares, securities, or obligations of an investment company which is not a bank holding company and which is not engaged in any business other than investing in securities, which securities do not include more than 5 per centum of the outstanding voting securities of any company and do not include any single asset having a value greater than 5 per centum of the value of the total assets of the bank holding company.    .

(6) to shares of any company all the activities of which are a financial fiduciary, or insurance nature and which the [Federal Reserve] Board . . . has determined to be so closely related to the business of banking or of managing or controlling banks as to be proper incident thereto . . .

(7) to any bank holding company which is a labor, agricultural, or horticultural organization and . . . exempt from taxation . . .

(8) to shares held or acquired by a bank holding company in any company which is organized under the laws of a foreign country and which is engaged principally in the banking business outside the United States.[28]

The attempt of the 1956 act to bring bank-holding companies in line with the restricted operations of state and federally chartered banks was successful only in part. It is quite clear that the operations of bank-holding companies were now subject to the Glass-Steagall provisions of the 1933 Banking Act and that Federal Reserve Board approval was now required before a bank-holding company could acquire more than 5 percent of the voting share of any bank or company. Moreover, it is evident that bank-holding companies were now restricted from moving across state lines unless specifically allowed by state statute. Nevertheless, there were still several areas in which breaches remained. First was the omission of one-bank-holding companies. Thus, bank-holding companies that controlled only a single bank could engage in activities generally not permissible to single banks or multibank holding companies. Second was the failure to give specific weights to the several factors used to determine the appropriateness of an acquisition of merger by a bank holding company. Whether the financial and managerial characteristics of the proposed partners, the needs and welfare of the defined community, or the degree of economic competition and concentration would be the primary determinant in any one decision was left in doubt.

**Douglas Amendment to BHCA of 1956.** In 1966, Congress amended the Bank Holding Company Act, filling at least part of the breach. Subsection c of section 3 of the 1956 Act was amended to read as follows:

The [Federal Reserve] Board shall not approve—
(1) any acquisition or merger or consolidation which would result in a monopoly, or which would be in furtherance of any combination or conspiracy to monopolize or to attempt to monopolize the business of banking in any part of the United States, or
(2) any other proposed acquisition or merger or consolidation . . . whose effect in any section of the country may be substantially to lessen competition, or to tend to create a monopoly, or which in any other manner would be in restraint of trade, unless it finds that the anti-competitive effects of the proposed transaction are clearly outweighed in the public interest by the probable effect of the transaction in meeting the convenience and needs of the community to be served.

In every case, the Board shall take into consideration the financial and managerial resources and future prospects of the company or companies and the banks concerned, and the convenience and needs of the community to be served.[29]

The emphasis here was on competitive factors. Clearly the Federal Reserve would not approve any acquisition, merger, or consolidation involving holding companies if it would substantially lessen competition, unless the anticompetition effects were overshadowed by the needs and convenience of the market served.

**Bank Holding Company Amendments of 1970.** The 1970 Amendments to the 1956 act finally resolved the issue of multi- versus one-bank holding companies. The key features of these amendments were as follows:

. . . "bank holding company" means any company which has control over any bank or over any company that is or becomes a bank holding company. . . .

. . . In the event of failure of the [Federal Reserve] Board to act on any application for approval under this section within the ninety-one-day period which begins on the date of submission to the Board of the complete record on that application, the application shall be deemed to have been granted. . . .

. . . a company covered in 1970 may also engage in those activities in which directly or through a subsidiary (i) it was lawfully engaged on June 30, 1968 . . . and (ii) it has been continuously engaged since June 30, 1968. . . .

[The prohibitions in this section shall not apply to] . . . any company the activities which the [Federal Reserve] Board . . . has determined . . . to be so closely related to banking or management or controlling banks as to be a proper incident thereto. In determining whether a particular activity is a proper incident to banking or managing or controlling banks the Board shall consider whether its performance by an affiliate of a holding company can reasonably be expected to produce benefits to the public, such as greater convenience, increased competition, or gains in efficiency, that outweigh possible adverse effects, such as undue concentration of resources, decreased or unfair competition, conflicts of interests, or unsound banking practices. . . .

. . . A bank shall not in any manner extend credit, lease or sell property of any kind, or furnish any service, or fix or vary the consideration for any of the foregoing, on the condition or requirement—

(1) that the customer shall obtain some additional credit, property, or service from such bank other than a loan, discount, deposit, or trust service;

(2) that the customer shall obtain some additional credit, property, or service from a bank holding company of such bank, or from any other subsidiary of such bank holding company;

(3) that the customer provide some additional credit, property, or service to such bank, other than those related to and usually provided in connection with a loan, discount, deposit, or trust service;

(4) that the customer provide some additional credit, property, or service to a bank holding company of such bank, or to any other subsidiary of such bank holding company; or

(5) that the customer shall not obtain some other credit, property, or service from a competitor of such bank, a bank holding company of such bank, or any subsidiary of such bank holding company, other than a condition or requirement that such bank shall reasonably impose in a credit transaction to assure the soundness of the credit.[30]

Thus, it is now the case that both multi-bank and one-bank holding companies are subject to the Bank Holding Company Act as amended. Further, the amended version specifically requires that the Federal Reserve act on all applications within ninety days of filing; otherwise the bank-holding company receives automatic approval. Also tie-in restrictions are now leveled at bank-holding companies. They are basically prohibited from requiring additional service lease or purchase as a condition of granting an initial such service request from a customer.

Finally, the Federal Reserve Board expressly reserves the right of determination as to those nonbanking activities that are "closely related to banking" and thus permissible to holding company operations (table 3-1). Through a grandfather clause, bank-holding companies, subject to Federal Reserve approval, can continue to engage in nonbank activities that would otherwise be prohibited, as long as those activities had been engaged in continuously since June 30, 1968.

It is apparent at this juncture that U.S. legislative actions had brought U.S. domestic banks and bank-holding companies to an even par with each other. However, foreign banks in the United States were still beyond the grasp of federal regulation, examination, and supervision, unless they controlled a U.S. subsidiary bank or became members of the federal reserve system. This issue was directly confronted by the International Banking Act of 1978.

*International Banking Act of 1978 (Public Law
No. 369, 95th Congress, Approved September 17, 1978)*

The growth in the number and size of foreign banking operations located in the United States during the 1970s was dramatic. Indeed, the U.S. banking industry expressed a great deal of concern regarding the significant competitive advantages believed to be accruing to foreign banking organizations during this period.

**Table 3-1**
**Summary of Nonbanking Activities Permitted and Prohibited to Bank-Holding Companies under Federal Reserve Board Interpretations of Section 4(c)(8) of the 1970 BHCA Amendments**

Activities permitted as closely related to banking:

Making loans for own account or account of others through dealing in bankers' acceptances, mortgage banking, finance-company operations, credit-card operations, and factoring

Acting as an industrial loan company or industrial bank, referred to as a Morris plan bank

Servicing loans for others

Conducting fiduciary activities (trust company operations)

Acting as investment or financial adviser to real-estate investment trusts and to investment companies under the Investment Company Act of 1940

Leasing personal and real property with full payout

Making equity and debt investments in corporations to promote community welfare

Providing bookkeeping or data-processing services

Operating insurance agencies or acting as an insurance broker, principally in connection with the extension of credit

Underwriting credit life, accident, and health insurance directly related to credit extensions by the bank holding company or one of its subsidiaries

Issuing and/or selling, at retail, money orders, travelers' checks, U.S. savings bonds, and other similar instruments

Trading and arbitraging gold and silver bullion

Operating limited courier services

Providing management-consulting services to nonaffiliated banks

Check verification activities

Acting as a futures commission merchant to execute futures contracts covering gold and silver bullion and coins

Underwriting certain federal, state, and municipal securities (types I, II, and II as according to the comptroller of the currency.

Activities prohibited as not closely related to banking:

Equity or insurance premium funding (combined sale of mutual funds and insurance)

Underwriting general life insurance not sold in connection with a credit transaction by a bank-holding company or one of its subsidiaries

Real-estate brokerage

Land development

Real-estate syndication

Management consulting

Property-management services

Underwriting mortgage-guarantee insurance

Providing computer output microfilm services without connection to any other permissable service

Operating a travel agency

Operating a savings and loan association

Sources: Gerald C. Fisher, "The Structure of the Commercial Banking System, 1960-1985," *Journal of Commercial Bank Lending* (September 1979):60; Regulation Y, "Bank Holding Companies," Board of Governors of the Federal Reserve System; and published interpretations of the Board of Governors of the Federal Reserve System.

Seemingly foreign banks had a great deal more latitude in their U.S. operations prior to 1978 than did their American counterparts. Only if they became members of the federal reserve system or controlled a subsidiary bank were foreign banks subject to the same competitive restrictions as U.S. banks. Otherwise, they benefited from the following advantages:

Cost advantage: Since most U.S. offices of foreign banks were not legally subject to the reserve requirements that the Federal Reserve imposes on its major competitor members, they had a significant cost advantage. Foreign banks also benefited from generally lower state-controlled capital requirements and, in the case of branches, the absence of insurance premium assessment on total deposits through FDIC insurance coverage.

Interstate branching: While the McFadden Act of 1927 and the Bank Holding Company Act of 1956, as amended, prevented full-service offices of U.S. banks from branching across state lines, no federal restrictions denied foreign banks the privilege of establishing agencies and branches in more than one state, as long as permitted by state law.

Nonbanking activities: U.S. commercial banks have generally been prevented from operating in investment banking. The Glass-Steagall provisions of the 1933 Banking Act were exacting in the limitations set up regarding securities activities of U.S. banking operations. U.S. banks could not underwrite new securities issues, with the exception of certain government securities, nor could they engage in securities brokerage and trading. Yet foreign branches and agencies in the United States were not covered by these restrictions, and thus they could hold equity in U.S. securities firms. Moreover, foreign-bank branches and agencies were not subject to the 1970 amendments to the Bank Holding Company Act, allowing them to engage in additional nonbanking activities forbidden to U.S. bank-holding companies.

In growing numbers, American bankers protested these competitive advantages enjoyed by foreign banks operating in the United States. However, they were split as to whether foreign-bank expansion should be controlled, and, if so, how such control should be manifested. While major money-center banks in New York, California, and Illinois faced direct competition from foreign banks in servicing both multinational customers and large U.S. firms, they questioned the extent to which foreign banks should be restricted in their U.S. operations. New restrictive regulation on foreign-bank expansion in the United States might well carry over to their own branches overseas. Thus, some foreign governments might retaliate, to the detriment of U.S. money-center worldwide branch activity. Also, the money-center banks felt that they could use the equity argument as leverage with federal banking authorities to seek similar advantages, especially in the areas of interstate branching and nonbanking securities activities.

On the other hand, regional and small banks believed that foreign banks should be restricted in their U.S. operations. These banks had little to fear from overseas retaliation because their foreign branching operations were quite limited. But they anticipated increasing regional and local competition from foreign banks and were disturbed by the possibility of large money-center banks securing these same competitive advantages.

Faced with these diverse views, the U.S. Congress considered various approaches to this fairness issue for several years. In 1966, the Joint Economic Committee of Congress undertook the first comprehensive study on activities of foreign banks in the United States.[31] It concluded that foreign banks did possess certain advantages and disadvantages due to disparate state and federal bank legislation. As a consequence, various legislative bills regarding the foreign-bank issue were put forth, but none was enacted.

It was not until 1978 and the passage of the IBA that the problems of foreign-bank competition within the U.S. market were directly confronted. The act set down comprehensive rules for foreign-bank operations in the United States. They were guided by a primary underlying principle: a national policy of equitable treatment for all banks in the United States or within a state. It was intended that both foreign and U.S.-owned banks be given the same banking powers and be subject to the same restrictions. Further, there would be a continuation of the dual banking system, whereby any bank in the United States, foreign or domestic, had an option of being state or federally chartered. Finally, recognition was given to the potential inequity of rule changes to the present or planned U.S. operations of foreign banks.

The IBA legislates and further empowers the Federal Reserve Board, the comptroller of the currency, and the FDIC to issue such rules, regulations, and orders as are necessary to carry out the mandate of national equitable treatment for all banks in the United States. To that end, significant changes in U.S. banking law are authorized in the areas of federal licensing and chartering; regulatory, supervisory, and examination authority; interstate banking; nonbanking activities; deposit insurance; Edge Act operations; and reserve requirements and interest-rate limitations.[32]

**Federal Licensing and Chartering.** Although all foreign banks operating in the United States are now required to register with the Federal Reserve Board, foreign agencies and branches (inclusive of commercial lending companies) are given the option of a federal or a state charter. Foreign subsidiary banks, like domestic U.S. banks, have always had the choice, but foreign agencies and branches had operated solely under state authority. This, therefore, preserves the duality of the U.S. banking system, giving foreign banks more latitude in their operations.

Section 4 of the IBA provides that subject to the approval of the comptroller of the currency, a foreign bank may establish a federal branch or agency only in a state where it does not already operate a state-licensed branch or agency and in which the establishment of such banking organization is not prohibited by state law. In furtherance of this allowance, the IBA provides that foreign banks may convert state branches, agencies, or commercial lending companies into federal branches or agencies. Nevertheless, foreign banks are prevented from operating both a federal branch and federal agency in the same state.

This section further subjects foreign branches and agencies to the branching restrictions and other conditions of the McFadden Act, but because they are offices of foreign banks and not separately incorporated, the limitations and restrictions on capital and surplus are directed toward the foreign parent bank. Also their capitalization requirements are distinctively circumscribed by the following:

> A federal branch or agency in any state . . . shall keep on deposit . . . with a member bank designated by such foreign bank, *dollar deposits or investment securities* of the type that may be held by national banks for their own account . . . in an amount as hereinafter set forth. . . .

> The aggregate amount of deposited investment, securities and dollar deposits for each branch or agency . . . shall not be less than the greater of (1) that amount of capital (but not surplus) which would be required of a national bank . . . or (2) 5 per centum of the total liability of such branch or agency, including acceptances, but excluding (A) accrued expenses, and (B) amounts due and other liabilities to offices, branches, agencies, and subsidiaries of foreign bank.[33]

Finally, section 2 of the act liberalizes the federal-charter option by permitting the comptroller to waive the requirement that all directors of a subsidiary of a foreign bank be U.S. citizens. Thus, a minority of such directors may be foreign, facilitating foreign-bank chartering and U.S. bank acquisition without undue compromise of the principle of local ownership and control.

**Regulatory, Supervisory, and Examination Authority**. Although several sections (6, 7, 11, and 13; see appendix B) deal in some manner with regulatory, supervisory, and examination authority of foreign banks, it is section 7 in which the primary framework may be found.

Section 7 provides that federal branches and agencies are to be supervised by the comptroller, federally insured state branches by the FDIC and state examining bodies, and nonfederally insured state branches and agencies and commercial lending companies by state examining bodies. In all cases, however, the Federal Reserve Board has residual authority for special examination of any and all foreign branches and agencies. This supervisory umbrella allows for a consolidated and consistent review of foreign-bank interstate networks. To facilitate this review, it is expected that the Federal Reserve will employ the reports of the other relevant examining bodies.

Moreover, section 7 provides that the Federal Reserve Board will establish reserve requirements for both federal- and state-licensed branches and agencies whose foreign parent banks have worldwide assets of at least $1 billion. For state licensees, this will be done in consultation and cooperation with state bank supervisory authorities. In return, these agencies and branches will have access to the Federal Reserve discount, borrowing, and clearing facilities, subject only to those restrictions as may be imposed by the Board.

**Interstate Banking**. Without question, the issue of interstate banking has been one of the most-controversial aspects of banking operations in the United States. The intent of the IBA was to deal with a growing multistate presence of foreign banks in a manner that would both balance and protect states' rights and the national interest. Notwithstanding, opinions were split as to whether foreign banks enjoyed a competitive advantage in multistate branching and, if so, in what manner parity should be established between foreign and domestic competitors in the United States.

The hub of this controversy centered around competitive equality for all banking competitors in the United States. A secondary consideration, although by no means less important, focused on the balance between state and national interests. In testimony before Congress, some argued that the restrictions of the McFadden and Bank Holding Company acts on domestic U.S. bank operations were largely fictional. At least the larger U.S. banks could move across state lines through Edge Act corporations, bank-holding companies, loan production offices, and correspondent banking activities. Yet the opposition asserted that the essence of banking lay in a bank's ability to receive deposits. In this arena, foreign banks enjoyed a significant competitive advantage over domestic banks, which could not accept deposits outside of their home state. Moreover, it was contended that the chiefly wholesale banking activities of foreign banks gave them a competitive advantage in the U.S. corporate market, enabling them better to meet the comprehensive banking needs of business firms across state lines.[34]

States were concerned that restricting foreign banks to a single state would result in a virtual monopoly of foreign banking by New York and California, the chief money-center areas of the country. This would serve to reduce the foreign capital inflows and consequent increases in economic activity in the remaining states. On the other hand, because not all branches of U.S. banks overseas were afforded equal treatment in their host countries, some believed that the U.S. market should limit such advantage to foreign competitors. Finally, some particular concern was manifested in the area of foreign-bank acquisition of U.S. banks. There was a degree of peril, it was believed, in the relatively unrestrained ability of a foreign bank to acquire a large U.S. bank, which could then be used as a center for interstate banking.[35]

The upshot of these various arguments was a balance of competitive equality between domestic and foreign banks and state and national interest, all contained within section 5 of the act.

Any foreign bank with offices in more than one state would now designate a home state. Thus, a subsidiary bank may not be operated outside of the home state, nor may federal and state branches and agencies. The latter group, however, may branch across state lines if expressly permitted by nonhome states; branches may accept just those deposits that Edge Act corporations are authorized to receive. The result is to bring foreign banks into line with the multistate restrictions of the Bank Holding Company Act.

Finally, section 5(b) further ensures a degree of fairness. It waives all deposit taking and branching restrictions for foreign banks that are already operating or have applied for permission to operate on or before July 27, 1978.

**Nonbanking Activities**. Section 8 of the act generally applies the restrictions of the Bank Holding Company Act, as amended, to the nonbanking activities of foreign banks and commercial lending companies operating in the United States. In addition, it specifically subjects these organizations to the anti-tie-in provisions of the holding-company legislation. By design, it is intended that foreign banks and companies be able to expand their bank-related activities in the United States in accordance with the same standards applicable to domestic bank-holding companies but that they not be restricted in their nondomestic business.

In particular, section 8(a) provides that a foreign bank or company shall be subject to the provisions of the Bank Holding Company Act of 1956, with the exception of section 3, and to sections 105 and 106 of the Bank Holding Company Act amendments of 1970. As a consequence, while these foreign organizations are denied the use of tying services, are restricted in branching and nonbanking activities, and are subject to the aggrieved-party rights of competitors when seeking Federal Reserve Board approval for U.S. bank acquisition, they are relieved from the criteria the Federal Reserve applies to bank acquisition by domestic bank-holding companies. This exemption did not resolve the equity issue of domestic-bank acquisition by foreign organizations.

Section 8(b), (c), and (d) entail grandfather provisions with regard to the nonbanking activities of foreign financial institutions in the United States. Nonbanking activities undertaken by September 17, 1978, the date of enactment of the IBA, may be retained until December 31, 1985. After December 31, 1985, nonbanking activities lawfully engaged in by July 26, 1978, may be continued unless the Federal Reserve deems it necessary to terminate this permission in order to prevent "undue concentration of resources, decreased or unfair competition, conflicts of interest, or unsound banking practices in the United States."[36]

Finally, section 8(e) amends 2(h) of the Bank Holding Company Act, which had allowed a bank-holding company operating in the United States, but primarily engaged in banking outside the United States, to hold equity in any foreign company that does business solely outside the United States. Under the new provisions, a foreign bank-holding company could hold equity in a foreign nonbanking company that also does business in the United States as long as the majority of the company's banking activities are conducted outside the United States, and additionally the nonbanking company could hold equity in a U.S. nonbanking company, as long as it is in the same general line of business. Recently, however, the Federal Reserve Board tightened its approach and issued new rules whereby a foreign institution's banking business outside the United States must exceed its worldwide nonbanking business to qualify for an exemption under section 8(e). Also, the Federal Reserve will now use the standard industrial classification system to determine whether a foreign bank-holding company's new business is that of a financial nature when applying for such federal exclusion.[37]

**Deposit Insurance**. Once again individuals and organizations were split over an issue regarding foreign banks. Some wanted insurance to be mandatory for all deposits in foreign banks; others, most notably the FDIC, pushed for voluntary insurance compliance, contending that there were sufficient legal controls over foreign parent banks to mandate a requirement. All involved, however, generally recognized that the majority of foreign branches' deposits were wholesale, while the primary concern in the United States had always been for the protection of the retail depositor.

Thus, section 6 of the IBA basically provides that all FDIC insurance of domestic-based deposits of U.S. branches of foreign banks would be voluntary. In instances where foreign branches accept deposits of less than $100,000, such deposits will be deemed to be retail, and thus FDIC insurance will be mandatory for all deposits in those branches. This requirement pertains to all federal branches and all state branches in those states where state-chartered banks are required to be insured. But before a branch can be so insured, the parent bank must pledge assets or provide a surety bond to the FDIC. This action is believed to protect against the perceived extra risk to the FDIC, a result of the jurisdictional difficulties inherent in a foreign bank with a large part of its activities, assets, and personnel outside the United States.

**Edge Act Operations.** Section 3 of the IBA contains the first revisions to section 25(a) of the Federal Reserve Act, popularly known as the Edge Act, since the section's passage on December 24, 1919. As will be recalled, 1957 and 1963 saw changes only in regulation K, not legislative amendments. In fact, Section 3 of this 1978 legislation was operationalized and clarified by further Federal Reserve revisions to regulation K on June 14, 1979.

Although it was generally agreed that Edge Act corporations had greatly aided in the financing of U.S. exports, it was also conceded that the antiquated statutory and regulatory framework under which they were required to operate had placed them at a competitive disadvantage relative to foreign banks. It was the purpose, therefore, of section 3(b) to make clear the intent of Congress for the furtherance of U.S. international trade:

> The Congress hereby declares that it is the purpose of this section to provide for the establishment of international banking and financial corporations operating under Federal supervision with powers sufficiently broad to enable them to compete effectively with similar foreign-owned institutions in the United States and abroad; to afford to the United States exporter and importer in particular, and to United States commerce, industry, and agriculture in general, at all times a *means of financing the international trade, especially United States exports; to foster the participation by regional and smaller banks throughout the United States in the provision of international banking and financing services to all segments of United States agriculture, commerce, and industry, and, in particular small business and farming concerns;* to stimulate competition in the provision of international banking and financing services throughout the United States; and, in conjunction with each of the preceding purposes, to facilitate and stimulate the export of United States goods, wares, merchandise, commodities, and services *to achieve a sound United States international trade position.* The Board of Governors of the Federal Reserve System shall issue rules and regulations [Regulation K] . . . in furtherance of the purposes described.[38]

Section 3(a) thus provides the three principal objectives of this amendment: elimination or modification of previous Edge Act provisions that (1) discriminate against foreign-owned banking institutions, that (2) disadvantage or unnecessarily restrict or limit Edge Act corporations in competing with foreign-owned banking institutions in the United States and abroad, or that (3) impede the attainment of congressional purposes aimed at achieving a sound U.S. trade position through Edge Act operations.

These new provisions and regulatory changes allowed Edges to expand their lending powers through singular incorporation and capitalization merger, increased leverage allowance, and more-varied financing capabilities. Further, reserve requirements were made more equitable, and foreign ownership of Edges was permitted. Together these modifications were expected to stimulate competition in the United States in the provision of international banking and financing services, to increase U.S. exports, and to provide a means for Edge corporations to compete more effectively with foreign banks worldwide.

**Reserve Requirements and Interest-Rate Limitations.** Although specific authorization for establishing reserve requirements for foreign banks is provided by section 7 of the IBA, no such direct authorization is provided with respect to interest-rate ceilings. Nonetheless, section 13 empowers the Federal Reserve Board to issue such rules, regulations, and orders as may be deemed necessary to carry out its duties and responsibilities inherent in the act. Thus, on July 23, 1979, the board proposed the imposition of not only reserve requirements but interest-rate ceilings on state and federal branches and agencies of foreign banks whose parent banks possessed worldwide assets of at least $1 billion.

The proposal, which has now become regulation, subjected the foreign banks to the same reserve requirements and interest-rate ceilings as member banks of the federal reserve. Therefore, as a means to facilitate monetary policy and to urge vigorous and equitable competition in international banking and financial services, foreign banks in the United States, Edge Act corporations, and U.S. member banks would be similarly treated.

**Further Recommendations of the International Banking Act.** Insofar as Congress recognized a need for further study and recommendation in the areas of national and worldwide banking, it mandated two arenas of notable concern for further review. First, it directed the secretaries of Treasury and of State, along with the Federal Reserve, the comptroller, and the FDIC, to review and study the extent to which U.S. banks operating overseas are afforded the same equitable treatment as foreign banks operating in the United States and the effects of foreign discrimination, if any, on U.S. exports. Second, it directed the president of the United States, in consultation with the attorney general, the secretary of the treasury, the board, the comptroller, and the FDIC to report back on the continued applicability of the McFadden Act to present-day banking structure in the United States—that is, whether it unreasonably restricts national banks in their ability to compete.[39]

These issues remain unresolved. They continue to be of primary concern to the U.S. banking community and are currently being reviewed by Congress.

**Remaining Advantages to Foreign Banks.** Foreign banks, either currently operating in the United States or contemplating such operation, still possess some competitive advantages relative to domestic banks.

First, the grandfather provisions of the act allow foreign banks in the United States an advantage in branching, deposit taking, and allowable nonbanking activities. Second, although the cost of funding to foreign branches and agencies in the United States has steadily increased due to the swelling costs of parent funding from abroad and the new reserve requirements imposed by this legislation, there have still been periodic cost advantages as a consequence of sometimes lower reserve and capital requirements on the funds of the foreign parent.

The ability of a foreign bank to acquire a U.S. bank that another U.S. bank is prevented from buying is a particularly important and controversial advantage. Although it is clear that a U.S. bank is prevented from purchasing a bank in another state by the restrictions of the McFadden and Bank Holding Company acts and may be denied acquisition rights of a target bank in the same state, there are no such restrictions on foreign banks. Thus, a foreign bank, not currently domiciled in any form in the United States, may purchase a U.S. bank in any state. It appears that even the Federal Reserve Board concurs in this policy. According to a statement by the board on January 20, 1980, regarding the acquisition of Eagle National Bank of Miami, Florida, by Banco de Colombia S.A., such an acquisition "would have no adverse effects on existing or potential competition and would not increase the concentration of resources in any relevant arena" because the bank-holding company does not conduct business in the United States at this time.[40] The result is that a foreign bank in this situation is not subject to McFadden because it is domiciled outside the United States, and it is not subject to the anti-competitive restrictions of the Bank Holding Company Act because foreign banks are exempted from that provision under section 8(a) of the IBA.

*Depository Institutions Deregulation and Monetary Control Act of 1980*
*(Public Law No. 221, 96th Congress, Approved March 31, 1980)*
*and the International Banking Facility of December 3, 1981*

Although the IBA extended the authority of the Federal Reserve Board over reserve requirements of foreign banks in the United States, it did not directly address the skittish issue of Eurodollar holdings. This was left to the Depository Institutions Deregulation and Monetary Control Act of 1980.

During the 1970s, the increasing costs of compliance with domestic banking regulations prompted many U.S. banks, like their foreign counterparts, to extend their international banking operations beyond national boundaries. U.S. banks found that they could avoid restrictive bank regulation and increase their profitability by channeling international borrowing and lending through foreign branch offices. These overseas banking operations dealt primarily in the Eurocurrency market, a $1.6 trillion market at the end of 1980 of which 75 percent was in Eurodollars.[41] Although all banks in the United States were required to hold reserves on their dollar deposits, no such regulation existed for Eurodollar holdings of U.S. bank branches overseas, nor was there much effective regulation of like funds controlled by foreign parent banks. Insofar as the absence of such regulation reduces the cost of doing business through Eurocurrency transactions, it was contended that foreign parent banks with operations in the United States and U.S. bank branches overseas possessed a cost of funding advantage over U.S. domestic banks. Further, the Federal Reserve Board argued that its monetary policy, based on effective reserve management, was being stifled.[42]

As a consequence of these arguments, the U.S. Congress attempted to extend reserve requirements to the Euromarket by passage of the Monetary Control Act of 1980. Under Title I of this legislation, section 103(b)(5) gives the Federal Reserve authority to impose a uniform reserve requirement on Eurocurrency liabilities of all foreign branches, subsidiaries, and international banking facilities of member and nonmember depository institutions.[43] This included borrowing from foreign sources, sales of assets by depository institutions in the United States to their foreign offices, and loans to U.S. residents made by foreign offices of depository institutions in the United States. The Federal Reserve Board, however, soon realized that imposing these reserve requirements unilaterally against U.S. branch banks overseas would make them uncompetitive in world markets when pitted against essentially unregulated foreign banks. Subsequently, two multilateral approaches to this Eurocurrency issue were proffered. First, it was asserted that all nations would agree to impose identical reserve requirements on the Eurobanking offices operating within their national boundaries, to be held by the host country's central bank. The second proposal would require each participating monetary authority to impose reserve requirements on all Eurobanking offices, wherever located, whose head offices were within their national boundaries. Nevertheless, these proposals were perceived to be impractical at best due to the profitability potential of nonparticipating countries and impossible as a challenge to home-country sovereignty.[44]

The realization of the impracticality of prior proposals spurred efforts to eliminate or at least to lower the reserve requirements on Eurodollar holdings of all banks operating in the United States. But it was not until the Federal Reserve authorized the establishment of international banking facilities (IBFs) on December 3, 1981, that the issue of competitive equity for all banking competitors was further resolved.[45] Thus, domestic banks along with foreign controlled banking operations in the United States could now more realistically compete worldwide by dealing in Eurocurrencies within the U.S. home market.

Prior to this time, a combination of U.S. goverment-imposed costs and controls made Eurocurrency bank dealings in the United States either impossible or, at the very least, noncompetitive. The reserve requirements of regulation D and interest-rate ceilings of regulation Q were two principal impediments. In addition, the board's long-standing policy of refusing to permit foreign-currency deposits in banks in the United States and the often-prohibitive state tax barriers helped to nullify the Euromarket aspirations of banks in the United States, leaving such dealings to offshore financial operations in locations like London, Paris, Nassau, the Cayman Islands, and Singapore.

Thus, beginning December 3, 1981, any U.S. depository institution, Edge or Agreement corporation, or U.S. office of a foreign bank could establish an IBF in any state that has enabling legislation. IBFs would be generally free of reserve requirements and interest-rate ceilings, operating somewhat as free trade zones for international banking services.

Under the board regulations, IBFs were permitted to accept deposits only from foreign residents, other IBFs, or their affiliates, but they would be exempt from regulation D reserve requirements. Deposits from foreign operations of foreign firms, banks, and governments and U.S. firms and banks are included, but deposits from U.S. offices of foreign firms and banks are not. Both deposits and withdrawals must be for at least $100,000; however, they will not be subject to the interest-rate ceilings of regulation Q. Although intrabank deposits may be on an overnight basis, other deposits from nonbanking sources must be for a minimum of two days. Negotiable certificates of deposit, bankers' acceptances, or other bearer instruments are prohibited; only nonnegotiable time deposits are allowed.

For the first time, banks were allowed to accept foreign-currency-denominated deposits in the United States. Thus, IBFs can directly participate in the Eurocurrency market from the United States. However, these funds may not be employed to support U.S. domestic economic activity. Loans can be made only to foreign residents as previously defined. If IBFs choose to lend funds to their own affiliates in the United States, the loans are treated like any other from a foreign branch.

To open an IBF, it is necessary only that the Federal Reserve and appropriate state authorities be notified two weeks in advance. The IBF need not be physically separate from the bank office, but its asset and liability accounts must be separately maintained. Moreover, although the IBF operations remain subject to federal taxation, they must be relatively free of additional state and local taxes to be competitively effective. To this end, the states of New York, California, Illinois, Florida, Connecticut, Maryland, Georgia, and North Carolina have passed legislation exempting these facilities from local and state taxes.

Overall it is expected that the creation of IBFs will enable banks in the United States to obtain a larger share of the Eurocurrency market and, thus, a larger competitive edge in the global market. Generally comparable terms for Eurocurrency deposits and loans and lower country risk should aid in attainment of these goals. There are still, however, several disadvantages to IBF operations that may affect their competitiveness within the global market. For instance, the minimum two-day booking period for nonbank depositors and the FDIC opinion subjecting these deposits to insurance premiums may serve to make IBFs somewhat less attractive to the depositor or the bank.[46] Furthermore, the inability to accept deposits from or make loans to U.S. residents, to issue negotiable instruments, or to finance activities in the United States is still a hindrance in an extremely competitive world market.

*State Banking Law*

Although foreign-bank competition in the United States is chiefly a phenomenon of the last twenty years, its origins can be traced back to the late 1800s when Japanese and Canadian banks began operations in the states of California, Oregon, and Washington.[47] The growth of foreign-bank operations in the United States followed a boom-and-bust pattern corresponding to both U.S. and worldwide economic trends. Indeed, it was not until the close of World War II that foreign interest in the U.S. banking market began to reappear.

Prior to the passage of the IBA in 1978, entry, regulation, supervision, and examination of foreign banks was left to the individual states. Although enabling legislation for foreign-bank operations was passed in Massachusetts as early as 1906, followed by Oregon in 1907, California in 1909, and New York in 1911, states were generally restrictive in this regard. It was not until January 1, 1961, that the first real impetus to foreign-bank competition in the United States arose when New York banking law was changed to permit foreign-branch operations within the states.[48] Before this, only agencies, representative offices, and foreign-bank subsidiaries were allowed, severely restricting deposit-taking opportunities of foreign competitors. This change was particularly significant in that New York City was a chief financial center of the United States and a principal financial center of the world. The attraction to foreign banks was therefore unequivocal. Yet a further state stimulus to foreign-bank activity was not far behind. In 1973, the state of Illinois passed the Foreign Banking Office Act, permitting foreign banks to operate a single branch in the Chicago Loop area.[49] Here again, foreign deposit-taking activity was liberalized by state law, but it was clear that the foreign-bank guests in Illinois would also enjoy the severely restrictive branching regulations applied to domestic banks in the state.

California, the remaining U.S. money and trade center, did not seek to loosen further what it considered an already liberal legislative environment for foreign banks. Indeed it was not until the passage of the IBA that foreign-branch banks could operate in California. Section 1756.1(a) of the California State Financial Code required that "a foreign banking corporation shall not commence to transact in this state the business of accepting deposits, or transact such business thereafter unless . . . it has been approved for Federal Deposit Insurance Corporation insurance."[50] Thus, because deposit taking, an important competitive function, required FDIC insurance and insofar as foreign-bank branches could not avail themselves of such insurance before 1978, only foreign agencies and subsidiaries could effectively operate in California. Subsidiaries could take deposits, but they required more-complicated state-chartering requirements and larger capital infusions than branch operations needed.

In general, states have zealously guarded their right to regulate entry and operations of foreign banks within their boundaries. Although many have looked favorably on the added economic activity generated by foreign banks, states have been cautious and commonly restrictive regarding foreign-banking operations, perhaps reflecting the concerns of their respective home-state banking communities.

Although the IBA has opened up additional avenues for foreign-bank competition in the U.S. market and a number of states have enacted legislation to correspond to the federal provisos, state banking commissions have not abdicated their regulatory roles. For instance, responding to our queries, Edward P. Eustace, the New York deputy superintendent of banks, indicated by letter of January 14, 1982, that

> a number of changes have been made in . . . [New York] laws and regulations relating to foreign banks. Some were influenced by the Federal legislation. Others were made as part of the continuing process of updating the regulatory structure in response to developments in the industry.
>
> Following is a list of the principal changes which have been enacted [in the last eighteen months]:
>
> (1) To permit agencies to issue certificates of deposits, other than to individuals, in either domestic or foreign markets, in amounts not less than $100 thousand. Prior to this change, agencies were not permitted to take any form of deposits.
> (2) To decrease the amount of eligible assets statutorily required to be maintained from 108% of liabilities to 100%, with a policy position that the ratio be maintained at a level approximately equal to capital ratios at domestic banks.
> (3) Broadened the category of assets that are eligible for deposit (pledge) by branches for the account of the [New York State] Superintendent of Banks. . . .
> (4) Broadened the definition of eligible assets . . . to include real estate, precious metals, etc.

(5) Issued various regulations to facilitate the establishment of International Banking Facilities (I.B.F.s) by branches and agencies and excluded I.B.F. liabilities from both asset maintenance and pledge of assets requirement for a one year period commencing 12-3-81.

(6) Revised [New York State] examination report forms for branches/ agencies to (a) accommodate Federal [Reserve] Requirements and (b) to make the reports more meaningful in satisfying [New York State] supervisory responsibility.

(7) Conformed state reserve requirements on deposits of branches to conform with the Federal Reserve Regulation D in order to avoid an overlapping of Federal-State Provisions.

(8) Entered into agreements with [the] Federal Reserve to count reserves maintained by New York branches with [them] purusant to Regulation D toward the New York State pledge of asset requirement.

As well, he suggested that in the opinion of the State Banking Department,

the perception that state banking laws do not have any significant impact on the operation of foreign banks [since passage of the International Banking Act in 1978] is entirely false—especially insofar as New York is concerned. The International Banking Act extended our dual banking system to foreign bank operations. . . . this is a healthy environment. The extent to which federal entry will or will not diminish the significance of state supervision in the future may depend largely on the policies of the various states. New York state policy is receptive to foreign bank entry. . . . the I.B.F. concept, which allows foreign banks to transact internationally oriented business at New York licensed offices on a reserve free basis and exempt from state and local taxes was spearheaded by New York, the first state to enact the enabling legislation.

Thus, it is clear that New York, while adhering to federal legislation, both encourages and controls foreign-banking activity within its own state boundaries.

Along these same lines, it is interesting to note some of the responses of the bank regulatory departments and agencies of the states of California, Florida, Missouri, and Illinois. The deputy, licensing and special programs, of the California State Banking Department, John R. Paulus, indicated that

we still regard ourselves [the State Banking Department] as the primary regulator of foreign banks in California, with the International Banking Act providing a federal option. . . .

Since passage of the International Banking Act, we have amended our law to provide options such as a wholesale branch, previously not contemplated by our Financial Code.

From the Office of the Comptroller of the State of Florida, the chief of the Bureau of International Banking, Wilbert O. Bascom, responded, "The

[Florida State] statutes, as noted, consider agencies as if they were state banks." A June 23, 1981, memorandum to the commissioner of finance of the state of Missouri, Kenneth W. Littlefield, specified:

> The International Banking Act of 1978 . . . is the federal law governing the establishment of subsidiaries, branches, and agencies of foreign banks. Prior to the passage of this Act, all banks of foreign countries that operated in the United States did so under the authority of state law. While the Act permits federal licensing of foreign banks, it does not . . . preempt state law. . . .
>
> . . . Section 362.925 [of the Missouri Annotated Statutes] prohibits a bank organized in any other state or country from taking deposits in Missouri. Therefore, under existing law, no foreign bank can establish a domestic deposit receiving office in Missouri. . . .
>
> . . . Since no foreign banks are permitted to accept deposits in Missouri, neither a federal nor a state branch is permissible in Missouri.

Of special interest is a recent letter to us from William C. Harris, the commissioner of banks and trust companies for the state of Illinois. Commenting on the Illinois State Foreign Banking Office Act of 1973 and the impact of the 1978 IBA, he suggests that the entry of two Australian branch banks into Illinois under the federal branch option was less than equitable:

> . . . Since the I.B.A. '78 and the regulations that followed were finalized there have been 8 foreign branch entries into Illinois. Six (6) of these chose the State of Illinois to be the licensing authority and regulator while 2 chose the Comptroller of the Currency. . . . It should be noted that the 2 licensed by the Comptroller were Australian banks which are not authorized by Illinois law to conduct business in Illinois because Australia is not reciprocal with Illinois. That is to say Illinois banks cannot conduct a general banking business in Australia. . . . The I.B.A. expressly provides that the Comptroller of the Currency cannot license a foreign bank unless expressly permitted by the State.
>
> A suit has been filed against the Comptroller and the Australian New Zealand Banking Group, Ltd., relating to this issue of his licensing of banks which are prohibited from doing a general banking business in Illinois under State Law.

What is discernible here is an attempt by the state of Illinois to maintain substantial control of foreign-bank entry even though a federal charter is involved. In accordance with this approach, the Conference of State Bank Supervisors in October 1981 sued the comptroller to prevent foreign-bank entry into states, exclusively under federal regulations. As in the Illinois case, the plaintiffs believed that the concept of reciprocity of operation would be neutralized if the states could not further regulate federally chartered foreign banks. A federal district court ruled in favor of the Comptroller, specifying that only if a state barred in toto a particular class of foreign-bank operation could it control entry of specific foreign banks on state terms.

The struggle between continued state control of foreign-bank entry and operation within state borders and the newer federal option continues. Table 3-2 shows those states, as of 1979, that specifically authorize or prohibit foreign branch and/or agency operations by state statute. Although only fifteen states expressly authorize such operation, seventeen specifically deny entry of branches and agencies of foreign banks. Eighteen states lack specific legislation. The result is a lack of state consistency and thus a less than common front aimed at foreign-bank competition, a primary reason behind the passage of IBA.

It is not likely that the states will easily surrender what they believe to be their sovereign authority to regulate financial activities within their borders. Close scrutiny of selected state statutes of those states expressly authorizing foreign-bank operations within their borders (table 3-3) will show that the concept of state control is strong. Clearly regulation, supervision, and exam-

**Table 3-2**
**States Authorizing and Prohibiting Foreign-Bank Operations, by Statute**

| *States Expressly Authorizing* | | | *States Expressly Prohibiting* | | |
|---|---|---|---|---|---|
| *Branches and Agencies* | *Branches Only* | *Agencies Only* | *Branches and Agencies* | *Branches Only* | *Agencies Only* |
| Alaska | Illinois | Florida | Arkansas | Florida | Nevada |
| California | Massachusetts | Georgia | Indiana | Georgia | Ohio |
| Mississippi | Oregon | Hawaii | Iowa | Hawaii | |
| New York | | Missouri | Maine | Missouri | |
| Pennsylvania | | | Maryland | | |
| South Carolina | | | Michigan | | |
| Utah | | | Minnesota | | |
| Washington | | | Montana | | |
| | | | New Hampshire | | |
| | | | New Jersey | | |
| | | | New Mexico | | |
| | | | North Carolina | | |
| | | | North Dakota | | |
| | | | Oklahoma | | |
| | | | Texas | | |
| | | | Vermont | | |
| | | | Virginia | | |

Source: Compiled from the "State Banking Law Service," *American Banker Association* (1979) and "A Profile of State-Chartered Banking," *Conference of State Bank Supervisors* (Washington, D.C., 1979).

Note. Sixteen other states do not expressly deny or authorize foreign-bank operations within their boundaries. They are: Alabama, Arizona, Colorado, Connecticut, Delaware, Idaho, Kansas, Kentucky, Louisiana, Nebraska, Rhode Island, South Dakota, Tennessee, West Virginia, Wisconsin, and Wyoming.

**Table 3-3**
**Selected State Statutes Authorizing Foreign-Bank Operations within State Boundaries**

| State | Statute Citation |
|-------|------------------|
| Alaska | Statutes: Section 06.05.367 |
| California | Financial code: Section 1750 |
| Florida | Code annotated: Sections 659.67 through 659.08 |
| Georgia | Code annotated: Sections 41A-3301 through 41A-3311 |
| Hawaii | Revised statutes: Section 403-16 |
| Illinois | Annotated statutes 16½: Sections 501, 519 |
| Massachusetts | Annotated laws: Chapter 167, section 37 |
| Missouri | Annotated statutes: Sections 362.420 through 362.455 |
| New York | Banking law: Section 200 |
| Oregon | Revised statutes: Section 713.010 |
| Pennsylvania | Laws 1977: Act 37 |
| South Carolina | Laws 1978: Rat. 801 |
| Washington | Revised code: Chapter 30.42 |

Source: "State Banking Law Service," *American Banker Association* (1979).

ination of U.S. banks, bank-related operations, and foreign banks operating in the domestic market are split (table 3-4). Although the comptroller of the currency primarily oversees U.S. national banks and federally chartered foreign branches and agencies, it splits its authority with state banking commissions in regulating federally insured foreign state branches. Similarly the FDIC shares its authority with the states regarding insured banks that are not members of the Federal Reserve. State banking commissions, however, maintain primary authority over the minority of U.S. and foreign banks that are state chartered and noninsured. This leaves the Federal Reserve Board. Although it maintains residual examining authority over all foreign banks in the U.S. and oversees the regulation of bank-holding companies and Edge and Agreement corporations, it shares such authority with states over U.S. state member banks.

Thus, it would appear that shared regulatory authority between state and federal agencies is well accepted. In fact, a perusal of both state and federal legislation would confirm this proposition. Yet such phenomena as the recent challenge by state banking supervisors to the chartering authority of the comptroller and the continual concern of state authorities regarding the lack of a reciprocity requirement in present federal legislation will most certainly maintain this controversy for some time to come.

**Further Legislative Directions**

Although probably there will be no major overhaul of foreign-bank legislation in the United States in the near future, there may be some further equitable adjustments, at least for the operations of U.S. domestic banks.

**Table 3-4**
**Regulatory, Supervisory, and Examination Authority of Banking Operations in the United States**

| Agency Authority | U.S. Banks | | | | Bank-Related Operations | | | Foreign Banks | | |
|---|---|---|---|---|---|---|---|---|---|---|
| | National Banks | State Member Banks | State Nonmember Banks — Insured | State Nonmember Banks — Noninsured[b] | Bank Holding Companies | Edge Corporations | Agreement Corporations | Federal Branches and Agencies | Federally Insured State Branches | Nonfederally Insured State Branches, Agencies, and Commercial Lending Companies |
| Federal Reserve Board[a] | | X | | | X | X | X | | | |
| Comptroller of the Currency | X | | | | | | | X | | |
| Federal Deposit Insurance Corporation | | | X | | | | | | X | |
| State Banking Commission | | X | X | X | | | X | | X | X |

[a] Although the IBA specifically provides the Federal Reserve Board with residual examining authority for foreign banks operating in the United States, no such provision exists for U.S. domestic banks. It is, however, apparent that the board, in one way or another, affects the operations of all U.S. banks. See Howard Crosse and George H. Hempel, *Management Policies for Commercial Banks*, 3d ed. (Englewood Cliffs, N.J.: Prentice-Hall, 1980), pp. 52-55.

[b] No more than 2 percent of all commercial banks in the United States fall into this category. See Eric N. Compton, *Inside Commercial Banking* (New York: John Wiley, 1980), p. 166.

The U.S. Congress is currently concerned with the problems inherent in domestic thrift and banking institutions. The result may well lead to new and more-competitive powers for all domestic depository institutions in the United States. In October 1981, the U.S. House of Representatives approved a bill designed to help ailing savings and loan associations and mutual savings banks.[51] The legislation would given them many of the powers and market capabilities now possessed by U.S. commercial banks. The Senate, however, delayed action on the bill until it could put together a more-comprehensive financial package. Its version, S. 1720, sponsored by Senator Jake Garn, R. Utah, chairman of the Senate Banking, Housing, and Urban Affairs Committee, essentially would allow commercial banks in the United States to underwrite municipal-revenue bonds and sponsor mutual funds and would permit them to acquire troubled financial institutions across state lines.[52] These proposed new powers are an attack on the prohibitions of the Glass-Steagall provisions of the 1933 Banking Act, the McFadden Act of 1927, and the amended version of the Bank Holding Company Act. Yet the effect would be to allow domestic banks to compete better with their foreign counterparts in the U.S. market. Although the Reagan administration has presented its own version of this bill, proposing that banks operate their new investment businesses through separate subsidiaries much like the securities industry, there is little question that such legislation would revolutionize the U.S. banking industry.[53] Although passage of either version of the Senate bill is not immediately expected, future enactment would serve to nullify the competitive advantages maintained by foreign banks in the United States through the grandfather clauses of the IBA and their ability to purchase U.S. banks in situations where other U.S. banks could not.

Somewhat secretive boardroom meetings have been taking place recently in the large money-center banks of the United States. Discussion has centered on the possibility of pushing for repeal of the grandfather clauses of the IBA—those dealing with interstate branching and nonbanking activities. Supposition seems to rest on either of two arguments. It may be that the money centers with the support of their state regulatory bodies desire only to limit the grandfather advantages to those foreign banks whose home countries abide by international reciprocity. On the other hand, this movement by the money centers could be a threat to the federal regulatory agencies and Congress, a threat to force them to accede to the principal provisions of S. 1720 and thus to give the U.S. banking industry increased competitive powers. Either way, it is probable that further legislative change regarding the banking industry in the U.S. will result within the 1980s.

**Notes**

1. U.S., Congress, House, *Bank Holding Company Act of 1956*, P.L. 511, 84th Cong., 2d sess., 1956, H.R. 6227, pp. 133-139.

2. Gerald H. Anderson, "Current Developments in the Regulation of International Banking," *Economic Review*, Federal Reserve Bank of Cleveland (January 1980):6.

3. U.S., Congress, House, *An Act to Provide for the Consolidation of National Banking Associations*, P.L. 639, 69th Cong., 2d sess., 1927, H.R. 2, pp. 1224-1234.

4. U.S., Congress, House, *Banking Act of 1933*, P.L. 66, 73d Cong., 1st sess., 1933, H.R. 5661, pp. 184-185, 188-190; U.S., Congress, House, *Banking Holding Company Act Amendments of 1970*, P.L. 91-607, 91st Cong., 2d sess., 1970, H.R. 6778, pp. 1760-1768.

5. U.S., Congress, House, *Federal Reserve Act*, P.L. 43, 63d Cong., 1913, H.R. 7837, pp. 1-27.

6. U.S., Congress, House, *An Act to Amend Certain Sections of the Act Entitled "Federal Reserve Act," Approved December 23, 1913*, P.L. 270, 64 Cong., 1916, H.R. 13391, pp. 43-48; U.S., Congress, Senate, *An Act to Amend the Act Approved December 23, 1913, Known as the Federal Reserve Act*, P.L. 106, 66th Cong., 2d sess., 1919, S. 2472, pp. 378-384.

7. U.S. Congress, House, *International Banking Act of 1978*, P.L. 95-639, 95th Cong., 2d sess., 1978, H.R. 10899, pp. 607-625.

8. U.S., Congress, House, *Depository Institutions Deregulation and Monetary Control Act of 1980*, P.L. 96-221, 96th Cong., 2d sess., 1980, H.R. 4986, pp. 132-193; Elijah Brewer, et al., "The Depository Institutions Deregulation and Monetary Control Act of 1980, *"Economic Perspectives* 4, Federal Reserve Bank of Chicago (September-October 1980):5.

9. Nicholas Carlozzi, "Regulating the Eurocurrency Market: What are the Prospects?" *Business Review*, Federal Reserve Bank of Philadelphia (March-April 1981):15-23.

10. "The Establishment of International Banking Facilities," *International Letter*, no. 450, Federal Reserve Bank of Chicago, Chicago, June 19, 1981, pp. 1-2; "International Banking Facilities Approved," *International Finance* Economics Group of the Chase Manhattan Bank, June 22, 1981, pp. 4-5.

11. Gordon Matthews, "Court Backs Comptroller's Powers over Foreign Banks," *American Banker*, October 9, 1981, p. 2.

12. Edward W. Reed, Edward K. Gill, and Richard K. Smith, *Commercial Banking*, 2d ed. (Englewood Cliffs, N.J.: Prentice-Hall, 1980), p. 427.

13. *Federal Reserve Act*, 1913, p. 26.

14. Neil Pinsky, "Edge Act and Agreement Corporations: Mediums for International Banking," *Economic Perspectives*, Federal Reserve Bank of Chicago (September-October 1978):25-26.

15. *Act to Amend Certain Sections to the Federal Reserve Act* (1916), p. 47.

16. Pinsky, "Edge Act and Agreement Corporations," p. 26.

17. *Act to Amend the Federal Reserve Act* (1919), pp. 378-384.

18. Board of Governors of the Federal Reserve System, "Corporations Doing Foreign Banking or Other Foreign Financing under the Federal

Reserve Act, Regulation K,'' *Federal Reserve Bulletin* (December 1956):1301-1311.

19. Board of Governors of the Federal Reserve System, "Corporations Engaged in Foreign Banking and Financing under the Federal Reserve Act, Regulation K, 12 CFR Part 211,'' *Federal Reserve Bulletin*, (September 1963):1239-1242.

20. Board of Governors of the Federal Reserve System, "International Bank Operations, Regulation K, 12 CFR Part 211,'' *Federal Reserve Bulletin* (June 1979):3-18.

21. *Act to Provide for the Consolidation of National Banking Associations* (1927), pp. 1228-1229.

22. Eric N. Compton, *Inside Commercial Banking* (New York: John Wiley, 1980), p. 160.

23. Eugene Carlson, *Wall Street Journal*, December 15, 1981, p. 31.

24. *Banking Act of 1933*, pp. 184-194.

25. Paul F. Jessup, *Modern Bank Management* (St. Paul, Minn.: West Publishing, 1980), pp. 178-179, 188-191.

26. Phil Battey, "Fed Tightens Restrictions on Outside Businesses Run by Foreign Banks in U.S.,'' *American Banker*, November 14, 1980, p. 11; Anderson, "Current Developments,'' p. 7.

27. Benton E. Gup, *Financial Intermediaries: An Introduction*, 2d ed. (Boston: Houghton-Mifflin, 1980), p. 244.

28. *Bank Holding Company Act of 1956*, pp. 133-137.

29. U.S., Congress, House, *To Amend the Bank Holding Company of 1956*, P.L. 89-485, 89th Cong., 2d sess., 1966, H.R. 7371, pp. 612-613.

30. *Bank Holding Company Act Amendments of 1970*, pp. 1760-1768.

31. U.S., Congress, Senate, *International Banking Act of 1978, A Report of the Committee on Banking, Housing, and Urban Affairs*, S. Rept. 1073 to accompany H.R. 10899, 95th Cong., 2d sess., 1978, pp. 1-2.

32. The *International Banking Act of 1978* is reprinted in its entirety in the Appendix.

33. *International Banking Act of 1978*, p. 611.

34. *International Banking Act of 1978, A Report of the Committee*, pp. 7-8.

35. Ibid., pp. 9-10.

36. *International Banking Act of 1978*, p. 622.

37. Battey, "Fed Tightens Restrictions,'' p. 11.

38. *International Banking Act of 1978*, pp. 608-609.

39. *International Banking Act of 1978, A Report of the Committee*, pp. 23-24.

40. "Foreign Banks Get New Florida Entree,'' *American Banker*, February 5, 1982, p. 2. For further insight, see Steven J. Weiss, "National Policies on Foreign Acquisitions of Banks,'' *Bankers Magazine* (January-February 1981):25-29.

41. *World Financial Markets* (New York: Morgan Guaranty Trust Co., March 1981), p. 13, and Julie Solomon, "Banks Can Do Euromart Business in U.S. after 'Free Trade' Zone Starts Thursday," *Wall Street Journal*, November 30, 1981, p. 4.

42. Carlozzi, "Regulating the Eurocurrency Market," pp. 17-19.

43. *Monetary Control Act of 1980*, p. 136.

44. Carlozzi, "Regulating the Eurocurrency Market," pp. 19-20.

45. "The Establishment of International Banking Facilities," pp. 1-2; and "International Banking Facilities Approved," pp. 4-5.

46. IBFs were exempted from FDIC insurance premiums on December 26, 1981, by the International Banking Facility Deposit Insurance Act, P.L. 97-110, 97th Cong., 2d sess., 1981, H.R. 4879, pp. 1513-1516.

47. Sarkis J. Khoury, *Dynamics of International Banking* (New York: Praeger Publishers, 1979), p. 86.

48. Ibid., pp. 87, 99.

49. Illinois, *Foreign Banking Office Act, Annotated Statutes* (August 17, 1973), P.A. 78-346, pp. 80-90; and Illinois, *An Act to Amend Sections 11, 13 and 15 of the "Foreign Banking Office Act," Approved August 17, 1973* (n.d.), ch. 16-1/2, pars, 511, 513, 515.

50. California, *State Financial Code* (January 1, 1981), ch. 14, art. 1, sec. 1756.1-1765, pp. 83-84.

51. U.S., Congress, House, *A Bill to Enhance the Competitiveness of Thrift Institutions, to Protect Depositors and Creditors of Such Institutions, and for Other Purposes*, H.R. 4724, 97th Cong., 1st sess., 1981, pp. 1-34.

52. U.S., Congress, Senate, *A Bill to Enhance the Competitiveness of Depository Institutions, to Expand the Range of Services Provided by Such Institutions, to Protect Depositors and Creditors of Such Institutions, and for Other Purposes*, S. 1720, 97th Cong., 1st sess., 1981, pp. 89-209.

53. U.S., Congress, Senate, Committee on Banking, Housing, and Urban Affairs, *Financial Institutions Restructuring Act of 1981, Hearings*, Statement of Donald T. Regan, Secretary, Department of Treasury, before the Committee, Senate, on S. 1720, 97th Cong., 1st sess., 1981, pp. 4-48.

# 4 Asset and Liability Management

The management of assets and the management of liabilities of international banks are interrelated. A bank's asset and liability structure directly affects its respective management. There are basically two types of risk in the asset and liability management of international banks: diversifiable or nonsystematic risk and nondiversifiable or systematic risk. The composition of assets and liabilities can be diversified in order to reduce risk, however, complications arise because diversified assets and liabilities are still vulnerable to external nondiversifiable factors such as inflation, interest-rate and exchange-rate changes, and other domestic and international financial market conditions. This chapter discusses the pertinent theoretical framework of asset and liability management from an international banker's point of view.

## The Role of the International Bank

An international bank, like a domestic bank, performs two basic functions: payment of business transactions and financial intermediation. A payment can be made through checks, cable, or Telex to a foreign customer to pay for goods and services through the international bank clearing system. The settlement of such international payments is achieved through the international banking system. International payments may arise from exports, imports, international loans, foreign direct and portfolio investment, and foreign-exchange dealings. Foreign banks must have a checking account at a U.S. bank in order to clear the international payments denominated in dollars, or U.S. banks must have a demand deposit with foreign banks if they want to settle the payment transactions denominated in non-U.S. dollar currencies. In other words, international banks serve as an agent to pay for and collect international payments through their worldwide international banking network.

The second function of the international bank is to transfer funds from savers (depositors) to investors (borrowers) on an international scale.[1] This financial intermediation function has become more important for international banks in recent years. Through their specialization, expertise, and experience, international banks have come to possess a comprehensive knowledge of the sources and uses of international funds. International bankers keep current with the financial and credit conditions of foreign individuals, business firms, and governments through their international financial information systems. Through financial intermediation, the international bank is able to pull financial resources together in large sums and loan them to borrowers who can utilize them most profitably and efficiently.

Domestic deposits do not normally match the domestic demand for loans because the availability of domestic funds is greater than the domestic demand for loanable funds. Particularly during a recessionary period in the United States, these excess funds are loaned out to foreign borrowers. Conversely, when domestic demand for funds is greater than the domestic sources of funds, usually during a boom period, the excess demand is financed by foreign sources of funds.

The typical sources of international funds are demand deposits, time deposits, repurchase agreements (RP), federal funds (FF), certificates of deposit (CD), bankers' acceptances (BA), commercial paper (CP), and Eurodollars held by foreign individuals, corporations, governments, and financial institutions. The deployment of these funds is found in such short-term investments as foreign exchange, foreign treasury bills, CDs, FFs, BAs, Eurodollar loans, and international loans to foreign individuals, business firms, governments, and financial institutions. The description of the international flow of funds is summarized in table 4-1.

Clearly an international bank does a substantial portion of its international banking business through foreign-exchange dealings, international transfer of funds, export-import financing, international deposit holding, and/or international loan making. Table 4-1 illustrates how an international bank accepts deposits from domestic sources and lends them out to foreign borrowers, or accepts deposits from foreign sources and loans them out to domestic borrowers. Furthermore, the table indicates the manner in which international banks borrow money in the federal funds market from domestic banks and lend them out to foreign borrowers. In other words, it is apparent that international financial intermediation takes place whenever an international bank develops a linkage between suppliers and users of funds on a global scale.

## Asset-Liability Gap Analysis

The gap between international assets and liabilities exists in terms of maturity, interest rates, and risk. It is relatively easy to understand the gap in maturities and interest rates between international deposits and international loans; however, it is much more difficult to comprehend the risk involved in international asset and liability holdings. For instance, foreign-exchange risk exists if the bank holds foreign-currency assets and liabilities

**Table 4-1**
**International Financial Intermediation**

| | International Bank | | |
| Uses of Funds | Uses of Funds | Sources of Funds | Sources of Funds |
|---|---|---|---|
| Domestic and Foreign Individuals Business Governments Financial institutions | Foreign exchanges (FX) Liquid assets (LA) Demand deposits (DD) Time deposits (TD) Federal funds (FF) Certificates of deposits (CD) Banker's acceptances (BA) Eurodollar loans ($EL) Other loans | Demand deposits (DD) Time deposits (TD) Federal funds (FF)[a] Repurchase agreements (RP)[b] Certificates of deposits (CD) Banker's acceptances (BA)[c] Commercial paper (CP)[d] Eurodollar deposits ($ED) | Domestic and Foreign Individuals Business Governments Financial institutions |

[a]Federal funds are excess reserves that banks lend to each other on a short-term basis, normally one day. Foreign banks in the United States participate in the market and contributed to the integration of the domestic interbank market into the international interbank markets.

[b]In a repurchase agreement, usually a bank borrows money by selling securities out of its portfolio to a buyer (creditor) and simultaneously agrees to repurchase back either on call or at a future date at a price to cover the agreed-upon yield.

[c]A banker's acceptance is a time draft arising from international trade drawn on and accepted by a bank to pay the face amount. A banker's acceptance may be discounted by the accepting bank or sold to another bank or investor, although the accepting bank continues to guarantee payment on maturity.

[d]Commercial paper is an unsecured note issued by well-known corporations or banks. It is probably the cheapest source of funds because it does not require a registration with Securities and Exchange Commission for a maturity of 270 days or less, and it is usually denominated in a large sum (several million dollars).

in different quantities. Additional risk exists if the loan portfolio is heavily concentrated in a few borrowers from one country instead of dispersed to many countries. Furthermore, if the bulk of funds come from a few large depositors in one country, the situation is considered risky. The danger of the asset-liability mismatch is found in its adverse impact on a bank's liquidity and profitability.

*International Liquidity*

The traditional definition of liquidity for a bank is shown by its ability to convert its short-term assets into cash without great loss. Banks in general, both domestic and international, need cash balances or primary reserves to pay for cash transactions such as wages, salaries, and other cash payments. The adequacy of a bank's cash balance is determined by its net cash flow, which is the difference between cash inflow and cash outflow. Banks also need cash balances for precautionary and speculative purposes. Aside from these traditional reasons for holding cash, an international bank also holds cash in the form of foreign exchange. Foreign exchange is normally used to meet customer demand for export and import payments, interest payments on foreign-currency loans, and foreign-currency-denominated loans. Furthermore, foreign exchange is used to cover forward market transactions and to invest in foreign short-term securities for liquidity purposes.

In the context of asset and liability management, an adequate amount of liquidity means the ability to borrow in money markets to smooth out volatile deposit withdrawals and loan demands. When a bank faces a net deposit withdrawal, which is the difference between the deposit inflow and outflow, the bank's liquidity is needed to meet such withdrawals; when loan demand is greater during a boom period, the bank's liquidity is used to meet that demand. Conversely, during a recessionary period when the loan demand is slack, temporarily idle cash is invested in short-term rather than long-term liquid assets. Because primary reserves are noninterest-earning assets, this is considered a better approach. Yet since liquidity serves as a temporary cushion for deposit and loan demand changes, this investment should be low risk, easily marketable, and have reasonable earnings.

*Maturity Gap*

In general, the international bank borrows short and lends long. In other words, the bulk of international funding comes from short-term deposits, and these funds are loaned out for long-term purposes.[2] Traditionally international bankers made short-term loans to finance trade in the form of letters of credit and other self-liquidating commercial loans. In recent years, however, the maturity of international loans has lengthened to five to ten years, particularly for foreign-government and private-project loans. Since a substantial commitment is made on long-term loans, banks generally dislike calling them back in order to continue business relationships with other customers. Therefore the bank has to depend on short-term funding on a continual basis. In domestic banking, the maturity gap can be managed by maintaining the captive depositors that have other banking business with the bank. In international banking, however, foreign depositors are usually large wholesale banks or corporations that may withdraw a large amount of deposits in a short time. If this happens, the bank has to replenish the deposit withdrawals by soliciting other international deposits or issuing CDs, BAs and other short-term money-market instruments.

Since international short-term funds are very sensitive to interest-rate differentials between countries, it is not unusual to see these funds moving from one country to another to take advantage of higher yields. Still, as long as withdrawals of foreign deposits are refinanced, the international banking business will continue. When foreign-deposit withdrawals cannot be financed, the squeeze on international liquidity will bring about a chain reaction on other international banks in the form of subsequent deposit withdrawals. This domino effect could eventually paralyze the whole international banking system.[3]

## Interest-Rate Gap

International banks, like domestic banks, depend on the interest-rate spread between loans and deposits for their profitability. The interest rate on Eurodollar deposits generally has been greater and the interest rate on Eurodollar loans loans has been lower than is the case for deposits and loans in the United States (refer back to table 1-7). This means that the interest-rate spread of the Eurodollar market is much smaller than that in U.S. loan markets. International banks have operated on a low margin, quite often as low as 1/8 percent. Nonetheless, it is difficult, if not impossible, to compare the interest-rate spread between the Eurodollar and U.S. prime loan markets because there is usually a compensating balance for U.S. loans, reserve requirements and deposit insurance for U.S. deposits, and a loan commitment fee for Eurodollar loans generally ranging from a quarter-percent to a half-percent; however, since the LIBOR is an interbank loan rate, the data in table 1-7 were adjusted for risk premiums for prime borrowers in order to make a meaningful comparison with the U.S. prime rates. In short, the data allow for a unique comparison of interest-rate spreads in U.S. and Eurodollar markets.

The interest-rate spread in the Eurodollar market is low because the market is basically efficient and competitive.[4] Unlike U.S. domestic banks, there are no legal restrictions on entry into the Eurodollar market. International banks do not require additional charters to participate in the international market. Through modern communication networks, international financial information is disseminated quickly and instantaneously throughout the international banking system. Because of the absence of reserve requirements and insurance assessments on Eurodollars in nearly all foreign countries, these banks can pay relatively higher interest rates on deposits, and because of their lower overhead costs, they can charge relatively lower interest rates on their loans. In essence, an efficient market means a narrower interest-rate spread between loan and deposit rates. This is what has been happening in the Eurodollar market. Although the interest-rate spread is narrower in terms of percentages, interest earnings in absolute terms are much greater because international banks are operating in the wholesale area where deposits and loans are usually in the millions. Because of the thin interest margin, however, a single default on an international loan could jeopardize a bank's profitability. Therefore, effective asset and liability management, with a special emphasis on the interest-rate gap, is of critical importance to international banks.

The Eurodollar market has operated relatively free from government regulation. Yet international banks still have to be cognizant of the crucial relationship of their assets and liabilities because their cost of funding directly affects their profitability margin from loans. Domestic banks, on the other hand, have been protected by government regulations in the form of regulation Q, which restricts the maximum interest payments on bank time and savings deposits. However, as regulation Q is slowly phased out and the cost of funding increases, domestic banks have begun to pay more attention to asset and liability management, with special reference to maturity and interest-rate mismatch.

The interest-rate gap analysis is particularly important because of fluctuations in interest rates in not only domestic but also foreign money markets. The international bank borrows short and lends long. If a long-term loan is made when interest rates are low and interest rates go up when short-term liabilities mature, the international bank manager is forced to borrow at higher rates, which may exceed the long-term loan rates made earlier. Banks may be capable of absorbing such interest-rate losses for a short period of time, but they cannot sustain such losses in the long run.[5]

Another risk in international asset and liability management is caused by the interest-rate discrepancy between domestic and foreign markets. During a recessionary period in the U.S. home market when credit demand and interest rates are low, international portfolio managers are most likely to make a loan abroad or invest in foreign short-term securities, which pay higher yields. But when domestic credit demand increases, they are faced with a dilemma: whether to borrow at higher rates at home or sell the liquid assets at a loss, which will further reduce the profit margin. Domestic banks are not accustomed to doing this.

The linkage between the U.S. money market and Eurodollar market has definitely affected profit margins of U.S. banks. According to a study by the Federal Reserve Board, the variability in U.S. short-term interest rates has closely matched the variability in Eurodollar rates. This conclusion is consistent with other studies. Patrick Hendershot, Sung Kwack, and Rodney Mills came to similar conclusions: the U.S. short-term rate is the primary determinant of the equilibrium Eurodollar rate.[6] The Eurodollar market is operating at low interest margins, and because of this competitive pressure, many U.S. banks have abandoned prime rates as a base for loans, employing the LIBOR, which is generally lower.

### Diversification of the Structure of Assets and Liabilities

An additional risk that international banks face lies in the concentration of its deposit holders and loan-portfolio structure. International banking is basically wholesale, and there are relatively fewer depositors as compared to domestic banking operations, which include retail functions. In domestic banking, if one depositor withdraws, the impact on overall deposits will be less because the average size of the individual deposit is small. Furthermore, there is more likelihood that additional deposits may be forthcoming with new depositors. In international banking, the withdrawal of one multi-million-dollar depositor will have a much greater impact on the overall deposit structure. Furthermore, the country origin of international depositors is concentrated in a few countries. Finally, domestic deposits are rather stable when compared to foreign deposits, which are more volatile since the supplier of international deposits may not be the user of international loans. Quite often funds come from foreign depositors and are loaned out to domestic borrowers. Conversely, funds are raised domestically and loaned out to foreign borrowers. This domestic and foreign mismatch of funds can be risky because foreign deposits may be more volatile and foreign borrowers may have additional country risk. Clearly it is much more difficult to predict the behavior of foreign depositors and borrowers as compared to their domestic counterparts.

Unless a bank has an unlimited amount of resources, it is difficult to diversify both deposits and loans in terms of country, region, and business types. It was estimated that over 70 percent of U.S. commercial bank loans to nonoil less-developed countries, (LDCs) were concentrated in ten countries in 1979: Brazil ($16.1 billion), Mexico ($13.1 billion), Korea ($7.6 billion), Taiwan ($4.9 billion), Phillippines ($4.7 billion), Spain ($4.5 billion), Argentina ($4.4 billion), Hong Kong ($3.4 billion), Greece ($2.9 billion), and Colombia ($2.56 billion).[7] Ideally though, it is desirable to have different types of international depositors and borrowers, such as foreign governments, banking institutions, and business firms. Moreover, further diversification of corporate business firms into industry groups such as shipping, steel, manufacturing, and trading will also spread the risk.

In summary, the main objective of the asset-liability gap analysis for an individual bank is to maintain proper balance among international liquidity, profitability, solvency, and operating efficiency. It is essential to have stable and continued sources of international funding and to maximize profitability through sufficient spreads between loan and deposit interest rates. Also, it is imperative for banks to diversify both their loan and deposit structure without too much concentration in any particular funding source or use. The success of asset and liability management of an individual bank depends on its skills, expertise, and experience. But there is an additional risk, which is unique to international banks: international banks face nondiversifiable market risks that are outside the individual bank's control.

**Changes in World Financial Markets**

International banks are supposed to manage their assets and liabilities under given conditions of world financial markets. Yet world financial markets have been greatly influenced by policies of major industrial countries in regard to official loans and changes in interest rates and inflation and exchange rates on an international scale. Individual banks, however, have to operate within the constraints that exist in these financial markets.

*Importance of Private International Loans*

From a historical perspective, the role of multinational commercial banks has gradually shifted from a meager participant to a more-vital and significant lender in the international loan market. In the 1950s, the major source of development loans came from government grants and official soft loans, mainly from the United States. Since Western Europe and Japan were still in the postwar reconstruction stage in the 1950s, the United States accepted the major responsibility of providing development loans to developing nations around the world. In regard to private international loans, U.S. banks again provided the bulk of short-term commercial loans to finance international trade between the United States and Western Europe. But during the 1960s, the United States began to experience balance-of-payments deficits, and the burden of foreign aid became obvious. Consequently the U.S. government switched its loan mechanism to multilateral development loans through the World Bank. In order to fill the gap created by this reduction in U.S. government aid and grants, U.S. and foreign commercial banks increased their loan amounts to LDCs.

The growth of private international loans accelerated in the 1970s, evidenced by the tremendous increase in the Eurodollar market. Net liabilities of the Eurodollar currency market increased from $65 billion in 1970 to $705 billion in 1980. Similarly the outstanding medium- and long-term debt of developing countries increased more than five fold, reaching $426.1 billion in 1980 compared with $77.9 billion in 1971. Of the total debt outstanding, the share of private debt, particularly from financial institutions, increased from 46 percent in 1970 to 63 percent in 1980.[8] The U.S. Department of Commerce estimates that banks in the United States and U.S. bank branches overseas accounted for about 25 percent of total private credit in 1980.[9]

Several interesting developments occurred in international banking in the 1970s. First, U.S. banks increased their share of international credit through their head offices as the U.S. government repealed foreign capital and credit controls in 1974. Second, European and Japanese banks increased their share of medium- and long-term loans to LDCs through Eurocurrency syndicate markets, the average size of such loans being generally much larger than those for commercial and industrial needs. Third, Eastern European countries increased their borrowings from the U.S. and other Western private banks. Fourth, international private loans were employed to finance economically and financially viable government projects and other private commercial and investment projects in the 1980s instead of just to support balance-of-payments deficits and social infrastructures, as was the case in the 1960s. Finally, as bilateral and multilateral public credit dwindled, international borrowers began to pay higher market interest rates for private loans without government subsidies.[10]

## Worldwide Inflation and Higher Interest Rates

The 1970s experienced an unprecedented period of volatile inflation and interest rates in both developing countries and advanced countries. Many developing countries, particularly the oil-importing countries of Argentina, Brazil, Colombia, Greece, Korea, Pakistan, and Turkey exhibited annual inflation rates of over 20 percent during the 1973-1980 period. Most advanced countries, with the exception of Germany, experienced double-digit inflation in the 1970s.[11] Such high inflation rates caused interest rates to rise proportionately.

The asset and liability management of international banks has become further complicated by volatile changes in inflation and interest rates. It has become very difficult to forecast future interest rates. Since the average maturity period of an international portfolio is longer than that of short-term liabilities, the rise in the cost of borrowing in the short run will squeeze interest-rate spreads because loan interest rates are generally fixed. In many instances, international banks rely on sources of short-term funding through federal funds, commercial paper, and security repurchase agreements whose interest rates may fluctuate more than one hundred basis points overnight. Therefore, many international banks have recently begun to use floating interest rates, which are reset more frequently, sometimes on a six-month basis. They have also begun to lengthen the maturities of both U.S. dollar and foreign-currency liabilities in international markets. For instance, international financial markets have started to witness such longer-term liabilities as five-year Eurodollar notes and Eurocurrency bonds denominated in British pounds, German marks, Japanese yen, and Swiss francs.[12] Furthermore, interest future markets have become a useful tool to hedge against interest-rate losses by predetermining future borrowing and lending rates. Worldwide fluctuations in inflation and interest rates affect an individual bank's profitability and also its asset and liability management.

**Foreign-Exchange Risk**

When the international monetary system was changed from a fixed-exchange-rate system to a floating-rate system in 1973, multinational banks were faced with greater foreign-exchange risks. With the fixed-rate system, exchange rates of most advanced countries, particularly the United States, were reasonably stable, although many developing countries experienced frequent devaluations. After 1973 the exchange rates of both developing and advanced countries exhibited wide bands of fluctuation.

Basically international banks are faced with three types of foreign-exchange risk: translation exposure, transaction exposure, and economic exposure.[13] These foreign-exchange exposures are often referred to as the accounting effect, financial effect, and economic effect.

*Translation Exposure*

Translation exposure deals with an accounting effect or the book value of a bank. The accounting or book value of an international bank may be affected by exchange-rate changes if the bank has foreign assets, liabilities, and capital accounts denominated in foreign currencies. If the bank's net position (assets greater than liabilities) is long, the depreciation in foreign currency will bring about a net loss in book value. Conversely, if the bank's net position is short (liabilities greater than assets), the depreciation in foreign currency will bring about a net gain in book value. For instance, if a multinational bank has foreign loans and deposits denominated in foreign currencies and exchange rates change, then it will have an accounting or book value gain or loss depending on the net position of its assets and liabilities. Furthermore, the accounting book value of foreign-currency holdings of the bank will also change in this situation. Therefore the translation effect deals with an unrealized gain or loss of the bank as a result of exchange-rate changes.

Before 1975, the Financial Accounting Standard Board (FASB) allowed international firms, including banks, to use three types of translation methods. The current and noncurrent method allowed the firm to translate current assets and liability items at current exchange rates and noncurrent items at historical rates. Under the monetary and nonmonetary method, monetary items such as cash, accounts receivable, and accounts payable were translated at current exchange rate, and nonmonetary items such as inventories and fixed assets were translated at historical rates. Under the current-rate method, all balance-sheet items could be translated at the current exchange rate. Under this three-method system, an international firm could select an appropriate method to translate foreign activities and to meet its special needs and smooth out the erratic impact of foreign-exchange rates of financial reporting on a consolidated basis. Depending on the type of industry—one with substantial fixed assets, current assets, or monetary assets—the selection of an appropriate translation method would reflect the meaningful value of foreign activities. Furthermore, under this rule, all translation gains and losses were recognized against current income or an appropriate reserve.

The uniform standard of translation method, however, became effective on January 1, 1976, under FASB 8. FASB 8 required that all U.S.-based multinational firms use the temporal method, somewhat similar to the monetary and nonmonetary method. The main difference between the two methods was found in the valuation of inventory and marketable securities, which were translated at the lower cost or market price under the temporal method. FASB 8 also required that all translation gains and losses be reported in the quarterly income statement, affecting earnings per share.[14]

According to an FASB survey, a majority of international business firms complained that the procedures under FASB 8, primarily due to volatile fluctuations in earnings per share, often had nothing to do with the economic reality of foreign operations. Consequently, on December 7, 1981, the FASB issued statement 52, substantially revising foreign-currency translation rules for financial statement presentations.[15] FASB 52 requires the use of current translation exchange rates for both the balance sheet and profit-and-loss statement. The significant difference in FASB 52 is that translation gains or losses are reported as a balance-sheet item under the equity account. The use of current exchange rates can cause variations in the amounts reported in the equity account, but generally those effects will not be as significant as a change in earnings per share. It is generally true that the impact of translation losses shown in earnings per share is much greater than that shown in the equity account; however, if foreign transla- tion losses become larger, then the decrease in the equity account will have a significant impact on not only shareholders but management also.

Generally all elements of a foreign entity's financial statement are translated into dollars using the current exchange rate. This means that the exchange rate in effect at the balance-sheet date is used in translating assets and liabilities and that a weighted average exchange rate is used to translate revenues, expenses, gains, and losses. All translation gains and losses are recorded in the equity account. There are a few exceptions, however. For in- stance, historical exchange rates are permitted for translation when foreign financial statements are not denominated in a functional currency and remeasurement is required. Furthermore, when foreign translations are not denominated in the functional currency, foreign transaction gains or losses may be reported in the income statement. A firm's functional currency would be the currency of the primary economic environment in which the firm operates; normally that is the currency of the environment in which the firm predominantly generates and expends cash.

*Transaction Exposure*

Transaction exposure is sometimes referred to as the financial cash-flow effect of exchange-rate changes since an actual financial transaction takes place. A financial transaction can be on a sight or time basis. International banks may buy or sell foreign exchange in the spot market or make an international loan agreement whose principal and interest payments will be made in the future. Exchange rates may change between the time the loan agreement is made and when actual payments of principal and interest take place. In the past, most international loans of U.S. banks were made in dollars; however, many U.S. multinational banks are now making international loans in denominating currencies other than U.S. dollars. If international loans are denominated in foreign currencies, exchange-rate changes will certainly affect the financial value of future principal and interest payments. Yet even if international loans are denominated in U.S. dollars, the financial value of the loan may be affected by exchange-rate changes if the borrower's currency value appreciates. Therefore, if the exchange rate of the borrower's currency appreciates, it is better to originate the international loan denominated in the borrower's currency than in U.S. dollars. This principle also applies to the liability side of a bank balance sheet when denominated in foreign currencies.

In order to reduce the transaction risk of exchange-rate changes, international banks may engage in forward contracts through foreign-exchange or interbank markets. One may avoid transaction exposure by hedging all future transactions and not taking an open position. By going into forward-exchange markets, a forward rate is selected for the delivery of foreign exchange in the future. A forward rate may be at discount, par, or premium. If the forward rate is lower than the spot rate, which is the current market rate, then it is at a discount. If the forward rate is the same as the spot rate, then it is at par. And if the forward rate is greater than the spot rate, then it is at a premium. The exchange rate can be expressed in two ways: by the number of foreign-currency units per U.S. dollar, or by the number of U.S. dollars per foreign-currency unit. But no matter the rate, a forward discount means that the value of a foreign currency is lower, and in the case of forward hedging, the overall pricing of a loan must take into account the forward cost (forward discount) or the forward gain (forward premium).

Transaction exposure of foreign rate changes can also be minimized by engaging in money markets. Let us assume a U.S. bank is making a foreign-currency loan in British pounds maturing in three months. The money-market hedge works as follows. A U.S. bank borrows British pounds for three months, converts the British pounds to dollars in the spot market, and then invests the dollars in the U.S. money market to earn interest. At the end of the three months, the U.S. bank receives the British pounds as loan payment and then pays back the loan with the British pounds. In this way, foreign risk is avoided.

If the U.S. bank does not wish to hedge its exchange-rate risk either through forward or money markets, then it is exposed to exchange-rate changes in the future. In fact, if the bank is exposed, its position is the same as a speculation because the bank is taking a chance in converting the British pounds at the future spot rate at the time the loan matures. If the actual future spot rate is greater than the forward rate, there is a gain through speculation. There is a possibility, however, that the actual future spot rate will be lower than the forward rate. Then there is a loss. According to Kohlhagen, Levich, Dufey, and Giddy, the forward rate has been an unbiased indicator of future spot rates in the long run.[16] Nonetheless, there are many instances in the short run where forward rates are not equal to future spot rates because there are many other factors affecting future exchange rates: price changes, interest rates, the balance-of-payments deficit, and international reserves.[17]

In the case of either forward hedging or money-market hedging, the ultimate test of transaction gains or losses in the British example depends on the relationships between the forward or future spot rates and the interest-rate differential between Great Britain and the United States. In the case of forward hedging, the interest earnings by the U.S. bank on a British pound loan must be large enough to cover the interest rate in the United States and forward discount of British pounds in the forward market. Theoretically the forward rate must reflect at least the spot rate plus interest earnings as a carrying cost because a portion of the interest could have been earned by investing money during the forward contract period. Putting the argument differently, the interest-rate differential between Great Britain and the United States must at least be equal to the forward premium or discount of the British pound. This argument can also be applied to the case of money-market hedging. The amount of British pound borrowing will be the amount of future pound receivables less the interest rate. The interest rate on British pound borrowing must at least equal the interest rate in the United States, plus the future spot rate change.

Multinational banks may invest temporarily idle foreign-exchange holdings through interest arbitrage. Interest arbitrage deals with purchases and sales of foreign exchange in spot and forward markets and simultaneous investment in short-term money markets. If a U.S. multinational bank has temporarily idle Swiss francs at a Swiss branch, they may opt for available alternatives in marketable securities in various countries, taking into account the forward exchange-rate changes. For instance, the bank may sell Swiss francs and buy British pounds in the spot market and invest the British pounds in a money-market instrument that yields the highest real return. At the same time, the bank matches the money-market instrument maturity with a forward sale of British pounds in the forward market. Again though, future British pounds may be exposed to exchange-rate changes if they are not hedged in the forward market. After paying taxes in both Great Britain and Switzerland, the bank realizes a net real return from the transaction. Similar calculations in such countries as Germany, France, and Italy would also result in a best-investment alternative yielding the highest net gain.

*Economic Exposure*

The economic effect of exchange-rate changes involves long-run effects in international money and capital markets. If the U.S. dollar depreciates, there will be an increase in U.S. exports and a reduction in U.S. imports, assuming the price elasticities of imports and exports are sufficiently high. The depreciation of the U.S. dollar will have varying effects on different banks depending on whether they are export oriented or import oriented. Generally the depreciation of the dollar will bring about larger foreign direct investment and portfolio investment in the United States because the value of the dollar will have declined relative to foreign currencies. In other words, foreign currencies would be able to purchase more U.S. goods and financial securities. Furthermore, there might be an increase in the demand for U.S. dollar loans because the interest payment in dollars would decline, although the initial value of the dollar loan would still have been lower in terms of foreign currencies.

Although FASB 52 addressed the issue of providing information compatible with the expected economic affects of exchange-rate changes, it is unlikely that an appropriate exchange rate could be found that would truly reflect the economic value of the firm. The exchange rate is basically determined by the supply of and demand for a foreign currency. The demand for a foreign currency may arise from international trade, travel, investment, or speculative purposes. The exchange rates may change in the short run regardless of fundamental factors of the economy, and exchange-rate changes in the short run may have no direct relationship to the economic earning power of a firm or a bank. The earning power of a firm depends on personnel, capital, and technology. In case of a bank, its ability to make profitable loans is premised on management skills and the competitive situation of funding and loan markets in both international and domestic arenas. Exchange-rate changes may affect international capital flows, but they should not directly affect the domestic sector's banking business where economic conditions are independent of changes in international markets.

The systematic change in world financial markets will affect each country differently. Most oil-importing developing countries rely on external debt to finance their capital and import requirements. Therefore an increase in international interest rates will exacerbate the debt-servicing problem of a borrowing country. As inflation spread worldwide because of higher oil prices, the effect was much more severe on countries that depended heavily on foreign oil but could not finance oil imports through export expansion. Furthermore, it is likely that the increase in exchange rates of advanced countries will further deteriorate the balance of payments of developing countries, which would have to expend more of their curriencies to import from the advanced countries.

## Country Risk Analysis

Many multinational banks analyze solvent country risk by utilizing both quantitative and qualitative methods. From a banker's point of view, country risk measures the creditworthiness of a country in international loan markets. The higher the country risk that is assigned to a nation, the higher the risk premium that will be charged to a borrower by both public and private creditors. In most developing countries, the governments themselves are substantial borrowers of private credit, which, in turn, is guaranteed by the state.

In order to insure credit extended by international banks, a weight system is commonly used in country risk analysis. National historical data regarding economic and financial variables are analyzed, and these historical trends are compared with those of other countries. Then a particular weight is assigned to each variable. For instance, if a country's inflation rate is much higher than that in other countries, a lower weight is assigned to its inflation variable. This process of analyzing different variables is repeated for such other factors as balance-of-payments deficits, international reserve positions, GNP growth rates, and international debt-service payments, including interest and amortization payments. For non-quantifiable factors such as political and social stability, an arbitrary weight is given.

One simple but useful country risk table (table 4-2) is that compiled by the monthly publication *Euromoney*.[18] The table lists sixty-seven countries using the floating rates indicated on loans. The countries are ranked from the best to the worst credit rating. The table is based on the interest-rate spread of the total volume of country loans in relation to the maturity of the loan. The index is then compared to the overall Euromoney index. For instance, according to the publication's 1980 country risk table, Australia was the best-risk country in the Euromarkets. The country had the lowest interest spread and the longest maturity period. As expected, most countries in the better-risk category were developed or energy-rich countries, such as France, Finland, Sweden, Denmark, Belgium, Canada, Malaysia, and Indonesia.

**Table 4-2**
**The Euromoney Index Groups**

*Group I*

Index weighting: 0.3267
Industrialized countries

| | | |
|---|---|---|
| Australia | Iceland | Sweden |
| Austria | Ireland | Switzerland |
| Belgium | Italy | United Kingdom |
| Canada | Japan | United States |
| Denmark | Luxembourg | Plus all supra- |
| Finland | Netherlands | national institutions |
| France | New Zealand | |
| Germany (Federal Republic) | Norway | |

*Group II*

Index weighting: 0.2845
Includes high- and upper-middle-income developing countries, plus capital-surplus oil exporters

High income (over $2,500)

| | | |
|---|---|---|
| American Samoa | Gabon | Martinique |
| Bahamas | Greece | Singapore |
| Bermuda | Greenland | Spain |
| Brunel | Israel | Venezuela |

Upper-middle income ($1,136-$2,500)

| | | |
|---|---|---|
| Argentina | Guadeloupe | Portugal |
| Bahrain | Hong Kong | Puerto Rico |
| Barbados | Iran | Reunion |
| Brazil | Iraq | South Africa |
| Cyprus | Lebanon | Surinam |
| Djibouti | Malta | Trinidad and Tobago |
| Fiji | Netherlands Antilles | Uruguay |
| French Guiana | Panama | Yugoslavia |

Capital-surplus oil exporters

| | | |
|---|---|---|
| Kuwait | Oman | Saudi Arabia |
| Libya | Qatar | United Arab Emirates |

*Group III*

Index weighting: 0.27
Intermediate middle income ($551-$1,135)

| | | |
|---|---|---|
| Algeria | Ecuador | Mexico |
| Antigua | Guatemala | Namibia |
| Belize | Ivory Coast | Nicaragua |
| Chile | Jamaica | Paraguay |
| China, Republic of | Jordan | Peru |
| Colombia | Korea, Republic of | Seychelles |
| Costa Rica | Macao | Syrian Arab Republic |
| Dominica | Malaysia | Tunisia |
| Dominican Republic | Mauritius | Turkey |

*Lower middle income ($281-$550)*

| | | |
|---|---|---|
| Angola | Grenada | Philippines |
| Bolivia | Guyana | St. Vincent |
| Botswana | Honduras | Senegal |
| Cameroon | Liberia | Sudan |
| Cape Verde | Mauritania | Swaziland |
| Congo | Morocco | Thailand |
| El Salvador | Nigeria | Western Samoa |
| Equatorial Guinea | Papua New Guinea | Zambia |
| Ghana | | Zimbabwe |

*Group IV*

Index weighting: 0.0309
Low income ($280 or less)

| | | |
|---|---|---|
| Afghanistan | Haiti | Pakistan |
| Bangladesh | India | Rwanda |
| Benin | Indonesia | Sierra Leone |
| Bhutan | Kampuchea | Somalia |
| Burma | Kenya | Sri Lanka |
| Burundi | Lao People's Democratic Republic | Tanzania |
| Central African Republic | Lesotho | Togo |
| Chad | Malalgasy, Republic | Uganda |
| Comoros | Malawi | Upper Volta |
| Egypt, Arab Republic of | Maldives | Viet Nam |
| Ethiopia | Mali | Yemen Arab Republic |
| Gambia, The | Mozambique | Yemen, People's Democratic |
| Guinea | Nepal | Republic of |
| Guinea-Bissau | Niger | Zaire |

*Group V*

Index weighting: 0.0879
Centrally planned economies

| | | |
|---|---|---|
| Albania | Czechoslovakia | Mongolia |
| Bulgaria | German Democratic Republic | Poland |
| China, People's Republic of | Hungary | Romania |
| Cuba | Korea, Democratic People's Republic | Soviet Union |

Source: *Euromoney* (October 1980):24.

Note: To weight the index, and to produce the subindexes, countries were placed in the groups shown here. The index weighting for each group is equal to that group's average share of borrowings in the syndicated Eurocurrency credit market over the five years 1975-1979.

The interest-rate spread of an individual country can be compared with the overall market index.[19] The overall Euromarket index is also published by *Euromoney*. The Euromoney index is a weighted average of interest-rate spreads in relation to maturities of all participating countries. The loans of borrowing countries are also weighted according to World Bank groups. The World Bank classifies borrowing countries in the following manner: group I, The industrial countries and supranational institutions; group II, the high- and upper-middle-income developing countries (per-capita GNP $1,136 or more in 1977); group III, intermediate and lower-middle-income countries ($281-$1,135); group IV, lower-income countries ($280 or less); group V, centrally planned countries. A list of each group's countries is shown in table 4-2.

The Euromoney index shows the direction and magnitude of changes in the market over time. In other words, it shows whether market conditions are tightening or relaxing. Individual borrowers can compare their financing costs with the overall market condition. A borrower can observe whether its terms are improving or deteriorating against the market. For instance, the interest-rate spread of Brazil was 1-7/8 percent over the LIBOR in April 1978 for a $250 million loan with a ten-year maturity. Then in April 1980, the interest-rate spread of Brazil declined to 0.9375 over the LIBOR for a similar loan. Consequently the Brazilian index fell 58 percent during this period. Meanwhile the Euromoney index also declined from $157.6 to $112.2, a 28.8 percent decline during the comparable period. The Brazilian index, however, declined at a greater rate than the overall market index. Therefore the market perception of Brazil improved during the period.

The analysis of country risk plays an important part in asset and liability management of multinational banks. Theoretically it is more desirable to diversify country risk by including a large number of countries in asset and liability composition. Because of capital constraints, however, many international banks cannot diversify country risk fully but are forced to concentrate their loan and liability structure within group I and II countries; Western Europe and higher- and upper-middle-income developing countries. With a given amount of capital, it is still worthwhile to diversify country risk by including as many countries as possible from groups I and II rather than concentrating on just a few countries. The rationale for such diversification is directly related to the unique nature of country risk, which entails the problems of nationalization, expropriation, labor unrest, exchange controls, and devaluations.[20] For instance, the Nigerian government nationalized all foreign commercial banks in 1977, and the Mexican peso was devalued twice in 1976 and again in 1982. As a result, U.S.-based Citicorp diversified its international asset and liability structure with respect to geography, industry, and currencies. It set a country risk limit that an individual country cannot exceed in its amount of borrowings. In fact, normally no single country outside the United States has more than 7 percent of the total commercial portfolio of Citicorp.[21]

According to Alan Rugman and others, American firms and banks with a large proportion of foreign operations are shown to have more-stable earnings than comparable firms selling mostly in the U.S. domestic market.[22] In one study, which focused on the stability of multinational businesses, U.S. banks exhibited less risk and more stability than those of U.S. manufacturing companies and banks doing domestic business alone. It is argued that this stability is mainly due to risk diversification. When the domestic demand for loans is sluggish and domestic earnings are low, international banks increase their loan offerings abroad.


**Capital Adequacy**

Historically capital requirements in the United States were instituted after the bank failures of the 1930s. Banking regulators felt that minimum capitalization rates such as 7 percent of total assets would serve as a cushion to absorb losses. This kind of regulatory framework worked well during the 1930s when banks were small and basically served the local market. Today U.S. banks are much larger and serve not only regional and national markets but also international markets. It is impossible for a bank to cover loan losses or deposit withdrawals with the equity capital account alone. This is especially true for international banks, which hold large deposits from single depositors and make large multimillion-dollar loans. For all practical purposes, the equity account is generally used for long-term capital assets such as buildings and equipment, and only small portions of the account are dispersed through loan demand or deposit withdrawals.

A true test of capital adequacy today would depend on a bank management's ability to provide liquidity, solvency, and profitability to manage properly the asset and liability structures of the institution. A fixed rate of capital requirement in relation to assets or deposits is arbitrary and unworkable. What would be an adequate amount of capital would depend upon the nature of a bank's business and specialization. In a recent study, Citicorp argued that the traditional definition of capital, which includes common stock, capital surplus, and retained earnings, is outdated; the modern definition should include preferred stocks and long-term debt with maturity of ten years or more.[23] Thus, the traditional definition of capital adequacy with a fixed rate of capital to risky assets cannot be applied to international operations because risk-free assets in domestic banking may turn out to be risky asets in international banking. For example, deposits due from foreign banks may be considered to be risk-free assets in domestic banking; however, if these deposits are due from LDCs with higher country risk, they can be very-high-risk assets.

There is no simple way to measure the capital adequacy level by a single ratio because adequate capital must be determined by a bank's ability to manage other items in the balance sheet efficiently. If the bank manages liquidity properly by acquiring funds through domestic as well as international money markets, the need for larger capital will be reduced. Today international liquidity can be measured by a bank management's ability to acquire short-term funds in international markets, either through deposit acquisition or purchased funds like CDs and BAs. International liquidity is attainable, yet the question remains as to how to acquire it quickly and efficiently. It is true that no amount of capital will salvage a grossly mismanaged bank.[24] But a well-managed bank can operate on a very thin capital base. If a bank is well managed, its earnings will grow, and a portion will be retained to contribute to the internal capital base. Then, externally, more investors will be willing to purchase the bank's stock, and the overall bank capital base will increase.

**Notes**

1. Gunter Dufey and Ian Giddy, *The International Money Market* (Englewood Cliffs, N.J.: Prentice-Hall, 1978), pp. 14-18.

2. Steven Davis, *The Management Function in International Banking* (New York: John Wiley, 1978), pp. 83-85.

3. J. Dean and I. Giddy, *Averting International Banking Crises* (New York: Graduate School of Business Administration, New York University, 1981), pp. 3-27.

4. Dufey and Giddy, *International Money Market*, pp. 54-64.

5. S.W. Kung, "Asset-Liability Management for Smaller Banks," *Bankers Magazine* (January-February 1981):78-81.

6. P. Hendershot, "The Structure of International Interest Rates," *Journal of Finance* (September 1967):455-465; S. Kwack, "The Structure of International Interest Rates," *Journal of Finance* (September 1971): 897-900; R. Mills, "Structural Change in the Eurodollar Market," Federal Reserve Board, November 1, 1973, pp. 1-23.

7. L.S. Goodman, "Can Risks in LDC Lending be Diversified?" *Business Economics* (March 1982):12-15.

8. Figures include the public and publicly guaranteed debt of ninety-eight developing countries plus estimates of private nonguaranteed debt. See World Bank, *Debt Service Tables* (Washington, D.C., 1981), p. xv.

9. U.S. Department of Commerce, *Survey of Current Business* (August 1981):28-38.

10. B. Nowzad, "Debt in Developing Countries: Some Issues for the 1980's," *Finance and Development* (March 1982):13-15; W.C. Williams, *International Capital Markets*, Occasional Paper 7 (Washington, D.C.: IMF, 1981), pp. 5-22.

11. Federal Reserve Bank of St. Louis, *International Economic Indicators*, (February 1982), and various issues of the IMF's *International Financial Statistics* (1972-1982).

12. G.M. Von Furstenberg, "Incentives for International Currency Diversification," *IMF Staff Papers* (September 1981):477-494.

13. A.R. Prindle, *Foreign Exchange Risk* (New York: John Wiley, 1976), pp. 21-36.

14. Financial Accounting Standards Board, "Statement of Financial Accounting Standards, No. 8" (Stamford, Conn., December 1975), pp. 3-88.

15. Financial Accounting Standards Board, "Statement of Financial Accounting Standards, No. 52" (Stamford, Conn., December 1981), pp. 5-32.

16. S. Kohlhagen, "The Performance of the Foreign Exchange Markets," *Journal of International Business Studies* (Fall 1975):33-39; I. Giddy and G. Dufey, "The Random Behavior of Flexible Exchange Rates," *Journal of International Business Studies* (Spring 1975):1-32; Richard M. Levich, "On the Efficiency of Markets for Foreign Exchange," in *International Economic Policy*, ed. R. Dornbush and J. Frankel (Baltimore: John Hopkins University Press, 1979).

17. R. Everett, A. George, and A. Blumberg, "Appraising Currency Strength and Weakness," *Journal of International Business Studies* (Fall 1980):80-91.

18. "The Country Risk League Table," *Euromoney* (October 1980):26-40.

19. "The Launch of the Eurocurrency Index," *Euromoney* (October 1980):15-25.

20. A. Angelini, M. Eng, and F. Lees, *International Lending Risks and the Eurodollars* (New York: John Wiley, 1979), pp. 89-97.

21. Citicorp, *Citicorp Annual Report and 10-K* (New York, 1980), pp. 15-30.

22. Alan Rugman, *International Diversification and the Multinational Enterprise* (Lexington, Mass.: Lexington Books, D.C. Heath and Company, 1979), pp. 15-37.

23. D.S. Howard and G.M. Hoffman, *Evolving Concepts of Bank Capital Management* (New York: Citicorp, 1980), pp. 7-27.

24. Justin Watson, "A Regulatory View of Capital Adequacy," *Journal of Bank Research* (Autumn 1975):170-172.

# 5 Empirical Comparison of Asset and Liability Structure

Differences exist between the operating structures of large U.S. banks and foreign banking competitors doing international banking business. Comparative analysis of the financial statements of these banking competitors indicates that foreign banks differ from each other and from their U.S. competitors with regard to methods of raising funds and using funds. The structural composition varies with respect to loan portfolios, deposits, liquidity and capital for foreign agencies, branches and subsidiary banks, and large U.S. commercial banks.

Comparison of the financial structure of foreign and U.S. banks, while invaluable for gauging competitor market movements, is fraught with problems. First, detailed and meaningful financial information for foreign banks is especially difficult to obtain. The statistical classification found in the Federal Reserve Board Call Report for foreign banks (see appendix D) is not identical with the format used for large U.S. banks. Furthermore, foreign-bank income statistics are meaningless because of conceptual problems in allocating costs and revenues on a domestic and foreign office basis. Second, even though foreign banking organizations in the United States are subject to U.S. banking laws and regulations, the U.S. and foreign banking systems are inherently different. Generally, foreign environments are characterized by nationwide branch banking, while the U.S. environment by statewide unit banking. In addition, it is quite common for major decisions of foreign-bank branches in the United States to be made by home-office top management. Even for foreign-bank subsidiaries, banking philosophy and policies are greatly influenced by the parent bank. Overall, it is generally agreed that the organizational structure of foreign banks is highly centralized.

## Banking Concentration

The majority of commercial banking assets in most advanced countries are controlled by a small number of banks (table 5-1). For instance, the five largest banks in Canada control 90 percent of the total commercial banking assets of that country. Nationwide branch banking is quite common to most of the rest of the world, yet the United States has basically a unit-banking system encompassing more than 14,000 individual banks scattered throughout the nation. Moreover, because of a grandfather clause in the 1978 IBA,

113

**Table 5-1**

**Indicators of Banking Concentration in Major Foreign Countries**

| Large Banks | Percentage of Commercial Banking Assets | Percentage of Total Banking Assets |
|---|---|---|
| Australia | | |
| 7 major trading banks | 88 | 49 |
| Belgium | | |
| 3 largest commercial banks | 80 | 32 |
| Canada | | |
| 5 largest chartered banks | 90 | 60 |
| France | | |
| 3 largest nationalized banks | 55 | 45-50 |
| Germany | | |
| 3 largest commercial banks | 42 | 10 |
| Italy | | |
| Big 5 banks | 47 | 28 |
| Japan | | |
| 13 city banks | n.a. | 53 |
| The Netherlands | | |
| 3 largest commercial banks | 60 | 41 |
| Spain | | |
| "Big seven" commercial banks | 58[a] | 34[a] |
| Switzerland | | |
| 5 big banks | n.a. | 48 |
| United Kingdom | | |
| 6 London clearing banks | 70 | n.a. |
| United States | | |
| 3 largest commercial banks | 18 | 12[b] |
| 10 largest commercial banks | 34 | 23[b] |

Source: Steven J. Weiss, "National Policies on Foreign Acquisitions of Banks," *Bankers Magazine* January-February 1981:29. Reprinted with permission by the publisher.

[a]Share of deposits.

[b]Includes savings and loan associations and mutual savings banks.

many foreign banks in the United States and their parent banks participate in nonbanking activities, helping to explain why the average size of foreign banks is much larger than that of U.S. banks.

Table 5-2 shows the twenty-five largest commercial banks outside the United States and the twenty-five largest American commercial banks, ranked in order by total deposit size. The deposit size of U.S. banks ranged from $5.0 billion to $89.3 billion in 1980, while the deposit size of foreign banks fell between $50.5 billion and $107.5 billion for the same period. Only three U.S. banks—Bank of America, Citibank, and Chase Manhattan—are large enough to be included in the twenty-five largest world banks.

Table 5-3 shows the ten largest U.S. banks that do the bulk of the international banking business. International banking is highly concentrated in New York, Los Angeles, San Francisco, and Chicago. Only in recent

**Table 5-2**
**Twenty-Five Largest Commercial Banking Companies inside and outside the United States, December 31, 1980**

| Outside the United States | Country | Assets[a] |
|---|---|---|
| Banque Nationale de Paris | France | 107,449,631 |
| Caisse Nationale de Crédit Agricole | France | 105,906,369 |
| Crédit Lyonnais | France | 98,147,449 |
| Société Générale | France | 90,164,865 |
| Barclays Banks | Britain | 88,624,733 |
| Dai-Ichi Kangyo Bank | Japan | 88,519,780 |
| Deutsche Bank | Germany | 88,468,402 |
| National Westminster Bank | Britain | 82,585,341 |
| Mitsubishi Bank | Japan | 76,433,197 |
| Fuji Bank | Japan | 75,396,945 |
| Sumitomo Bank | Japan | 73,459,526 |
| Sanwa Bank | Japan | 70,268,863 |
| Dresdner Bank | Germany | 62,595,548 |
| Midland Bank | Britain | 60,543,710 |
| Industrial Bank of Japan | Japan | 60,475,895 |
| Westdeutsche Landesbank Girozentrale | Germany | 57,898,325 |
| Cie Financiere de Suez | France | 57,279,713 |
| Bank of Tokyo | Japan | 55,861,833 |
| Royal Bank of Canada | Canada | 53,462,183 |
| Mitsubishi Bank | Japan | 52,821,868 |
| Cie Financiere de Paris et des Pays-Bas | France | 52,282,105 |
| Banco do Brazil | Brazil | 52,238,425 |
| Tokai Bank | Japan | 50,998,711 |
| Commerzbank | Germany | 50,685,657 |
| Algemene Bank Nederland | Netherlands | 50,576,613 |

| Inside the United States | Assets[a] |
|---|---|
| Bank of America NT&SA, San Francisco | $89,265,951,000 |
| Citibank NA, New York | 72,503,974,000 |
| Chase Manhattan Bank N.A., New York | 58,698,641,000 |
| Manufacturers Hanover Trust Co., New York | 40,924,368,000 |
| Morgan Guaranty Trust Co., New York | 35,704,230,000 |
| Chemical Bank, New York | 30,156,770,000 |
| Continental Illinois NB&T Co., Chicago | 27,109,836,000 |
| Bankers Trust Co., New York | 23,942,285,000 |
| First National Bank, Chicago | 21,417,484,000 |
| Security Pacific National Bank, Los Angeles | 21,183,852,000 |
| Wells Fargo Bank N.A., San Francisco | 17,360,398,000 |
| Crocker National Bank, San Francisco | 14,952,078,000 |
| Marine Midland Bank N.A., Buffalo, N.Y. | 14,200,612,000 |
| Irving Trust Co., New York | 12,567,302,000 |
| United California Bank, Los Angeles | 12,445,019,000 |
| Mellon Bank N.A., Pittsburgh | 11,757,544,000 |
| First National Bank, Boston | 10,384,685,000 |
| Bank of New York | 8,319,164,816 |
| Seattle-First National Bank | 7,164,166,000 |
| National Bank of Detroit | 7,151,516,000 |
| First National Bank, Dallas | 6,534,133,000 |
| Republic National Bank, Dallas | 6,319,702,000 |
| First City National Bank, Houston | 5,440,983,000 |
| North Carolina National Bank, Charlotte | 5,071,204,000 |
| Union Bank, Los Angeles | 4,999,282,000 |

Sources: Moody's Bank and Finance Manual, 1981, and "The Fortune Directory of the 50 Largest Commercial-Banking Companies outside the United States," *Fortune,* August 10, 1981.

[a]Millions of dollars.

**Table 5-3**
**Foreign Net Income and Foreign Loan Portfolios of the Ten Largest U.S. Banks**
*(thousands of U.S. dollars)*

| | Foreign Loans as Percent of Total Loan Portfolio | | Total Foreign Loans | Total Net Income | | Percentage of Contributions from Foreign Operations | |
|---|---|---|---|---|---|---|---|
| | 1980 | 1979 | 1980 | 1980 | 1979 | 1980 | 1979 |
| Bank America | 38 | 41 | 23,670,000 | 645,003 | 600,155 | 45 | 38 |
| Citicorp | 31.2 | 40 | 4,600,000 | 507,000 | 544,192 | 62.1 | 64.5 |
| Chase Manhattan | 48.6 | 44.7 | 16,742,000 | 364,654 | 311,228 | 48.4 | 40.6 |
| Manufacturers Hanover | 51 | 51 | 14,300,000 | 230,177 | 211,281 | 49.5 | 48.7 |
| Morgan Guaranty | 40.9 | 54.5 | 14,605,000 | 367,682 | 288,298 | 57.6 | 52.2 |
| Continental Illinois | 31.5 | 30.7 | 7,684,000 | 224,143 | 194,126 | 41.0 | 40.0 |
| Chemical New York | 42.2 | 41.7 | 9,436,988 | 175,183 | 142,308 | 38.0 | 34 |
| Bankers Trust | 48.1 | 45.0 | 7,813,639 | 214,019 | 113,738 | 52.0 | 50.0 |
| Western Bancorporation | 29 | 24.2 | 8,854,320 | 233,400 | 214,900 | 29.0 | 24.0 |
| First Chicago | 39 | 61 | 6,547,284 | (63,008) | 112,041 | (9.5) | 4.0 |

Source: Moody's Bank and Finance Manual, 1980 and 1981 editions, in addition to data extracted from corporate annual reports.

years, as domestic markets have become saturated and international banking more lucrative, have regional banks ventured into international banking operations. According to a recent study by Robert Morris Associates, the average compound growth rate of earnings from international operations for the ten largest banks was 22.8 percent in the 1972-1977 period compared to 4.4 percent for earnings from domestic operations.[1]

Foreign loans and income from foreign operations of large U.S. banks were a substantial share of the total banking business in 1980 (table 5-3). Major U.S. multinational banks with a large proportion of foreign loans in their portfolios experienced higher earnings in 1979 and 1980 when the domestic loan market was slow. For instance, Bank of America, the nation's largest commercial bank, registered international income of $292 million, which was 45 percent of the bank's total income in 1980, up from 38 percent the previous year. The bank is represented in 94 countries through a network of 113 overseas branches, 19 corporate and representative offices, and more than 270 subsidiaries and affiliates abroad. Foreign loans constituted 38 percent of the Bank of America's loan portfolio, and foreign deposits comprised the largest source of the corporation's funds—35.6 percent in 1980. Moreover, Citicorp, the nation's second largest bank, registered net income from international operations as $315 million in 1980 which was 62.1 percent of total corporate net income. Citicorp's overseas loan portfolio averaged $4.6 billion in 1980, or 31.2 percent of the total portfolio, and its international operations were spread through 1,300 overseas offices located in 92 countries.

## Comparison of Asset and Liability Structure

Tables 5-4, 5-5, and 5-6 present major balance-sheet items of large U.S. banks, foreign subsidiary banks, and foreign-bank agencies and branches in the United States for the 1976-1980 period. These tables show the composition of assets and liabilities of these three banking groups and illustrate funding sources and fund applications. Standard banking assets—defined as total assets minus clearing balances due to directly related institutions—increased rapidly for all three groups during the period. The increase in standard banking assets of foreign-bank agencies and branches, however, is much more dramatic, with $30.3 billion in 1976 and $93.6 billion in 1980, an almost threefold increase. Consequently the ratio of standard banking assets of foreign-bank agencies and branches as a percentage of the same assets for large U.S. banks also increased from 8.1 percent in 1976 to 16.7 percent in 1980. Meanwhile standard banking assets of foreign-bank subsidiaries increased 104 percent, from $10.8 billion in 1976 to $21.9 billion in 1980. This increase is also reflected in the standard banking-asset ratio relative to large U.S. banks showing 2.9 percent in 1976 and 3.9 percent in 1980.

**Table 5-4**

**U.S. Large Commercial Banks: Summary of Assets and Liabilities**

*(millions of dollars)*

| Category | May 1976 | May 1977 | May 1978 | May 1979 | May 1980 |
|---|---|---|---|---|---|
| Standard banking assets | 374,559 | 413,705 | 485,023 | 500,721 | 559,188 |
| Commercial and industrial loans | 99,621 | 103,392 | 118,450 | 134,078 | 148,918 |
| U.S. residents | n.a. | n.a. | n.a. | 124,490[l] | 138,361[a] |
| Foreign residents | n.a. | n.a. | n.a. | 6,068[l] | 5,747[a] |
| Other loans | 126,308 | 138,544 | 159,189 | 187,232 | 208,724 |
| Interbank loans and deposits[b] | 17,938 | 21,183 | 23,337 | 26,710 | 30,413 |
| U.S. | 12,619 | 15,531 | 17,391 | 20,534 | 23,139 |
| Foreign | 5,319 | 5,652 | 5,946 | 6,176 | 7,276 |
| Securities | 80,410 | 89,740 | 89,520 | 96,715 | 102,484 |
| Other assets | 50,282 | 60,846 | 94,527 | 55,986 | 68,649 |
| Clearing balances[c] | 55,570 | 56,141 | 66,139 | 97,329 | 109,027 |
| Due from related institutions[d] | | | | | |
| U.S. | | | | | |
| Foreign | | | | | |
| Total assets/total liabilities | 430,129 | 469,846 | 551,162 | 598,050 | 668,215 |
| Standard banking liabilities | 349,745 | 375,479 | 437,349 | 464,092 | 503,776 |
| Deposits and credit balances of | | | | | |
| nonbanks | 283,657 | 296,879 | 343,538 | 348,158 | 377,875 |
| U.S. residents | 282,551 | 295,766 | 341,896 | 345,952 | 376,266 |
| Foreign residents[c] | 1,106 | 1,113 | 1,642 | 2,203 | 1,609 |
| Interbank liabilities[f] | 62,225 | 74,539 | 87,293 | 100,399 | 112,053 |
| U.S. | 52,784 | 65,540 | 78,902 | 94,442 | 105,967 |
| Foreign | 9,441 | 8,999 | 8,391 | 5,957 | 6,086 |
| Other Liabilities | 3,863 | 4,061 | 6,518 | 15,535 | 13,848 |
| Clearing liabilities | 32,348 | 34,389 | 48,411 | 42,585 | 54,153 |
| Demand deposits due to | | | | | |
| U.S. banks | 20,838 | 21,941 | 33,228 | 29,279 | 34,721 |
| Demand deposits due to | | | | | |
| foreign banks | 4,845 | 5,656 | 7,742 | 7,143 | 11,500 |
| Others[g] | 6,665 | 6,892 | 7,441 | 6,163 | 7,932 |
| Due to directly related institutions[d] | | | | | |
| U.S. | | | | | |
| Foreign | | | | | |
| Residual[h] | 48,036 | 59,978 | 77,000 | 91,373 | 110,286 |

Source: Federal Reserve Board, Washington, D.C. 1981.

[a]Does not include acceptances and commercial paper: 1979 = $3,520 million and 1980 = $4,810 million. No details were available for previous years.

[b]Includes federal funds sold (purchased) and time deposits but not demand deposits, due from (to) banks.

[c]Includes cash items in process of collection, demand balances due from U.S. banks, and (when available) deposits due from banks in foreign countries.

[d]Net assets (net liabilities) due from (to) own foreign branches are reported as part of other assets (other liabilities) on the weekly report of condition.

[e]Represent demand deposits of foreign governments and official institutions.

[f]Includes federal funds purchased, securities sold under agreements to repurchase, and time deposits due to the banks. Excludes demand deposits.

[g]Includes certified and officers' checks, letters of credit, and so forth.

[h]Total assets minus total liabilities. This amount includes but is not equal to capital accounts and reserves.

**Table 5-5**

**U.S. Commercial Banking Subsidiaries of Foreign Banks: Summary of Assets and Liabilities**

*(millions of dollars)*

| Category | May 1976 | May 1977 | May 1978 | June 1979 | May 1980 |
|---|---|---|---|---|---|
| Standard banking assets | 10,768 | 12,503 | 16,551 | 20,701 | 21,982 |
| Commercial and industrial loans | 3,658 | 4,111 | 5,287 | 6,082 | 6,270 |
| U.S. residents | 3,242 | 3,484 | 4,547 | 5,277 | 5,239 |
| Foreign residents | 416 | 627 | 740 | 805 | 1,031 |
| Other loans | 2,711 | 3,369 | 4,073 | 5,871 | 6,384 |
| Interbank loans and deposits | 1,048 | 1,030 | 1,499 | 2,053 | 2,015 |
| U.S. | 911 | 854 | 1,194 | 1,594 | 1,609 |
| Foreign | 137 | 176 | 305 | 459 | 406 |
| Securities | 2,421 | 2,807 | 3,454 | 4,068 | 4,333 |
| Other assets | 930 | 1,186 | 2,238 | 2,627 | 2,980 |
| Clearing balances | 1,447 | 2,015 | 2,939 | 2,911 | 3,429 |
| Due from related institutions | 358 | 648 | 822 | 727 | 1,133 |
| U.S. | 84 | 144 | 163 | 146 | 212 |
| Foreign[a] | 274 | 504 | 659 | 581 | 921 |
| Total assets/total liabilities | 12,573 | 15,166 | 20,312 | 24,339 | 25,623 |
| Standard banking liabilities | 10,389 | 12,443 | 16,283 | 19,844 | 21,412 |
| Deposits and credits of nonbanks | 8,656 | 9,780 | 12,545 | 15,996 | 16,085 |
| U.S. | 7,838 | 8,779 | 11,348 | 14,753 | 14,923 |
| Foreign | 818 | 1,001 | 1,197 | 1,243 | 1,162 |
| Interbank Liabilities | 729 | 787 | 904 | 1,546 | 1,842 |
| U.S. | 554 | 558 | 653 | 1,365 | 1,629 |
| Foreign[b] | 175 | 229 | 251 | 181 | 213 |
| Other liabilities | 1,004 | 1,876 | 2,834 | 2,382 | 3,485 |
| Clearing liabilities | 429 | 739 | 1,593 | 1,436 | 1,210 |
| Demand deposits due to U.S. banks | 92 | 257 | 794 | 445 | 257 |
| Demand deposits due to foreign banks | 131 | 141 | 342 | 242 | 398 |
| Other | 205 | 341 | 457 | 749 | 555 |
| Due to directly related institutions | 477 | 502 | 555 | 940 | 730 |
| U.S. | 322 | 280 | 162 | 145 | 86 |
| Foreign | 155 | 222 | 393 | 795 | 644 |
| Capital account and reserves | 1,279 | 1,482 | 1,881 | 2,119 | 2,271 |

Source: Federal Reserve Board, Washington, D.C., 1981 and Abdalla M. Eldarrat, "Operating Characteristics of U.S-owned Banks and U.S. Offices of Foreign Banks: A Comparative Financial Analysis" (Ph.D. diss., St. Louis University, 1982).

[a]In May 1978 foreign-bank subsidiaries had an unusually high claims on head office or parent of about $700 million. For purposes of more-meaningful comparison, this amount was replaced with that year's average of about $41 million.

[b]Includes deposits of foreign governments and official institutions.

**Table 5-6**

**U.S. Branches and Agencies of Foreign Banks: Summary of Assets and Liabilities**
*(millions of dollars)*

| Category | May 1976 | May 1977 | May 1978 | May 1979 | May 1980 |
|---|---|---|---|---|---|
| Standard banking assets | 30,300 | 35,637 | 46,472 | 81,781 | 93,548 |
| Commercial and industrial loans | 15,637 | 16,557 | 21,444 | 31,956 | 40,045 |
| U.S. residents | 11,516 | 11,866 | 15,494 | 21,206 | 25,767 |
| Foreign residents | 4,121 | 4,691 | 5,950 | 10,751 | 14,278 |
| Other loans | 1,183 | 1,703 | 3,330 | 5,980 | 8,584 |
| Interbank loans and deposits | 8,632 | 12,105 | 17,483 | 32,376 | 31,282 |
| U.S. | 5,743 | 7,396 | 10,720 | 17,485 | 20,409 |
| Foreign | 2,889 | 4,709 | 6,763 | 14,892 | 10,873 |
| Securities | 1,354 | 1,426 | 2,001 | 2,599 | 3,126 |
| Other assets | 3,494 | 3,846 | 2,214 | 8,870 | 10,511 |
| Clearing balances | 5,366 | 6,733 | 13,929 | 12,168 | 13,871 |
| Due from related institutions | 12,934 | 11,218 | 17,918 | 26,402 | 38,535 |
| U.S. | 5,399 | 4,596 | 6,529 | 7,578 | 13,572 |
| Foreign | 7,535 | 6,622 | 11,389 | 18,826 | 24,963 |
| Total assets/total liabilities | 48,600 | 53,588 | 78,319 | 120,353 | 145,954 |
| Standard banking liabilities | 23,881 | 27,661 | 49,368 | 56,263 | 73,728 |
| Deposits and credits of nonbanks | 7,158 | 9,081 | 12,739 | 19,209 | 19,245 |
| U.S. residents | 3,091 | 4,382 | 7,725 | 13,948 | 14,402 |
| Foreign residents | 4,067 | 4,699 | 5,014 | 5,261 | 4,843 |
| Interbank Liabilities | 12,235 | 15,020 | 22,050 | 24,566 | 44,378 |
| U.S. | 9,683 | 12,237 | 18,422 | 23,445 | 35,851 |
| Foreign | 2,552 | 2,783 | 3,628 | 6,810 | 8,527 |
| Other liabilities | 4,488 | 3,560 | 4,579 | 6,799 | 10,105 |
| Clearing liabilities | 3,524 | 4,941 | 6,766 | 14,539 | 9,369 |
| Demand deposits due to U.S. banks | 597 | 1,103 | 1,840 | 5,029 | 3,406 |
| Demand deposits due to foreign banks | 1,454 | 2,045 | 1,800 | 1,604 | 2,436 |
| Others | 1,473 | 1,793 | 3,126 | 7,907 | 3,527 |
| Due to directly related institutions | 21,583 | 20,298 | 31,435 | 48,593 | 61,649 |
| U.S. | 5,482 | 4,731 | 6,861 | 8,199 | 14,114 |
| Foreign | 16,101 | 15,567 | 24,574 | 40,394 | 47,535 |
| Capital accounts and reserves | 612 | 688 | 750 | 928 | 1,208 |

Source: Federal Reserve Board, Washington, D.C., 1981.
Note: Includes New York investment companies and agreement corporations.

The loan structures of large U.S. banks and foreign-bank subsidiaries are somewhat similar, while foreign-bank agencies and branches are clearly different (table 5-7). The average commercial and industrial loan of large U.S. banks and foreign subsidiary banks accounted for 22.3 percent and 26.3 percent of total assets, respectively, in the period 1976-1980, while the average ratio for foreign-bank agencies and branches was 28.9 percent in the same period. The average ratio of other loans, which include consumer loans, real-estate loans, and other types of loans, was 30.1 percent for large U.S. banks, 22.6 percent for foreign-bank subsidiaries, and only 4.2 percent for foreign-bank branches in the 1976-1980 period.

Clearly foreign-bank agencies and branches are catering to large multinational corporations for their internationally related trade and business financing. In comparison, a relatively substantial portion of the loan portfolio for large U.S. banks and foreign-bank subsidiaries is relegated to individual consumer loans and real-estate loans. The importance of commercial and industrial loans for foreign-bank agencies and branches is evidenced by a 26.9 percent share of total commercial and industrial loans of large U.S. banks in 1980. Another interesting comparison is that the bulk of U.S. and foreign bank subsidiaries' commercial loans is made to domestic customers, while a substantial portion (30.4 percent) of foreign-bank agency and branch commercial and industrial loans is made to foreign customers. Furthermore, when domestic loan demand and economic activity were sluggish, as in 1976-1977 and 1979-1980, the loan ratio of U.S. banks and foreign-bank subsidiaries declined, whereas the loan ratio of foreign-bank agencies and branches expanded to foreign customers.

Another unique asset structure of these three banking groups is found in interbank loan deposits and securities holdings. As explained in table 5-4, interbank loans and deposits consist largely of federal funds and time deposits, including Eurodollar deposits with commercial banks. In the 1976-1980 period, the average ratio of interbank loans and deposits as a percentage of total assets was relatively low for U.S. banks (4.4 percent) and for foreign subsidiary banks (7.7 percent), while the same ratio was comparatively greater for foreign-bank agencies and branches (22.2 percent). On the other hand, the average ratio of securities as a percentage of total assets is much greater for U.S. banks (17.1 percent) and foreign subsidiary banks (17.7 percent) but much lower for foreign-bank agencies and branches (2.5 percent). This means that foreign-bank agencies and branches hold their liquidity in interbank loans and deposits primarily at U.S. banks rather than in U.S. and municipal government securities. In fact, foreign banks maintain their liquidity through other financial institutions as a convenience inasmuch as government securities require additional professional personnel whom they lack.

In comparing the liability structures of the three banking groups, there appears to be a reasonable resemblance again between large U.S. banks and foreign-bank subsidiaries, while a striking contrast tends to predominate for foreign-bank agencies and branches. The single most important source of funds results from deposits and credit balances of nonbanks, representing 61.2 percent of large U.S. bank assets and 64.7 percent of foreign-bank subsidiary assets in the 1976-1980 period but only 15.5 percent of the total

**Table 5-7**
**Comparative Percentage Composition of Major Assets and Liabilities, 1976-1980 Average**

| Items | Large U.S. Banks — Percentage of Total Assets | U.S. Subsidiaries of Foreign Banks — Percentage of Total Assets | U.S. Subsidiaries of Foreign Banks — Percentage of Large U.S. Banks | U.S. Branches and Agencies of Foreign Banks — Percentage of Total Assets | U.S. Branches and Agencies of Foreign Banks — Percentage of Large U.S. Banks |
|---|---|---|---|---|---|
| Standard banking assets | 86.1 | 84.5 | 3.4 | 64.0 | 11.9 |
| Commercial and industrial loans | 22.3 | 26.3 | 4.2 | 28.9 | 20.1 |
| U.S. residents | 20.8 | 22.7 | | 20.2 | 17.8 |
| Foreign residents | 1.6 | 3.6 | 15.6 | 8.7 | 212.8 |
| Other loans | 30.1 | 22.6 | 2.7 | 4.2 | 2.3 |
| Interbank loans and deposits | 4.4 | 7.7 | 6.3 | 22.2 | 80.8 |
| U.S. | 3.3 | 6.3 | 6.5 | 13.6 | 62.9 |
| Foreign | 1.1 | 1.5 | 4.8 | 7.2 | 141.7 |
| Securities | 17.1 | 17.7 | 3.7 | 2.5 | 2.3 |
| Other assets | 12.4 | 9.7 | 3.0 | 6.9 | 8.1 |
| Clearing balances | 13.8 | 12.9 | 3.3 | 12.2 | 13.6 |
| Due from related institutions | | 3.6 | | 23.7 | |
| U.S. | | .8 | | 8.7 | |
| Foreign | | 2.9 | | 15.0 | |
| Total assets | 100.0 | 100.0 | 3.5 | 100.0 | 15.8 |
| Standard banking liabilities | 78.7 | 82.0 | 3.7 | 52.2 | 9.4 |
| Deposits and credits of nonbanks | 61.2 | 64.7 | 3.8 | 15.5 | 4.0 |
| U.S. residents | 60.9 | 59.0 | 3.5 | 9.2 | 2.5 |
| Foreign residents | .3 | 5.7 | 73.1 | 6.3 | 323.0 |
| Interbank liabilities | 16.0 | 5.8 | 1.3 | 26.4 | 25.9 |

| | | | | | |
|---|---|---|---|---|---|
| U.S. | 14.4 | 4.7 | 1.1 | 22.1 | 23.8 |
| Foreign | 1.5 | 1.1 | 2.8 | 5.3 | 71.1 |
| Other liabilities | 1.5 | 11.6 | 31.2 | 7.6 | 78.2 |
| Clearing liabilities | 7.8 | 5.3 | 2.5 | 6.6 | 18.1 |
| Demand deposits due to U.S. banks | 5.1 | 1.8 | 1.2 | 2.0 | 8.1 |
| Demand deposits due to foreign banks | 1.3 | 1.3 | 3.3 | 2.7 | 26.6 |
| Others | 1.3 | 2.1 | 6.7 | 3.2 | 52.6 |
| Due to directly related institutions | | 3.3 | | 41.0 | |
| U.S. | | 1.2 | | 9.1 | |
| Foreign | | 2.1 | | 31.9 | |
| Capital and reserves | 14.1 | 9.2 | | .9 | |

Source: Federal Reserve Board, Washington, D.C., 1981.

assets of foreign-bank agencies and branches. Although large U.S. banks relied heavily on U.S. customers for over 99 percent of nonbank deposits, foreign-bank subsidiaries relied on foreign depositors for only about 10 percent of their total. However, the deposit rate of foreign customers for foreign bank agencies and branches was about 40 percent in the same period. Still, the deposit ratio of domestic customers for foreign-bank agencies and branches has increased over the years. This means that even though large U.S. banks continue to enjoy relatively cheaper sources of funds through deposit holdings of U.S. domestic customers, foreign banks have definitely penetrated the domestic deposit market.

Demand deposits represent a major source of funding for large U.S. banks, ranging between 41 percent and 44 percent of total deposits in the 1976-1980 period (table 5-8). Foreign subsidiary banks and branches and agencies, however, rely on time deposits as the major source of funds. Although foreign subsidiary banks engage in retail banking to some extent, they are like foreign-bank agencies and are very active in wholesale deposit efforts. As the cost of money increased in the later 1970s, corporate treasurers began to worry about interest rates on their deposits; they economized, keeping minimum cash balance whenever possible and investing in interest-earning deposits for profit. This is the reason why the share of time deposits has increased substantially over the years for all three banking groups. Thus, competition has become much stronger among these groups in attracting not only demand deposits but also time deposits. The impact of high-interest-paying time deposits on bank profitability has resulted in a narrower interest spread, particularly for foreign banks, which have a larger proportion of costly time deposits in their liability structure.

Both large U.S. banks and foreign-bank agencies and branches rely more heavily on interbank sources of funds than do foreign-bank subsidiaries. The average ratio of interbank liabilities as a percentage of total assets was 14.4 percent for large U.S. banks and 22.1 percent for foreign-bank branches and agencies in the 1976-1980 period but only 4.7 percent for foreign-bank subsidiaries. This seems to indicate that foreign-bank subsidiaries are a separate entity both legally and financially, depending less on interbank money-market activities. From the viewpoint of the net position of interbank assets and liabilities, however, both large U.S. banks and foreign-bank agencies and branches appear to be net borrowers in U.S. domestic money markets. Furthermore, it would appear that foreign subsidiary banks rely very little on their parent-bank institutions as a source of funds, while foreign-bank agencies and branches draw most heavily from them. In fact, the average ratio of borrowing from related institutions was 3.3 percent for subsidiary banks assets and 41 percent for branch and agency assets in the 1976-1980 period, with 39.1 percent of the latter total from the parent operations.

**International Liquidity**

The main objective of asset and liability management is to obtain and retain a maximum amount of low-cost funds and to invest these funds in a manner that will yield maximum returns while maintaining adequate liquidity. An equilibrium balance between liquidity and profitability is probably the most-important function of international banks because too much liquidity will reduce profitability and too little liquidity will interrupt transaction and intermediary functions. Liquidity needs and profit-maximization objectives depend on several pertinent factors, such as management objectives, the regulatory environment, financial market conditions, and customer needs. Banks derive their income primarily from loans, which bring in the largest yield to the bank. At the same time, international banks must hold cash for liquidity purposes. The proper distribution of bank funds among maximum-profit-producing loans and liquid assets will have a decisive impact on a bank's profitability and liquidity. The maintenance of a maximum spread between interest earnings on loans and interest payments on funding sources has become a critical task for banks as the cost of funding continues to increase over the years. Yet a maximum interest spread is a prerequisite for adequate profitability because salary costs and other overhead also spiral upward.

Two liquidity ratios used in table 5-9 are the ratio of cash assets plus short-term government securities to total assets and the ratio of cash plus short-term treasury securities and federal funds sold to total assets. It appears that large U.S. banks tend to have higher liquidity ratios of this nature as compared to foreign subsidiary banks and foreign-bank agencies and branches, particularly with regard to the latter. However, since foreign-bank agencies and branches rely on parent-banking institutions for a larger proportion of their funding, the liquidity ratios are not really indicative of their liquidity positions. Still, when net transactions with related institutions are added to the liquidity ratios, foreign-bank agencies and branches seem to possess higher liquidity as compared to large U.S. banks and foreign-bank subsidiaries.

The traditional way of measuring liquidity to satisfy bank regulatory agencies has become obsolete in an environment where the definition and scope of financial markets has expanded from the local community to national and international arenas. Traditional liquidity ratios are static and partial in nature, measuring isolated balance-sheet items at a given point in time. A modern and workable concept of liquidity relates to a bank's ability to acquire necessary funds quickly and efficiently in both domestic and global financial markets. Furthermore, it is premised on a bank's ability to manage its assets and liabilities efficiently and properly in terms of asset

**Table 5-8**
**Distribution of Deposits and Credit Balances**
*(millions of dollars)*

| | 1976 | | 1977 | | 1978 | | 1979 | | 1980 | |
|---|---|---|---|---|---|---|---|---|---|---|
| | *Amount* | *Percent* | *Amount* | *Percent* | *Amount* | *Percent* | *Amount* | *Percent* | *Amount* | *Percent* |
| Large U.S. banks | | | | | | | | | | |
| Demand | 136,960 | 42.1 | 142,925 | 41.0 | 177,454 | 44.3 | 170,301 | 42.4 | 213,896 | 42.2 |
| U.S. residents | 131,009 | 40.2 | 136,974 | 39.3 | 168,070 | 42.0 | 160,955 | 40.1 | 202,563 | 40.0 |
| Foreign residents | 5,951 | 1.8 | 5,951 | 1.7 | 9,384 | 2.3 | 9,346 | 2.3 | 11,333 | 2.2 |
| Savings | 64,130 | 20.0 | 75,276 | 21.6 | 73,959 | 18.5 | 71,056 | 17.7 | 67,120 | 13.2 |
| U.S. residents | n.a. | | n.a. | | n.a. | | n.a. | | n.a. | |
| Foreign residents | n.a. | | n.a. | | n.a. | | n.a. | | n.a. | |
| Time | 124,366 | 38.2 | 130,266 | 37.4 | 149,126 | 37.2 | 160,521 | 39.9 | 225,917 | 44.6 |
| U.S. residents | 114,595 | 35.2 | 121,267 | 34.8 | 140,735 | 35.1 | 154,564 | 38.4 | 219,231 | 43.2 |
| Foreign residents | 9,771 | 3.0 | 8,999 | 2.6 | 8,391 | 2.1 | 5,957 | 1.5 | 6,686 | 1.3 |
| Total | 325,685 | 100.0 | 348,467 | 100.0 | 400,539 | 100.0 | 401,878 | 100.0 | 506,933 | 100.0 |
| U.S. Subsidiaries of foreign banks | | | | | | | | | | |
| Demand | 3,347 | 33.4 | 3,976 | 34.1 | 5,981 | 38.7 | 6,027 | 35.5 | 5,678 | 30.3 |
| U.S. residents | 2,998 | 30.0 | 3,648 | 31.3 | 5,354 | 34.6 | 5,234 | 30.8 | 4,946 | 26.4 |
| Foreign residents | 349 | 3.5 | 328 | 2.8 | 627 | 4.1 | 793 | 4.7 | 732 | 3.9 |
| Savings | 2,022 | 20.2 | 2,555 | 21.9 | 2,783 | 18.0 | 2,488 | 14.6 | 2,201 | 11.7 |
| U.S. residents | 1,889 | 18.9 | 2,366 | 20.3 | 2,613 | 16.9 | 2,365 | 13.9 | 2,111 | 11.2 |
| Foreign residents | 133 | 1.3 | 189 | 1.6 | 170 | 1.1 | 123 | 0.7 | 90 | 0.5 |
| Time | 4,638 | 46.3 | 5,131 | 44.0 | 6,695 | 43.3 | 8,478 | 49.9 | 10,886 | 58.0 |
| U.S. residents | 4,172 | 41.7 | 4,506 | 38.6 | 5,953 | 38.5 | 7,775 | 45.8 | 10,148 | 54.1 |
| Foreign residents | 466 | 4.7 | 625 | 5.4 | 742 | 4.8 | 703 | 4.1 | 738 | 3.9 |
| Total | 10,007 | 100.0 | 11,662 | 100.0 | 15,459 | 100.0 | 16,993 | 100.0 | 18,765 | 100.0 |
| U.S. Branches and agencies of foreign banks | | | | | | | | | | |
| Demand | 4,708 | 38.8 | 6,226 | 41.5 | 8,300 | 39.2 | 11,414 | 37.9 | 11,080 | 34.4 |
| U.S. residents | 2,811 | 23.3 | 3,793 | 25.3 | 5,857 | 27.7 | 8,576 | 28.5 | 7,898 | 24.5 |
| Foreign residents | 1,897 | 15.6 | 2,433 | 16.2 | 2,443 | 11.5 | 2,838 | 9.4 | 3,182 | 9.9 |

|  | | | | | | | | | | |
|---|---|---|---|---|---|---|---|---|---|---|
| Savings | 294 | 2.4 | 495 | 3.3 | 766 | 3.6 | 1,261 | 4.2 | 283 | 0.9 |
| U.S. residents | 94 | 0.8 | 128 | 0.9 | 457 | 2.2 | 1,010 | 3.4 | 112 | 0.3 |
| Foreign residents | 200 | 1.6 | 367 | 2.4 | 309 | 1.5 | 251 | 0.8 | 171 | 0.6 |
| Time | 7,127 | 58.8 | 8,294 | 55.2 | 12,106 | 57.2 | 17,406 | 57.9 | 20,838 | 64.7 |
| U.S. residents | 3,703 | 30.5 | 4,450 | 29.6 | 8,044 | 38.0 | 13,705 | 45.6 | 17,012 | 52.8 |
| Foreign residents | 3,424 | 28.2 | 3,844 | 25.6 | 4,062 | 19.2 | 3,701 | 12.3 | 3,826 | 11.9 |
| Total | 12,129 | 100.0 | 15,015 | 100.0 | 21,172 | 100.0 | 30,081 | 100.0 | 32,201 | 100.0 |

Source: Federal Reserve Board, Washington, D.C., 1982.
Note: Figures may not add to totals due to rounding.

**Table 5-9**
**Liquidity Ratios**

| | Average | 1976 | 1977 | 1978 | 1979 | 1980 |
|---|---|---|---|---|---|---|
| Large U.S. banks | | | | | | |
| (Cash + U.S. government securities)/total assets(TA) | 20.5 | 20.8 | 20.4 | 18.4 | 22.1 | 20.7 |
| (Cash + broker loans + treasuries + federal funds sold)/TA | 25.3 | 15.6 | 25.0 | 23.7 | 27.5 | 24.8 |
| U.S. Subsidiaries of foreign banks | | | | | | |
| (Cash + U.S. government securities)/TA | 18.4 | 16.4 | 19.8 | 20.2 | 17.8 | 18.0 |
| (Cash + brokers loans + treasuries + federal funds sold)/TA | 22.2 | 19.9 | 21.8 | 24.7 | 21.8 | 22.2 |
| U.S. Branches and agencies of foreign banks | | | | | | |
| (Cash + U.S. government securities)/TA | 13.8 | 12.4 | 14.2 | 19.2 | 12.5 | 10.8 |
| (Cash + U.S. government securities + net due from directly related institutions)/TA | 31.8 | 30.2 | 31.2 | 36.4 | 31.0 | 26.6 |
| (Cash + broker loans + treasuries + federal funds sold)/TA | 20.0 | 17.4 | 21.3 | 25.2 | 20.4 | 15.9 |
| (Cash + broker loans + treasuries + federal funds sold + net due from directly related institutions)/TA | 32.8 | 35.2 | 38.3 | 42.4 | 38.9 | 32.8 |

Source: Tables 5-4, 5-5, 5-6, 5-7.

and liability maturities and quality. The traditional liquidity ratios are only a partial indication of a bank's liquidity position and are not absolute. What is truly needed is dynamic management of assets and liabilities, monitoring cash inflows and outflows and analyzing interest and maturity gaps in relation to risk and return trade-offs.

**Maturity and Interest-Gap Analysis**

Generally banks do not singularly match the maturity of each asset and liability item on a one-to-one basis; however, a wide maturity gap will result in not only liquidity but also profitability problems during periods of widely fluctuating interest rates. Foreign-bank agencies and branches tend to have a more-balanced position, matching the maturities of assets and liabilities closely. It appears that in the case of foreign-bank agencies and branches, short-term assets are financed mainly by short-term liabilities. Furthermore, foreign-bank agencies and branches seem to have relatively larger proportions of short-term assets and liabilities. In contrast, the maturity of long-term assets for large U.S. banks exceeds the maturity of short-term liabilities. In other words, large U.S. banks borrow shorter and lend longer as compared to foreign banks. Foreign-bank subsidiaries fall somewhere in between the two groups, with a slightly greater proportion of short-term liabilities than U.S. banks.

Generally a matched or balanced position of maturities is less vulnerable to interest-rate risk because the interst-rate spread is fixed for a given period of time. It can, however, be beneficial to take advantage of an opportunity to maximize profitability under conditions of rapidly changing interest rates. A longer maturity position with long-term assets exceeding short-term liabilities may optimize the interest-rate spread in a period of an upward sloping yield curve where interest return is greater than interest cost. When a yield curve is upward sloping where the long-term interest rates are greater than short term, banks may increase profitability by borrowing short and lending long. This situation may exist when an economy is coming out of a recession and expects a boom in the future with a greater demand for loans. But there is a danger that a mismatched position may be trapped by sudden interest-rate changes. For instance, if interest rates on long-term loans are fixed and short-term interest rates are rising, the bank will face a negative interest-rate spread. In this situation, the bank should reverse the gap position by lending short at higher interest rates and borrowing long if interest rates on long-term maturities are favorable. In short, maturity gap positions create liquidity and profitability risks and therefore require appropriate management skills for financial resource allocation and market access to adequate funding.

Statistical information on income statements of foreign banks proved to be unavailable either on an individual or an aggregate basis. Most foreign banks left such reply space blank in their Federal Reserve call reports. Previous attempts by other researchers to obtain foreign-bank profit figures were also unsuccessful.[2] Consequently, only an estimate on interest-rate spreads of foreign banks can be made by analyzing asset and liability structures and applying relevant interest rates.

By classifying bank assets and liabilities broadly on the basis of interest-rate sensitivity, an interest-spread table can be constructed (table 5-10). Returns on mortgages and other long-term and intermediate-term assets are assumed to be fixed or less sensitive to interest-rate changes in contrast to returns on commercial and industrial loans and other short-term assets like federal funds sold and interbank loans. Similarly, interest rates on demand and savings deposits are assumed to be fixed and less interest sensitive as compared to interest rates on short-term deposits and other short-term purchased funds such as federal funds and overnight borrowings.

Although the interest-rate spread table relies on averages, it provides some noteworthy information regarding interest spreads of large U.S. banks, foreign subsidiary banks, and foreign-bank agencies and branches in the United States. The table reveals that large U.S. banks have a comparatively greater spread, foreign-bank branches and agencies a substantially narrower spread, and foreign-bank subsidiaries fall somewhere in between. The explanation of these differences is directly related to the asset and liability structure of the banks. It is reasonable to conclude that foreign banks in general operate on a thin interest margin because they have relatively larger proportions of high-cost, interest-sensitive liabilities, whereas U.S. banks have relatively larger proportions of low-cost liabilities such as demand and savings deposits and higher fixed returns on long-term activities in real-estate and consumer loans.

Although it has been assumed that U.S. and foreign banks alike charge similar prime rates on commercial and industrial loans, in practice, that is not the case. Interviews with international bankers revealed that foreign banks will sacrifice profit margins and charge somewhat lower interest rates in order to penetrate markets. Furthermore, in many instances foreign banks have to pay a higher rate on their borrowings because of higher risk premiums on their credit standing, forcing them to cut margins to remain competitive.

Still, foreign banks can well afford narrower interest spreads, at least in the early stages of their banking business in the United States. First, most foreign banks came to the United States initially to serve their home-country business firms. If profits from U.S. operations are insufficient, they can make up the difference by charging higher interest rates or fees in their home country or in other international markets. Second, it is generally agreed that foreign-bank branches do receive some form of subsidy from their parent banks. Third, direct and indirect overhead costs of foreign-bank

**Table 5-10**
**Interest-Spread Estimates**
*(percentages)*

| | Large U.S. Banks | | | | | | U.S. Subsidiaries of Foreign Banks | | | | | | U.S. Branches and Agencies of Foreign Banks | | | | | |
|---|---|---|---|---|---|---|---|---|---|---|---|---|---|---|---|---|---|---|
| | 1976 | 1977 | 1978 | 1979 | 1980 | Average | 1976 | 1977 | 1978 | 1979 | 1980 | Average | 1976 | 1977 | 1978 | 1979 | 1980 | Average |
| C&I = total assets (TA) × prime rate[a] | 1.58 | 1.70 | 1.95 | 2.84 | 3.40 | | 1.98 | 1.85 | 2.36 | 3.17 | 3.74 | | 2.19 | 2.11 | 2.48 | 3.37 | 4.18 | |
| + Other loans = TA × mortgage rate | 2.64 | 2.67 | 2.76 | 3.14 | 4.47 | | 1.94 | 2.01 | 1.92 | 2.42 | 3.57 | | 0.22 | 0.29 | 0.81 | 0.50 | 0.85 | |
| + Interbank loans = TA × federal funds rate | 0.21 | 0.25 | 0.33 | 0.50 | 0.52 | | 0.42 | 0.38 | 0.59 | 0.94 | 0.94 | | 0.90 | 1.25 | 1.77 | 3.01 | 2.43 | |
| + Securities = TA × treasury bill (TB) rate | 0.98 | 1.66 | 1.23 | 1.63 | 1.74 | | 1.02 | 1.02 | 1.29 | 1.68 | 1.92 | | 0.15 | 0.15 | 0.22 | 0.22 | 0.24 | |
| + Clearing balances = TA × commercial paper rate | 0.68 | 0.66 | 0.95 | 1.79 | 2.06 | | 0.60 | 0.74 | 1.15 | 1.32 | 1.72 | | 0. | 0.70 | 1.41 | 1.11 | 1.20 | |
| + Due from related institutions = TA × Eurodollar rate | | | | | | | 0.16 | 0.25 | 0.35 | 0.36 | 0.62 | | 1.48 | 1.26 | 2.00 | 2.62 | 3.70 | |
| = Weighted average return on assets | 6.09 | 6.14 | 7.22 | 9.9 | 12.19 | 8.31 | 6.12 | 6.25 | 7.66 | 9.89 | 12.51 | 8.48 | 5.32 | 5.76 | 8.28 | 10.89 | 12.60 | 8.51 |
| Deposits of nonbanks = TL × rate on U.S. savings deposits[b] | 3.30 | 3.15 | 3.12 | 3.06 | 2.97 | | 3.44 | 3.23 | 3.09 | 3.45 | 3.30 | | 0.74 | 0.85 | 0.82 | 0.84 | 0.69 | |
| + Borrowing from nonbanks = TL × federal funds rate | 0.05 | 0.06 | 0.10 | 0.29 | 0.24 | | 0.40 | 0.69 | 1.11 | 1.10 | 1.54 | | 0.46 | 0.37 | 0.79 | 0.63 | 0.78 | |
| + Interbank liabilities = TL × federal funds rate | 0.73 | 0.83 | 1.25 | 1.88 | 1.91 | | 0.29 | 0.29 | 0.43 | 0.72 | 0.82 | | 1.27 | 1.55 | 2.24 | 2.28 | 3.45 | |
| + Clearing balances = TL × 3 months commercial paper rate | 0.39 | 0.40 | 0.97 | 0.78 | 1.03 | | 0.18 | 0.27 | 0.62 | 0.65 | 0.60 | | 0.38 | 0.51 | 0.68 | 1.33 | 0.81 | |
| + Due to related institutions = TL × Eurodollar rate | | | | | | | 0.21 | 0.20 | 0.24 | 0.47 | 0.39 | | 2.47 | 2.29 | 3.50 | 4.83 | 5.41 | |
| = Weighted average interest cost | 4.47 | 4.45 | 5.44 | 6.10 | 6.15 | 5.33 | 4.52 | 4.68 | 4.49 | 6.39 | 6.65 | 5.35 | 5.30 | 5.57 | 8.03 | 9.91 | 11.64 | 8.09 |
| Estimated spread | 1.62 | 1.65 | 1.78 | 3.80 | 6.04 | 2.98 | 1.60 | 1.57 | 3.17 | 3.50 | 5.86 | 3.13 | 0.32 | 0.19 | 0.25 | 0.98 | 0.96 | 0.42 |

Source: Federal Reserve Board, Washington D.C., 1981.

Note: The format of interest-spread calculation is adopted with modification from L. Goldberg and A. Saunders, "The Growth of Organizational forms of Foreign Banks in the U.S.," Working Paper No. 221 (New York: Solomon Brothers Center, New York University, 1980), p. 15.

[a]C&I = commercial and industrial loans.

[b]TL = total liabilities.

branches and agencies are much lower than those of large U.S. banks. Salaries paid to foreign banking officers are less than those paid to their U.S. counterparts. Furthermore, foreign banks lack the high costs associated with brick and mortar and extensive computer facilities, generally needed for retail operations. However, interest-rate spread is only one aspect of bank profitability and pricing. Yet effective interest spreads will be different if we take into account reserve requirements, deposit insurance fees and compensating balances, and other financial advisory services that may be provided.

## Capital Adequacy Test

It is difficult to develop any single ratio that will signify adequate depositor protection against possible loan losses or risky assets, particularly when we include foreign deposits and loans outside U.S. banking jurisdiction. For comparison purposes however, three basic bank capital ratios are calculated in table 5-11: capital to total assets, capital to risky assets, and capital to deposits. In the period 1976-1980, the mean ratios of total capital to total assets, total capital to risky assets, and total capital to total deposits were,

**Table 5-11**
**Capital Ratios**

|  | Average | 1976 | 1977 | 1978 | 1979 | 1980 |
|---|---|---|---|---|---|---|
| Large U.S. Banks |  |  |  |  |  |  |
|   Capital to total assets[a] | 14.1 | 11.2 | 12.8 | 14.0 | 15.3 | 16.5 |
|   Capital to risk assets[b] | 17.6 | 14.1 | 16.0 | 17.1 | 19.6 | 21.0 |
|   Capital to deposits | 19.1 | 14.8 | 17.2 | 19.2 | 22.7 | 21.8 |
| U.S. Subsidiaries of foreign banks |  |  |  |  |  |  |
|   Capital to total assets | 9.2 | 10.2 | 9.8 | 9.3 | 9.7 | 8.9 |
|   Capital to risk assets | 11.5 | 12.2 | 12.2 | 11.6 | 10.5 | 10.8 |
|   Capital to deposits | 12.5 | 12.8 | 12.7 | 12.2 | 12.5 | 12.1 |
| U.S. Branches and agencies of foreign banks |  |  |  |  |  |  |
|   Capital to assets | 0.9 | 1.3 | 1.3 | 1.0 | 0.8 | 0.9 |
|   Capital to risk assets | 1.2 | 1.4 | 1.5 | 1.2 | 0.9 | 1.2 |
|   Capital to deposits | 4.6 | 5.0 | 4.6 | 3.5 | 3.1 | 3.8 |
|  | *Adjusted for Net Advances from Parent Institutions* | | | | | |
|  | 6.3 | 6.2 | 6.6 | 5.7 | 6.8 | 6.0 |
|  | 7.3 | 7.1 | 7.7 | 7.1 | 7.7 | 6.7 |
|  | 24.3 | 25.0 | 23.6 | 21.1 | 24.6 | 27.0 |

Source: Tables 5-4, 5-5, 5-6, 5-7.

[a]Capital is defined to include funded debt.

[b]Risk assets = total assets − (cash + treasury securities).

respectively, 14.1 percent, 17.7 percent, and 19.1 percent for large U.S. banks; 9.2 percent, 11.5 percent, and 12.5 percent for foreign-bank subsidiaries; and 0.9 percent, 1.2 percent, and 4.6 percent for foreign branches and agencies.

Since the Federal Reserve Board recognizes that foreign-bank branches and agencies are not separately incorporated entities in the United States, it made an exception to the general rule and allowed them to include in their capital calculations 8 percent of standard banking assets or total net borrowings from directly related institutions. This exception to the rule seems to be in accordance with the board's position that net borrowings of agencies and branches from related banking institutions abroad be exempt from reserve requirements up to 8 percent of standard banking assets since member banks are not required to hold reserves against their capital.[3] Adjusting for net borrowings from related institutions abroad, all three capital ratios of foreign-bank agencies and branches have improved substantially, particularly the ratio of capital to deposits, showing a mean ratio of 24.3 percent with adjustments and only 4.6 percent without adjustment.

No single ratio will meet the test of capital adequacy when all functions are considered: depositor protection, loss absorption, and maintenance of operational facilities. Moreover, this test issue is further complicated by the inclusion of foreign loans and deposits. On the surface, international loans have done extremely well as compared to domestic loans. Average earnings, including interest fees and commissions from international banking operations of U.S. commercial banks, increased at over 20 percent per year in the 1970s while the figure for domestic banking operations was about 4.5 percent. International loan losses in relation to average loans have been almost nonexistent at less than 0.5 percent, whereas the ratio for domestic loans has been much greater.[4] It seems that in the aggregate, the capital to total asset ratio of 14 percent for large U.S. banks covers foreign loans quite adequately because they constitute no more than about 2.5 percent of total assets. However, on an individual bank basis, the amount of foreign loans for each of the ten largest U.S. banks is greater than 100 percent of their respective capital amounts. Over 66 percent of non-OPEC, LDC loans are made by U.S. banks and almost two-thirds of the twenty-five major LDC loans are made by just six large U.S. banks. Furthermore, the bulk of U.S. bank loans to LDCs is concentrated in only a few countries, such as Brazil, Mexico, South Korea, Taiwan, and the Philippines. Nonetheless, as long as international trade and investment is operating smoothly and all participating countries remain confident of the international banking system, there is less of a risk of international loan default. If unforeseen and unpredictable changes take place in international financial markets due to political and social unrest as evidenced in Poland, Iran, Zaire, and El Salvador, a domino

**Table 5-12**
**International Loan Rescheduling, 1956-1982**
*(billions of dollars)*

| | | |
|---|---|---|
| 1956 | Argentina | 500 |
| 1959 | Turkey | 440 |
| 1961 | Brazil | 300 |
| 1962 | Argentina | 270 |
| 1964 | Brazil | 270 |
| 1965 | Argentina | 274 |
| | Turkey | 220 |
| | Chile | 90 |
| | Total, 1965 | 584 |
| 1966 | Indonesia | 310 |
| | Ghana | 170 |
| | Total, 1966 | 480 |
| 1967 | Indonesia | 110 |
| 1968 | Indonesia | 180 |
| | Peru | 120 |
| | Ghana | 100 |
| | India | 100 |
| | Total, 1968 | 500 |
| 1969 | Peru | 100 |
| 1970 | Indonesia | 2,090 |
| | Ghana | 18 |
| | Total, 1970 | 2,108 |
| 1971 | India | 100 |
| 1972 | Chile | 258 |
| | Pakistan | 236 |
| | Cambodia | 2 |
| | Total, 1972 | 496 |
| 1973 | India | 340 |
| | Pakistan | 107 |
| | Total, 1973 | 447 |
| 1974 | Pakistan | 650 |
| | Chile | 460 |
| | India | 194 |
| | Ghana | 190 |
| | Total, 1974 | 1,494 |
| 1975 | India | 248 |
| | Chile | 230 |
| | Total, 1975 | 478 |
| 1976 | Zaire | 280 |
| | India | 200 |
| | Total, 1976 | 480 |
| 1977 | Zaire | 210 |
| | India | 120 |
| | Sierra Leone | 52 |
| | Total, 1977 | 382 |
| 1978 | Peru | 1,212 |
| | Turkey | 1,100 |
| | Total, 1978 | 2,312 |
| 1979 | Turkey | 3,200 |
| | Zaire | 1,000 |
| | Sudan | 500 |
| | Togo | 220 |
| | Total, 1979 | 4,920 |
| 1980 | Turkey | 3,000 |
| | Nicaragua | 562 |
| | Yugoslavia | 420 |
| | Zaire | 402 |
| | Sierra Leone | 40 |
| | Liberia | 35 |
| | Total, 1980 | 4,459 |
| 1981 | Poland | 4,300 |
| | Turkey | 3,200 |
| | Uganda | 730 |
| | Sudan | 500 |
| | Zaire | 500 |
| | Bolivia | 460 |
| | Pakistan | 250 |
| | Togo | 242 |
| | Nicaragua | 180 |
| | Madagascar | 140 |
| | Jamaica | 103 |
| | Senegal | 75 |
| | C.A.R. | 72 |
| | Liberia | 34 |
| | Total, 1981 | 10,786 |
| 1982 | Argentina | 5,000 |
| | Peru | 4,800 |
| | Poland | 4,600 |
| | Romania | 4,000 |
| | Vietnam | 3,500 |
| | Costa Rica | 2,600 |
| | Sudan | 600 |
| | Zaire | 530 |
| | Bolivia | 450 |
| | Pakistan | 447 |
| | Togo | 340 |
| | Senegal | 300 |
| | Honduras | 220 |
| | Madagascar | 120 |
| | Guyana | 110 |
| | Malawi | 98 |
| | Sierra Leone | 68 |
| | Uganda | 60 |
| | Liberia | 58 |
| | C.A.R. | 12 |
| | Total, 1982 | 27,913 |

Source: *Euromoney* (August 1982).
Note: Amount rescheduled by country and year.

effect of international loan default could wipe out the international banking system because of the large size of international loans. In other words, credit analysis of the individual borrower alone is not good enough because of country risk and other risks involved in international markets. According to some authors, such as Dhonte, many LDCs have reached an excessive debt ratio of debt service on international loans to export earnings. Indeed, eight of the thirteen countries with debt-service ratios of nearly 13 percent were forced to reschedule their loans to achieve longer maturities.

Because of the U.S. recession, worldwide trade repercussions, and Polish debt problems, a number of major U.S. multinational banks have experienced a sharp increase in nonperforming loans, those where problems of interest payment have led to deferral or rescheduling. For instance, over 500 participating U.S. and international banks were forced to reschedule the Polish debt, originally due in 1981, over a seven and a half year period, with higher interest rates.[5] Thus, such U.S. banks as Chase Manhattan, Morgan Guaranty Trust, Marine Midland, Irving Trust, and Manufacturers Hanover have begun to take a more-critical view of their involvement in similar situations.[6] An example of how the problem of rescheduling has grown is illustrated in table 5-12.

### Notes

1. Steven Davis, *The Management Function in International Banking* (New York: John Wiley, 1979), pp. 94-96.

2. L.G. Goldberg and A. Saunders, "The Growth of Organizational Forms of Foreign Banks in the U.S.," Working Paper No. 221 (New York: Salomon Brothers Center, New York University, August 1980), pp. 5-21.

3. Sidney Key and James Brundy, "Implementation of the International Banking Act," *Federal Reserve Bulletin* (October 1979):792.

4. Davis, *Management Function*, pp. 95-97.

5. *International Newsletter*, Federal Reserve Bank of Chicago, April 9, 1982, and *Wall Street Journal*, April 7, 1982.

6. *Wall Street Journal*, March 18, 1982.

# 6 Market Structure of the International Banking Industry

Unquestionably the international banking market in the United States has become complex in recent years. Although money-center banks have long been involved in international bank offerings both in the United States and overseas, it is only since about 1970 that intense rivalry for domestic business has forced at least the large regional banks to seek out foreign trade opportunities. Moreover, the explosive entry of foreign banks into the U.S. market in the 1970s served to squeeze further profit margins for all competitors. Correspondingly, U.S. banking deregulation, which has historically proceeded slowly, has begun to clear the throttled channels of competition.

U.S. money-center banks began their modern global efforts after 1945. Today they possess extensive networks of both domestic and offshore branches offering a myriad of international financial products. Yet the demand for international banking services in many parts of the United States has grown so rapidly that many regional banks have entered into the fray. Moving beyond the simple international transactions of issuing travelers' checks and letters of credit, they are getting involved in foreign lending, currency exchange, and, in some cases, Eurodollar management. Many regional banks that had been purely domestic in their outlook have now entered the world of international transactions, and those that already had some experience in international offerings have expanded aggressively, often meeting money-center banks in head-on competition. The competitive face of the international banking market in the United States has been further inflamed by the heavy foreign-bank presence. The sophistication and aggressiveness with which the foreign banks have approached international banking opportunities in the United States have forced many U.S. banks to reevaluate their marketing efforts. As a consequence, many U.S. money-center and regional banks have attempted to increase and refine their international bank offerings and restructure their pricing systems to meet the competition better.

To understand the competitive structure of the international banking industry in the U.S. is to be able to compete better. Therefore this chapter provides some insight into the evolution of marketing competition in the U.S. banking industry and the status of the U.S. market structure in which the offering of international financial products takes place. For this purpose, the results of a 1981-1982 study are reviewed, illustrating the prevalent marketing practices of international banking competitors in the United States.

**Background**

The marketing function of a banking organization should serve to deliver the right financial products to the right customers at the right place at the right time at the right price. Normatively, it would cut across the linear functional areas of the organization, integrating such line and staff operations as customer calling, loan processing and servicing, funding, research, and promotion. Accordingly the marketing function would follow a financial product from development to commercialization and the customer. In this manner, the four basic economic utilities from which buyer satisfaction is derived—form, time, place, and possession—are provided.

Marketing is much more than just selling and advertising. In the competitive environment of worldwide economic exchange, bankers must realize that marketing is nothing more nor less than the performance of business activities that direct the flow of products or services from producer-originator to customer-user so as to satisfy the user at a profit.[1] These business activities include product development, market information, buying and selling, pricing, distribution, promotion, credit, and risk taking. Moreover, the satisfaction of the customer-user at a profit, known as the marketing concept, holds the key to achieving organizational goals.[2] Thus, a banking organization would determine the needs and wants of its customer target markets and then adapt itself to delivering the desired satisfaction more effectively and efficiently than its competitors, constrained only by the externalities of regulatory standards and economic viability and its internal expertise and capital strength. Both long-range and short-range corporate planning are implicit in this approach.

This concept of modern marketing has had a spasmodic and often-fragmented acceptance within the U.S. banking industry. Although there are a number of extremely innovative and carefully planned banking operations, many are still characterized by performance more reminiscent of bank organizations in the pre-1960 atmosphere of prescribed markets and anticompetitiveness. Marketing came late to the banking industry. This is not surprising inasmuch as the utility of the marketing function increases dramatically with an increase in an industry's customer market base and a corresponding rise in competition for that customer purchasing power. This is predominantly what transpired in the U.S. markets for financial services. Beginning in the mid-1960s with retail bank offerings, the increased affluence and sophistication of consumers and the competitive thrusts of thrift institutions into what was once the sole domain of banks led the commercial banking industry to push out to its retail customers by the use of at least rudimentary marketing practices.[3]

The initiation of marketing practice in the retail side of the banking industry mirrors the marketing evolution that first took place in the manufactured-goods industries in the United States. The acceptance and implementation of modern marketing practice was first observed midway through this century in consumer packaged-goods companies where competition was the most severe. Rapidly spreading to consumer durables, marketing awareness has only recently penetrated the business strategies of wholesale and industrial firms where customer market segments are smaller and competition often less rigorous. Similarly, the banking industry today has only scratched the surface of comprehensive marketing planning strategy for the offering of its corporate financial products and services. While a legacy of anticompetitive regulatory standards, initiated in the early decades of this century, had served to stifle competition in past years and, thus, limit marketing rivalry between corporate financial offerings of banking competitors, the present-day situation is a far cry from those days.

In recent years there have been increasingly successful challenges to the artificial regulatory barriers surrounding the financial product offerings of the banking industry in the United States. As competition and costs have intensified for retail offerings, domestic banks increasingly have sought other sources of income. This situation has led many U.S. banks to place more emphasis on their corporate offerings. Yet as business operations continue to become more global in nature, these corporate financial offerings translate into international banking services. As a consequence, the complexity of competition is increased further by foreign-bank operations in the U.S. market. Now cognizant of the increased foreign trade emanating from U.S. boundaries, U.S. and foreign banks are competing among each other for lucrative shares of the international banking business. Although it is clear that strategic marketing planning is imperative within extremely competitive environments, it is not at all clear as to how and to what degree such planning has been implemented by the various international banking competitors in the United States.

**The Study**

Through the auspices of the Bankers' Association for Foreign Trade, we conducted in 1981-1982 a study of the major banking institutions in the continental United States that provide international banking services. The study was based on a mail survey of these banking institutions and personal interviews with selected banking officers and financial officers of several major corporations (see appendix A). A majority of the study population was drawn from the 1980-1981 membership roster of the Bankers' Association. Additional nonmember banks offering international banking services were obtained from a 1978 listing, "International Activities of United States Banks," and a 1979 listing, "Activities of Foreign Banks in the United States" provided by the *American Banker*.

The survey was directed to the executive officers of 466 banking organizations, inclusive of U.S. money-center banks, U.S. regional banks offering international financial products, Edge Act corporations, foreign-bank branches, and foreign-bank subsidiaries. It was estimated that these institutions were responsible for more than 95 percent of the international banking activities in the United States. We excluded foreign representative offices and agencies and investment companies because we believed that their limited functions or differing operations would allow little or no effective comparison. Further insight into the marketing practices of the international banking industry in the United States was provided by personal interviews with international banking officers of twenty-nine U.S. money-center and regional banks, foreign branches and subsidiaries, and Edge Act corporations. Finally, a balanced viewpoint was maintained through interviews with financial officers of several major corporations in the United States that purchase these international financial products.[4]

**Market Analysis**

The following analysis is based on survey and interview data provided by the different types of banking organizations operating in the U.S. market: U.S. money-center banks, U.S. regional banks, Edge Act corporations, foreign-bank branches, and foreign-bank subsidiaries. Data were elicited regarding their primary motivational factors for offering international banking services, the major types of international financial products offered, their marketing strategies, pricing determinants, present and future target markets, market advantages, and their beliefs concerning the impact of U.S. legislative actions.

*Business Motives*

When all respondent banking institutions are considered, serving existing customers and new business opportunities are found to be the primary motivating factors for providing international banking services (table 6-1).[5] Also it is evident that both Edge Act corporations and U.S. money-center banks significantly differ with U.S. regional banks in regard to most of the motivational factors.

Because most Edges are subsidiary extensions of U.S. money-center banks, it is not surprising that the two banking entities exhibit similar rankings. Both consider new business opportunities the dominant force behind their international banking activities, a result embodied in the legislative structure of the Edge Act and the most-recent pronouncements and market actions of the money centers. Edge Act corporations, however, do evidence a higher mean rating for profitability than do any other banking com-

# Table 6-1
## Motivations for Offering International Banking Services

| Motivations | Total Population (N = 160) | | U.S. Money-Center Banks (N = 9) | | U.S. Regional Banks (N = 83) | | Edge Act Corporations (N = 13) | | Foreign-Bank Subsidiaries (N = 13) | | Foreign-Bank Branches (N = 39) | | Analysis of Variance | Significantly Different Groups |
|---|---|---|---|---|---|---|---|---|---|---|---|---|---|---|
| | $\bar{x}$[a] | $s^2$[c] | $\bar{x}$ | $s^2$ | $\bar{x}$ | $s^2$ | $\bar{x}$ | $s^2$ | $\bar{x}$ | $s^2$ | $\bar{x}$ | $s^2$ | $F$[d] | Duncan, p ≤ .10 |
| Higher profitability | 3.56 | 1.20 | 4.11 | .86 | 3.42 | 1.03 | 4.38 | .75 | 3.85 | .47 | 3.38 | 1.82 | 4.03 | (1-5) (1-2) (3-5) (3-2) |
| New business opportunities | 4.10 | .86 | 4.44 | .28 | 4.01 | .72 | 4.54 | .44 | 4.38 | .59 | 3.97 | 1.49 | 1.55 | (3-2) (3-5) |
| Legal advantages | 1.63 | 1.14 | 2.11 | 2.36 | 1.43 | .71 | 1.77 | .52 | 2.15 | 1.64 | 1.62 | 1.45 | 1.65 | (1-2) (4-2) |
| Geographic proximity to customers | 3.02 | 1.72 | 3.44 | 1.53 | 2.72 | 1.52 | 3.92 | .74 | 3.08 | 1.24 | 3.23 | 2.34 | 3.46 | (3-2) |
| Serving existing customers | 4.16 | 1.35 | 4.22 | 1.69 | 4.46 | .93 | 3.62 | .92 | 4.46 | .27 | 3.62 | 1.98 | 4.32 | (2-3) (2-5) (4-3) (4-5) |

[a] Each factor was rated from the least important (1) to the most important (5), resulting in a reported mean rating (x) for the total bank population and for each bank group according to each factor.

[b] N = population. The difference between the total population (160) and the sum of the individual groups is due to the inability to identify specific bank types for three of the responses.

[c] $s^2$ = variance of scores from the mean.

[d] $F$ = calculated value to test the homogeneity of variance and determine whether a significant difference exists between bank groups.

petitors. This is consistent with the goals of money-center banks that establish Edges to cross state lines to meet the short-run goal of immediate profit maximization, primarily through multiple offerings of noninterest income fee services. Foreign-bank branches rank profitability third in importance as a motivating factor. Interviews with several international banking officers and U.S. corporate financial officers confirm the fact that foreign banks operate with a global approach to the marketing of their international financial products. Thus, foreign banks tend to accentuate asset growth, sacrificing shorter-run profit maximization in order to establish a market presence for long-term expansion.

Both the survey data and banking interviews indicate that U.S. regional banks are motivated to provide international banking services principally to serve existing customers. Largely concentrated in short-term trade financing, these services are provided to existing domestic customers who have expanded their business into foreign countries, many for the first time. This reflects the U.S. regional bank's need to service and maintain its present market share more than to establish a broader base of business opportunities for higher profitability. Foreign-bank subsidiaries, although similar in profit and market outlook to U.S. regional banks at the time of acquisition, slowly evolve over time to mirror the foreign parents' managerial objectives. As a consequence, greater emphasis is placed on international financing and foreign-exchange dealings with gradual changes in the bank's portfolio. Although data in table 6-1 indicate that foreign branches consider new business opportunities somewhat more important than serving existing customers, banking-industry interviews clearly distinguish between those foreign-bank branches that have entered U.S. markets to accommodate existing home-country transactions and those spurred by new business opportunities. Thus, many Japanese branches continue to concentrate on home-country subsidiaries operating in the United States and U.S. corporations doing business with Japan, while many British and Canadian branches have sought to expand their international financial offerings to appeal to both U.S. domestic business needs and worldwide requirements.

Edge Act corporations exhibit a higher mean rating for geographical proximity to customers than any of their competitors. Although not a prime motivating factor, such proximity seems to manifest some importance to Edges as legally adjustable delivery systems, enabling movement across state lines to better meet customer demand for international banking services. This advantage, moreover, has been recognized by foreign banks. Under the provisions of the 1978 IBA, foreign banks were given the authority to establish Edge corporations and most recently have chosen to do so, especially where they otherwise would be denied entry under state law.[6]

It is clear from the data that basic business factors are much greater motivators for offering international banking services than are legal advantages. The low rank order generally given to this factor indicates that the legal environment is considered no more than a conduit to achieve the business objectives of meeting customer demand, expanding market opportunities, and achieving higher profitability. Nonetheless, U.S. money-center banks and foreign-bank subsidiaries did rank legal advantages somewhat higher than other competitors did. But large money-center banks have little difficulty in meeting the legal minimum capital requirements for establishing Edges and now enjoy the additional legal privilege of IBFs. In the case of foreign banks, they believe that the legal requirements for establishing banking operations in the U.S. are much more lenient than that in many foreign countries.

## International Financial Products

Although all banking competitors were heavily involved in export-import financing, data in table 6-2 suggest that more-significant differences exist between banks in the offering of other specialized international banking services. For instance, Edge Act corporations rated foreign-exchange dealings lower than all other competitors, with significant differences at the 0.10 level. However, it is the Edge parent, chiefly the money-center bank or in some cases a very large regional, that has the staff and expertise to conduct foreign-exchange management, while the Edge more appropriately limits itself to trade financing and account clearing activities. Conversely, the data indicate that foreign branches are deeply involved in foreign-exchange dealings. Personal interviews with several U.S. bankers reflected a belief by the U.S. banking community that this is one area where foreign banks have made a definite and positive contribution. Foreign banks have not only satisfied a market need previously avoided by U.S. banks but have created new business opportunities for the entire U.S. international banking industry. Discussions with corporate financial officers further reveal that it is predominantly the foreign branch and the money-center bank that possess the personnel and expertise to provide the most-sophisticated financial products. Not only can they provide foreign-exchange management, but they have the necessary expertise to meet the market needs of major multinational corporations in the product areas of international cash management, performance bonds, and export insurance loans. Foreign-bank branches have tended to specialize more in wholesale banking functions, concentrating on corporate commercial and industrial loans and deposits and fee services.

The data indicate that U.S. regional banks exhibit a higher mean rating for export-import trade financing than any of their competitors, with the exception of the Edge Act corporation. Although significant differences at

**Table 6-2**
**Primary International Financial Products**

| International Financial Products | Total Population (N = 160) | | U.S. Money-Center Banks (N = 9) | | U.S. Regional Banks (N = 83) | | Edge Act Corporations (N = 13) | | Foreign-Bank Subsidiaries (N = 13) | | Foreign-Bank Branches (N = 39) | | Analysis of Variance | Significantly Different Groups |
|---|---|---|---|---|---|---|---|---|---|---|---|---|---|---|
| | $\bar{x}^a$ | $s^2$ | $\bar{x}$ | $s^2$ | $\bar{x}$ | $s^2$ | $\bar{x}$ | $s^2$ | $\bar{x}$ | $s^2$ | $\bar{x}$ | $s^2$ | $F^d$ | Duncan, $p \leq .10$ |
| Foreign loans | 3.32 | 2.03 | 4.56 | .53 | 3.05 | 2.07 | 3.62 | 1.76 | 3.31 | 2.56 | 3.54 | 1.83 | 2.37 | (1-2) (1-4) (1-5) |
| Export-import financing | 4.23 | .90 | 4.11 | .86 | 4.43 | .66 | 4.62 | .26 | 3.62 | .76 | 3.85 | 1.03 | 3.71 | (2-4) (2-5) (3-4) (3-5) |
| Funds transfer | 3.31 | 1.41 | 3.44 | 1.78 | 3.47 | 1.30 | 3.46 | 1.60 | 3.00 | 1.67 | 2.92 | 1.34 | 3.25 | (2-5) |
| Foreign-exchange dealings | 3.15 | 1.61 | 3.11 | 2.36 | 3.24 | 1.31 | 2.08 | 2.74 | 3.00 | 2.00 | 3.33 | 1.39 | 6.01 | (4-3) (1-3) (2-3) (5-3) |
| Non-commercial banking services | 1.46 | .70 | 2.67 | 2.00 | 1.28 | .44 | 1.46 | .60 | 1.31 | .56 | 1.62 | .72 | 6.77 | (2-5) (1-2) (1-4) (1-3) (1-5) |

Note: See table 6-1 for explanation of column headings.

the 0.10 level are found only with regard to foreign-bank subsidiaries and branches, inverviews with both international banking officers and corporate financial officers disclosed that this is one area in which regional banks are quite functional and have the opportunity to excel. Such short-term financing is more in keeping with regional capitalization and lending limits.

The only banking institution to rank foreign jumbo loans first in product emphasis was the U.S. money-center bank. Its extremely large capitalization and worldwide network of support enable the money center to deal quite readily with financial products of this size. One major U.S.-based multinational indicated that of $750 million in needed credit in 1981, over 60 percent was met by just a few U.S. money-center banks.

Noncommercial banking services were considered the least-important international financial products by all respondents. This is not very suprising. Generally commercial banks in the United States are legally prohibited from conducting nonbanking business except under such limited legal entities as Edge Act investment corporations and bank holding companies. Since investment Edges and large holding companies are primarily the offspring of U.S. money-center banks, it is clear why the mean rating exhibited by the money center is slightly higher and significantly different from the means of competitor institutions. Nonetheless, the second highest mean rating for such services is exhibited by foreign-bank branches. Yet, it may be, as one corporate treasurer indicated, that these branches are moving more aggressively to meet the global needs of very sophisticated U.S.-based companies with such nonbanking services as Eurobond placement and foreign investment advice.

*Marketing Strategies*

All respondent banking institutions considered customer need satisfaction to be the primary force in the marketing of their international financial products. This result reflects an adherence to basic marketing principles and strategy. More precisely, data in table 6-3 indicate that U.S. banks as a whole appear to value customer satisfaction to a higher degree than do their foreign counterparts. Yet many foreign banks located in the United States are primarily to serve their home-country customers, a ready-made market for which competition was considerably less. Also, as regulatory limitations increasingly disappear from the U.S. market, U.S. banks in particular are forced to operate in a more-competitive environment and follow the basic business philosophies necessary for success in a free-enterprise system. The effectiveness with which this marketing concept is practiced will be determined primarily by the long-term profitability engendered by these banking institutions.

**Table 6-3**
**Marketing Strategies for International Financial Products**

| Marketing Strategies | Total Population (N = 160) | | U.S. Money-Center Banks (N = 9) | | U.S. Regional Banks (N = 83) | | Edge Act Corporations (N = 13) | | Foreign-Bank Subsidiaries (N = 13) | | Foreign-Bank Branches (N = 39) | | Analysis of Variance | Significantly Different Groups |
|---|---|---|---|---|---|---|---|---|---|---|---|---|---|---|
| | $\bar{x}$[a] | $s^2$[c] | $\bar{x}$ | $s^2$ | $\bar{x}$ | $s^2$ | $\bar{x}$ | $s^2$ | $\bar{x}$ | $s^2$ | $\bar{x}$ | $s^2$ | $F$[d] | Duncan, p ≤ .10 |
| Product (service) packaging | 3.39 | 1.48 | 3.33 | 2.50 | 3.36 | 1.18 | 3.76 | 1.19 | 3.62 | 1.59 | 3.28 | 1.94 | 4.69 | |
| Customer need satisfaction | 4.41 | .95 | 4.89 | .71 | 4.52 | .84 | 4.46 | .60 | 3.85 | 2.14 | 4.28 | .89 | 3.22 | (2-4) (1-4) |
| Market segmentation | 2.92 | 1.41 | 3.11 | 1.11 | 2.90 | 1.41 | 3.46 | 1.10 | 3.00 | 2.50 | 2.67 | 1.18 | 1.93 | (3-5) |
| Promotion of Products | 3.24 | 1.29 | 3.33 | 1.75 | 3.18 | 1.47 | 3.38 | .92 | 3.00 | 1.67 | 3.38 | .98 | .82 | |
| Pricing to customer | 3.42 | 1.11 | 3.78 | 1.19 | 3.34 | 1.10 | 3.38 | 1.09 | 3.38 | 2.26 | 3.51 | .89 | 1.08 | |
| Proximity to customer | 3.06 | 1.70 | 3.22 | 1.44 | 3.05 | 1.83 | 3.31 | .56 | 2.62 | 1.59 | 3.08 | 1.65 | .44 | |

Note: See table 6-1 for explanation of column headings.

Price competition became an important consideration in the marketing strategies of U.S. bank competitors in the early 1970s as a consequence of the increased foreign-bank presence in the United States. Interest-rate margins narrowed due to foreign-bank competition. In recent years, however, costs of funding have increased for U.S. and foreign banks alike. In particular, increasing costs of parent funding from abroad and changes in U.S. international banking laws, chiefly as a result of the IBA, have compelled foreign banks to seek new sources of funding in competition with U.S. banks. Nevertheless, price competition continues to be a viable marketing strategy for at least some banking institutions. Interviews with banking officers of foreign branches and several of the more-aggressive U.S. regional banks reveal that price cutting is still used to differentiate financial products effectively when coupled with reduced margin spreads.

Personal interviews with banking competitors further indicate that money-center banks attempt to differentiate their international financial offerings on the basis of global service, supported by a worldwide network of branch offices. Through this network they believe they can more effectively satisfy customer needs by offering exceptional product quality, characterized by sophisticated technology and expertise and swift communication to customers. Regional banks and foreign-bank subsidiaries also tend to concentrate more on nonprice differentiation. Regional banks in particular believe that they excel in integrated product packaging. Thus, they rely on a total banking relationship whereby their selected customers are given personalized service for almost all of their needs. It is readily apparent that foreign-bank branches believe their mainstay is in pricing strategy. While the larger branches also accentuate their worldwide networks, the foreign branches in general continue to rely on lower prices through reduced profit margins. There is a particular point of disagreement on this matter of pricing strategy, however. Discussions with U.S. regional bankers indicate that they believe that such price cutting is a temporary market aberration and, at most, an entry strategy for foreign branches. They believe it cannot continue because the cost of funds pressure is too severe. Many foreign branches, however, advocate continuing price competition as a long-term market operating strategy. They claim that their marketing-oriented approach of asset growth, as opposed to the shorter-term profit tendencies of U.S. banks, will enable them to continue to differentiate their offerings on price. This is a strategic marketing orientation in which short-term profitability is sacrificed for long-term gain. The eventual realization of either side of the argument would have far-reaching consequences: complete nonprice competition for foreign banks or severe profitability pressures for all international banking competitors in the U.S. market.

Data in table 6-3 show that banking respondents view market segmentation as of little consequence in the marketing of their international financial products. This is somewhat surprising because customer-need satisfaction and market segmentation normally go hand-in-hand. A dominant concept in the marketing of goods and services, market segmentation serves to identify and consolidate prospective customer groups with similar needs to be satisfied, encouraging efficient and profitable allocation of organization resources.[7] The importance of segmenting customer markets increases with a rise in competition.

Banking industry interviews shed some light on this curious result. Although most U.S. regional banks clearly direct their resources toward medium and, sometimes, small-sized business firms, they tend to concentrate on total bank positioning. Already positioned by size of market and, in a few cases, by type of industry, they feel that with limited product offerings, their best strategy is to provide a total banking relationship to their customers with an integrated package of all their products. Therefore, to segment their markets further for particular products would be counterproductive. Interestingly not all regional banking officers completely understood the concept of market segmentation, leaving some question as to the survey results.

U.S. money-center banks and Edge Act corporations exhibited higher mean ratings for segmentation than did other competitors, although no significant differences were found at the 0.10 level. Discussions with banking officers of these institutions revealed that they understood the importance of the concept and did segment their markets to gain efficiencies in resource allocation. While money-center banks seemingly pursue all possible market options, Edges increasingly have sought to satisfy the middle-sized corporate market. Yet a close look at the customer market of the money-center bank reveals that the greatest proportion lies with large private multinational firms, demanding similar services. Therefore, there may be less need to segment this market, other than for creditworthiness, a point of understanding that would mitigate the survey results. Foreign-bank branch officers, moreover, indicate that their institutions fully agree with the need for effective segmentation of their markets. The survey results do not completely support this contention, however. Still, one may be reminded that many foreign-bank branches continue to concentrate on home-country customers, a previously segmented market.

*Pricing Determinants*

Banks in general consider the cost of raising funds and competition to be the two principal factors in determining the price of their international financial products (table 6-4). Foreign-bank branches in particular seemed to indicate that the cost of funding has had a considerable impact on their pricing strategy, forcing them to reduce margins whenever they attempted to remain price competitive. In the past, these branches received subsidies from their foreign parent or home government when worldwide interest rates were relatively low. In recent years, however, interest rates on Eurodollars have risen, making it extremely difficult for parent organizations to continue to fund branch subsidies over any extended period. Thus, foreign-bank branches have been thrust into U.S. money markets to compete with other U.S. financial institutions. Similarly, they have sought to issue certificates of deposit, bankers' acceptances, and other common money-market instruments at prevailing U.S. rates. Yet banking industry interviews reveal that foreign branches have been at a competitive disadvantage with respect to their U.S. counterparts. Lack of recognition by the U.S. financial community and higher country risk have made it more difficult and thus more expensive to raise such funds. Furthermore, because foreign banks typically possess a lower deposit-asset ratio as compared to U.S. banks, they are forced to resort to more-expensive money-market instruments to a greater degree. As one major Canadian bank recounted, "The Yankee [U.S.] banks are favored; we are no more risky, but we pay 1/4 to 3/8% of a point more in U.S. money-markets." The only moderating force in this cost spiral is found in the Eurodollar holdings of the foreign parent. Here reserve requirements in the home country are negligible in comparison to the United States, and should the decision be made to transfer any of these funds to a U.S. branch office, there could be a cost benefit.

Interestingly U.S. banks, including foreign subsidiaries under U.S. charter, rated competition significantly higher at the 0.10 level than did foreign-bank branches. But as industry interviews have confirmed, a number of foreign-bank branches still concentrate on serving existing home-country customers in the United States or U.S. firms doing business with the home-country market, a situation that is somewhat less competitive due to the branch advantages of knowledge and expertise in the area. The fact that foreign branches rated the cost of funds as the primary price determinant for their products was not unexpected. Those branches that have attempted to penetrate deeply into U.S. markets continue to stress price competition, whereby the increasing cost of funds serves to erode already slim profit margins.

Another point of interest is the extremely high mean rating and rankings given to long-run profit objectives by U.S. money-center banks. Seemingly they consider this factor to be much more important to their pricing policy than do their competitors. The statistically significant difference between the mean ratings exhibited by the U.S. money-center and regional banks is especially meaningful. Thus, it is readily perceived that the highly competitive money-center bank is much more willing to suffer risk in return for long-term market benefit than is the case for regional banks. Banking industry interviews substantiate this result. While U.S. money-center strategy is based on corporate strategic plans of up to ten years in the future and most foreign banks on extended plans of as many as five years, a number of U.S. regional banks admit to no more than three years. Some regional

**Table 6-4**
**Pricing Determinants for International Financial Products**

| Pricing Determinants | Total Population (N = 160) | | U.S. Money-Center Banks (N = 9) | | U.S. Regional Banks (N = 83) | | Edge Act Corporations (N = 13) | | Foreign-Bank Subsidiaries (N = 13) | | Foreign-Bank Branches (N = 39) | | Analysis of Variance | Significantly Different Groups |
|---|---|---|---|---|---|---|---|---|---|---|---|---|---|---|
| | $\bar{x}^a$ | $s^{2c}$ | $\bar{x}$ | $s^2$ | $\bar{x}$ | $s^2$ | $\bar{x}$ | $s^2$ | $\bar{x}$ | $s^2$ | $\bar{x}$ | $s^2$ | $F^d$ | Duncan, p ≤ .10 |
| Capital requirements | 2.34 | 1.64 | 3.67 | .33 | 2.78 | 2.69 | 2.16 | 1.28 | 2.62 | 1.92 | 2.38 | 2.14 | .702 | |
| Cost of raising funds | 3.94 | 1.49 | 4.11 | 1.11 | 3.73 | 1.56 | 3.62 | 1.42 | 3.92 | 1.74 | 4.49 | .73 | 2.99 | (5-3) (5-2) |
| Short-run profit objectives | 3.29 | 1.09 | 3.44 | 1.28 | 3.36 | 1.04 | 3.46 | .94 | 3.00 | 1.00 | 3.21 | 1.27 | 1.16 | |
| Long-run profit objectives | 3.76 | 1.09 | 4.44 | .53 | 3.69 | 1.21 | 3.46 | .60 | 3.85 | .97 | 3.82 | 1.05 | 2.95 | (1-2) (1-3) |
| Customer risk differentials | 3.59 | 1.03 | 3.67 | 1.00 | 3.47 | .98 | 3.62 | .59 | 3.77 | 1.69 | 3.64 | 1.03 | 1.55 | |
| Competition | 3.84 | 1.23 | 4.44 | .53 | 3.95 | 1.05 | 4.31 | .73 | 4.15 | .47 | 3.41 | 1.19 | 4.26 | (1-5) (2-5) (3-5) (4-5) |

Note: See table 6-1 for explanation of column headings.

banks even contend that the present economic environment is so volatile that it is extremely difficult to establish corporate plans for more than one operating year. Although they may attempt long-term planning, U.S. regionals concede that more often than not they are forced into substantial revisions.

*Present Target Markets*

Generally the primary customer organizations of U.S. money-center banks, Edge Act corporations, and foreign banks are other commercial banks and large private businesses or multinationals (table 6-5). On the other hand, U.S. regional banks concentrate much more on medium-sized or, sometimes, small private firms. The fact that money-center banks exhibit a much higher mean rating for commercial banks than do other bank competitors substantiates banking industry interviews. Clearly money-center banks provide substantial financial services to other U.S. and foreign correspondent banks in the form of check clearing, bank loans, cash management, and various other types of financial advising. Nevertheless, discussions with several international banking officers disclosed that money-center-owned Edges and a number of the more-aggressive foreign banks were increasingly positioning themselves for the middle-sized U.S. corporate market. As one German bank put it, "First, the Fortune 500, second, the Fortune 1000, and then the middle market." This should place even more competitive pressure on U.S. regional banks for the mainstay of its corporate customer base.

Although government agencies were not considered to be very important as a source of business for any of the banking competitors, some importance was reflected in the mean rating exhibited by the money-center bank. This was probably due to the great asset size, specialized expertise, and personal contacts possessed by this type of banking institution, making it unique among competitors.

*Market Advantages*

Overall, personalized services, specialized expertise, and knowledge of customer business needs were seen as contributing the most to competitive market advantage. Contrary to what might be expected, lower financing costs and the availability of large amounts of funds were not considered competitive advantages by anyone in the industry. Because all banking competitors now compete in essentially the same funding arena, it would appear that none of the institutions any longer believes it enjoys a competitive advantage in the cost of funds. U.S. money-center banks do not consider their huge asset size to be any great advantage (table 6-6). However, interviews

**Table 6-5**
**Present Target Markets: Organizational Type**

| Customer Types | Total Population (N = 160) | | U.S. Money-Center Banks (N = 9) | | U.S. Regional Banks (N = 83) | | Edge Act Corporations (N = 13) | | Foreign-Bank Subsidiaries (N = 13) | | Foreign-Bank Branches (N = 39) | | $F^d$ | Analysis of Variance Significantly Different Groups Duncan, $p \leq .10$ |
|---|---|---|---|---|---|---|---|---|---|---|---|---|---|---|
| | $\bar{x}^a$ | $s^{2c}$ | $\bar{x}$ | $s^2$ | $\bar{x}$ | $s^2$ | $\bar{x}$ | $s^2$ | $\bar{x}$ | $s^2$ | $\bar{x}$ | $s^2$ | | |
| Government agencies | 2.22 | 1.72 | 3.00 | 2.00 | 2.11 | 1.54 | 2.08 | 1.41 | 3.15 | 1.64 | 1.89 | 1.62 | 3.22 | (1-5) (3-4) (4-2) (4-5) |
| Commercial banks | 3.72 | 1.23 | 4.33 | 1.00 | 3.81 | 1.26 | 4.00 | 1.33 | 4.00 | 1.10 | 3.44 | 1.04 | 1.57 | (1-5) (1-4) |
| Other financial institutions | 2.66 | 1.36 | 3.22 | 1.19 | 2.51 | 1.35 | 2.77 | 2.53 | 2.77 | 1.36 | 2.72 | 1.05 | .79 | |
| Large private businesses | 3.88 | 1.18 | 1.22 | .69 | 3.69 | 1.12 | 4.08 | .91 | 4.23 | .53 | 4.15 | 1.03 | 2.20 | |
| Small to Medium-Sized private businesses | 3.42 | 2.03 | 2.56 | 1.78 | 3.88 | 1.94 | 2.85 | 1.81 | 3.62 | 1.42 | 3.00 | 1.21 | 5.45 | (1-4) (4-3) (4-5) (2-5) (2-3) |

Note: See table 6-1 for explanation of column headings.

with international banking officers of several U.S. regional and foreign banks seem to refute these conclusions. They contend that the asset size and financial reputation of money-center banks allow not only a funding cost edge but participation in much larger loan requests. Nevertheless it seems that U.S. money-center banks believe that their market advantage lies in nonprice differentiation for their international financial products: global service, expertise, and efficiency.

Data in table 6-6 also suggest that regional banks are actually at a disadvantage when it comes to ample funds, placing them in a difficult position to accomplish what many of their competitors have. But this implication would only support the corporate market thrust that most U.S. regional banks have already taken. Thus, with more-limited capital, it is quite fitting that U.S. regional banks should concentrate on the international corporate needs of the middle-level market, in both the United States and overseas, expanding their market share within this segment rather than to other market segments beyond their capability to serve profitably. It is also meaningful to note the higher mean rating given to personalized services by U.S. regional banks as compared to other banking institutions. This is consistent with arguments often expressed in interviews with regional bank officers. They believe their competitive advantage lies with the personalized and total banking relationship they are able to offer to the market. An acute knowledge of their customers' industries and needs, a totally integrated group of products, a stable and consistent calling program, and a lack of bureaucracy, they believe, all coalesce to provide the regional bank a profitable appeal, especially to middle-sized firms.

In recent years, debates within the U.S. banking community and testimony before U.S. congressional committees have focused on the more-aggressive nature with which foreign banks have marketed their financial products. Yet data in table 6-6 suggest that U.S. banks believe they are at least as vigorous in their pursuit of the market. Banking industry interviews, however, reveal that not all competitors view the aggressive pursuit of markets in exactly the same way. Although nearly all competitors consider a vigorous and coordinated call officer program essential to achieving their objectives, the money-center banks and the more-aggressive regional and foreign banks believe new product innovation is essential to meet the rapidly evolving needs of today's corporate market. Edge Act corporations, due to their unique legal charter, indicate that aggressive calling efforts will be fruitful only if accompanied by effective delivery vehicles through strategic locations. Finally, the overwhelming majority of foreign banks, particularly branches, view aggressive marketing heavily in terms of margin discounts and lower penetration pricing. Although different views exist, it is apparent that the present level of competition in the U.S. international banking industry has brought about a degree of market aggression previously unknown. Most likely, market share, return on assets, and overall long-term profitability will be the final arbiters of future success.

**Table 6-6**
**Market Advantages over Competitors**

| Market Advantages | Total Population (N = 160) | | U.S. Money-Center Banks (N = 9) | | U.S. Regional Banks (N = 83) | | Edge Act Corporations (N = 13) | | Foreign-Bank Subsidiaries (N = 13) | | Foreign-Bank Branches (N = 39) | | Analysis of Variance | Significantly Different Groups |
|---|---|---|---|---|---|---|---|---|---|---|---|---|---|---|
| | $\bar{x}$[a] | $s^2$[c] | $\bar{x}$ | $s^2$ | $\bar{x}$ | $s^2$ | $\bar{x}$ | $s^2$ | $\bar{x}$ | $s^2$ | $\bar{x}$ | $s^2$ | $F$[d] | Duncan, $p \leq .10$ |
| Availability of large funds | 2.94 | 1.73 | 3.00 | 2.00 | 2.34 | 1.43 | 3.31 | 1.73 | 3.62 | 1.26 | 3.67 | 1.12 | 7.49 | (3-2) (4-2) (5-2) |
| Personalized services | 4.29 | .97 | 4.22 | .94 | 4.52 | .81 | 4.23 | .53 | 4.31 | .56 | 3.87 | 1.33 | 9.81 | (2-5) |
| Specialized expertise | 4.12 | .95 | 4.22 | .94 | 4.05 | 1.24 | 4.23 | .69 | 4.54 | .60 | 4.08 | .44 | 4.24 | |
| Lower financing cost | 2.80 | 1.47 | 3.22 | 1.94 | 2.57 | 1.32 | 2.85 | 1.31 | 3.23 | 1.03 | 2.97 | 1.55 | 1.45 | (2-4) |
| Knowledge of customer needs | 4.14 | .92 | 4.67 | .25 | 4.13 | .77 | 4.54 | .44 | 4.15 | .64 | 4.15 | .71 | 3.51 | |
| Aggressive marketing | 3.67 | 1.25 | 4.00 | 1.00 | 3.67 | 1.03 | 3.85 | 1.31 | 4.00 | 1.67 | 3.59 | 1.25 | 2.72 | |

Note: See table 6-1 for explanation of column headings.

## U.S. Legislative Impact

Direct business incentives such as profitability and market opportunities seem to outweigh both the past and present legal environment as causal factors in the expansion of international banking services in the United States. Nevertheless, conclusions drawn from banking industry interviews indicate that U.S. regional banks believe that the IBA did have an impact that was more favorable to the operations of foreign-bank branches and U.S. money-center banks than to their own. This view may not be completely unrealistic in light of the grandfather clauses within the act. It will be recalled that foreign branches in existence before legislative enactment were allowed to continue interstate banking activities without new deposit-taking and branching restrictions. Also, they could keep certain nonbanking functions that they had already begun. In addition, inherent in the provisions of the IBA is the concept of reciprocity, which, regional banks contend, serves to the distinct advantage of the money-center bank with its great asset size and number of overseas branches. Thus, any beneficial impact accruing to foreign banks in the United States as a result of the act would be in the best interests of the large U.S. money-center banks, which would expect comparable treatment of their own branches abroad. Finally, it is apparent that U.S. regional banks feel that the foreign-bank presence in the United States will increase business opportunities for the money-center bank more than for any other competitor. It is believed that only the money-center bank is large enough with sufficient staff expertise and automated facilities to provide such needed services to the foreign-bank branch as correspondent banking, automated check clearing, data processing, and other related functions. Discussions with banking officers of Edge Act corporations and foreign-bank branches did reveal that their international banking business had grown to such an extent that there was enough extra business for U.S. regionals. New business that could not be handled due to the type or the amount of the transaction flowed to the regional bank.

Data in table 6-7 show, not surprisingly, that U.S. banks consider Edge Act legislation to be of greater importance in the expansion of their international banking business than do foreign banks. The intent of the legislation was to provide an effective means of competing with foreign-banking institutions in the United States. Most recently though, foreign banks have begun to establish Edges, but primarily as vehicles to circumvent state laws denying entry to foreign branches and agencies.

Although respondent banking institutions were generally neutral regarding the impact of the Monetary Control Act of 1980, banking industry interviews did disclose some interest regarding the effects of the recently authorized IBFs on December 3, 1981. Overall it is expected that these facilities will enable U.S. banks, chiefly money centers, to obtain a larger share of the Eurocurrency market and, thus, better compete in the global arena.

**Table 6-7**
**Impact of U.S. Legislation on International Banking Business**

| U.S. Legislative Actions | Total Population (N = 160) | | U.S. Money-Center Banks (N = 9) | | U.S. Regional Banks (N = 83) | | Edge Act Corporations (N = 13) | | Foreign-Bank Subsidiaries (N = 13) | | Foreign-Bank Branches (N = 39) | | Analysis of Variance | |
|---|---|---|---|---|---|---|---|---|---|---|---|---|---|---|
| | $\bar{x}$[a] | $s^2$[c] | $\bar{x}$ | $s^2$ | $\bar{x}$ | $s^2$ | $\bar{x}$ | $s^2$ | $\bar{x}$ | $s^2$ | $\bar{x}$ | $s^2$ | $F$[d] | Significantly Different Groups Duncan, $p \leq .10$ |
| International Banking Act | 3.21 | 1.74 | 3.22 | 1.44 | 2.86 | 1.44 | 3.23 | 2.03 | 3.31 | 2.06 | 3.85 | 1.77 | 4.10 | (2-5) |
| Edge Act and amendments | 2.84 | 1.99 | 3.56 | 1.78 | 2.90 | 1.67 | 4.23 | 1.19 | 2.38 | 2.76 | 2.10 | 1.46 | 8.25 | (5-2) (1-5) (3-2) (3-5) |
| Omnibus Banking Act, 1980 | 2.69 | 1.48 | 3.56 | 1.53 | 2.67 | 1.00 | 2.46 | 1.44 | 2.31 | 2.23 | 2.72 | 2.26 | 2.33 | (1-2) (1-3) (1-4) (1-5) |
| Capital outflow restrictions, 1960 | 2.14 | 1.94 | 3.44 | 4.78 | 1.96 | 1.49 | 2.38 | 1.76 | 2.23 | 2.36 | 2.13 | 1.69 | 3.69 | (1-2) (1-5) (1-4) (1-3) |
| Floating exchange rates | 2.51 | 1.89 | 3.56 | 2.03 | 2.46 | 1.49 | 2.54 | 2.27 | 2.46 | 2.94 | 2.46 | 1.83 | 1.90 | (1-2) (1-4) (1-5) (1-3) |

Note: See table 6-1 for explanation of column headings.

Restrictions on U.S. capital outflows in the 1960s and the establishment of floating exchange rates in 1973 were two factors generally considered less important in the expansion of international banking operations. Only money-center banks differed significantly with all competitors in this regard. However, in order to circumvent the capital outflow restrictions of the 1960s, U.S. money-center banks moved abroad to take advantage of Eurodollar markets. Furthermore, they sought to participate more vigorously in foreign-exchange markets to reduce the risk inherent in floating rates.

*Future Target Markets*

Market blueprints for the 1980s become quite clear when data in table 6-8 are examined. First, it can be seen that U.S. money-center banks are quite aggressive and broadly based in their future market outlook. They desire to expand their coverage to all possible geographic segments of the market, including local, national, and international customers. While banking institutions overall consider developing countries rather unimportant as future customer prospects, U.S. money-center banks hold the opposite view. They have been willing to take on riskier markets and probably will continue to do so in return for both worldwide political and economic leverage and worthwhile long-run profits.

Second, as could be expected, U.S. regional banks concentrate primarily on local or regional customers. Foreign banks emphasize not only local but national and interstate customers doing business with their home countries. In fact, several corporate financial officers of major U.S. multinational firms indicate that they find foreign-bank expertise and knowledge of home-country business operations and customer credit ratings invaluable.

Finally, foreign-bank subsidiaries consider advanced countries to be fairly important future customer prospects. This is easily construed in light of the fact that most foreign-bank subsidiaries in the United States are owned by parent banks from such industrialized countries as Great Britain, Japan, Germany, France, Canada, and Switzerland.

**Conclusion**

It is quite clear that the U.S. market environment for international financial products has become increasingly competitive. While various banking organizations have established particular niches for their products, often they overlap. Thus, market rivalry is accentuated, and pressure builds to alter existing marketing strategies. The success or failure of these marketing strategies is affected by the prevailing cost of funds, staff expertise, managerial competence, and the U.S. legal environment. What is the future for

**Table 6-8**
**Future Target Markets: Geographic Type**

| Customer Segments | Total Population (N = 160) | | U.S. Money-Center Banks (N = 9) | | U.S. Regional Banks (N = 83) | | Edge Act Corporations (N = 13) | | Foreign-Bank Subsidiaries (N = 13) | | Foreign-Bank Branches (N = 39) | | Analysis of Variance | |
|---|---|---|---|---|---|---|---|---|---|---|---|---|---|---|
| | $\bar{x}$[a] | $s^2$[c] | $\bar{x}$ | $s^2$ | $\bar{x}$ | $s^2$ | $\bar{x}$ | $s^2$ | $\bar{x}$ | $s^2$ | $\bar{x}$ | $s^2$ | $F$[d] | Significantly Different Groups Duncan, p ≤ .10 |
| Local or regional customers | 4.23 | .99 | 4.00 | 1.00 | 4.69 | .31 | 3.85 | 1.47 | 4.00 | .67 | 3.54 | 1.41 | 15.27 | (2-5) (2-3) (2-1) (2-4) |
| National or interstate customers | 3.57 | 1.19 | 4.00 | 1.25 | 3.29 | .96 | 3.62 | 1.42 | 3.85 | .97 | 3.95 | 1.47 | 3.54 | (2-5) (2-1) |
| Foreign customers (advanced countries) | 3.31 | 1.27 | 4.00 | .75 | 3.07 | 1.07 | 3.46 | .94 | 4.00 | .83 | 3.38 | 1.51 | 3.83 | (2-1) (2-4) |
| Foreign customers (LDCs) | 3.25 | 1.81 | 3.67 | 2.00 | 3.34 | 1.74 | 3.77 | 1.53 | 3.15 | 1.47 | 3.03 | 1.66 | .89 | |

Note: See table 6-1 for explanation of column headings.

this industry? What form will competition take? What type of financial and legal environment will reign? This is the subject of the final chapter.


**Notes**

1. Adapted from the official definition of marketing as set forth by the American Marketing Association in Committee on Definitions, Ralph S. Alexander, Chairman, *Marketing Definitions: A Glossary of Marketing Terms* (Chicago: American Marketing Association, 1960), p. 15.

2. See Philip Kotler, *Principles of Marketing* (Englewood Cliffs, N.J.: Prentice-Hall, 1980), p. 22; John B. McKitterick, "What Is the Marketing Management Concept," in *The Frontiers of Marketing Thought and Action* (Chicago: American Marketing Association, 1957), pp. 71-82; Fred J. Borch, "The Marketing Philosophy as a Way of Business Life," in *The Marketing Concept: Its Meaning to Management,* Marketing Series, No. 99 (New York: American Management Association, 1957), pp. 3-5; Robert J. Keith, "The Marketing Revolution," *Journal of Marketing* (January 1960): 35-38.

3. N.W. Pope, "Put Marketing in Its Place," *American Banker,* August 11, 1976; Jack W. Whittle, "You Have to Pay the Fiddler," *American Banker,* January 19, 1977; Leonard L. Berry, "Era of Competition," *American Banker,* July 13, 1977. All are found in the reprint series of *American Banker's Marketing Management,* vol. 1, August 1976-April 1977, and vol. 2, May 1977-December 1977 (New York).

4. A complete list of international banking officers and corporate financial officers interviewed, along with their corresponding institutions, may be found in appendix A.

5. The reported data for tables 6-1 through 6-8 are based on 160 usable responses from the banking institutions surveyed. This is a response rate of 34.3 percent. A one-way analysis of variance (ANOVA) was used to determine whether the mean ratings of the factors significantly differed at the 0.10 level across the five major bank types. The Duncan's new multiple range test was then used to adjust the level of significance to reduce the influence of chance due to multiple comparisons. In this way, it could be determined between which bank types the significant differences existed. For further exposition of these techniques, see Schurfler W. Huch, William H. Cornier, and William G. Bounds, Jr., *Reading Statistics and Research* (New York: Harper and Row, 1974), pp. 58-72.

6. Report of a 1982 survey by the *American Banker,* indicating that by the end of 1981, foreign banks owned sixteen of the sixty-eight banking Edges in the United States, or 4 percent of the total. Furthermore, the findings showed that 7 of the sixteen Edge corporations were opened in 1981, primarily as vehicles to enter those states that do not permit foreign branches and agencies.

7. For additional insight, see Philip Kotler, *Marketing Management: Analysis, Planning, and Control,* 4th ed. (Englewood Cliffs, N.J.: Prentice-Hall, 1980), p. 197; Jean-Marie Choffray and Gary L. Lilien, "A New Approach to Industrial Market Segmentation," *Sloan Management Review* (Spring 1978): 17-29; and Donald W. Scotten and Ronald L. Zallocco, *Readings in Market Segmentation* (Chicago: American Marketing Association, 1980), pp. 1-198.

# 7

## Future Trends in International Banking

The macroenvironment in which international banking competitors in the United States offer their financial products is a complex, evolving one. Microlevel decisions involving asset and liability management appropriate to the environment and marketing planning that strategically enhances the banking institutions's competitive position are imperative.

The need for international banking services will continue to grow as a reflection of the increasingly global nature of trade. This growth, coupled with a concentration of trading power in the United States, a vibrant U.S. capital market, and continual worldwide reliance on the U.S. dollar as the prime medium of exchange, provided increased international banking opportunities within the United States for domestic and foreign banks alike.

The adequacy of corporate strategic planning presupposes a knowledge of the future. For the rest of the 1980s, foresight into the future trends and consequences inherent in the U.S. legal environment, competitive market structure, and financial environment will be critical to the market success of all banking competitors.

### U.S. Legal Environment

The business incentives of market opportunity and profitability have led international banking competitors in the United States to seek ways to circumvent much of the anticompetitive regulatory restrictions that still remain. Thus, rather than being led by the restrictive standards of the U.S. legal environment, the banking industry has directed its competitive actions to correspond to the basic business philosophies necessitated by an aggressive, competitive system. Progressive U.S. banks, with some support from Congress and the executive branch, have persisted in chipping away at the anticompetitive banking restrictions mired in the McFadden and Bank Holding Company acts and the Glass-Steagall provisions of the 1933 Banking Act. These prohibitions against interstate banking and nonbanking commercial activities are outdated, and we believe that these restrictions should and will be removed.

Whether Senator Garn's bill, S. 1720, the Reagan administration's version as espoused by Treasury Secretary Donald Regan, or some other compromise achieves successful passage, it is surely time to allow banks in the

161

United States to move across state lines and to enjoy equity participation for more-efficient and aggressive competitive confrontation. Indeed it can be expected that in the not-too-distant future, banks will be permitted to move across state boundaries and to merge with not only financially troubled institutions but healthy ones as well. The prohibitions of McFadden and the amended version of the Bank Holding Company Act regarding interstate banking are rooted in the philosophy that bigness is anticompetitive and riskier to bank customers. We believe, however, that larger bank operations are more efficient and will increase benefits to customers and that such integrated operations will allow U.S. banks to compete more effectively with foreign banks in the U.S. market.

Increasing costs of banking operations make economies of scale something to be desired. Integration of banking organizations across state lines can achieve such economies and make available to customers such specialized financial products as those dealing with international trade that smaller local banks cannot provide. Although it is argued that Edge Act facilities and other holding-company affiliates already permit interstate financial offerings, there are still several competitive advantages to be achieved through genuine interstate operations. First, for banks to compete fully, it is generally agreed that unrestricted interstate deposit taking is necessary, a function not currently allowed. Second, even though Edge Act corporations can deal in an array of international financial products across state lines, they are capitalized separately and thus are limited in the size of their loan offerings, a situation not found with foreign branches and agencies whose capitalization is based on the larger foreign parent. Therefore true interstate banking operations would improve the financial product offerings to all customers and allow more-competitive pricing, conceivably improving profitability and market position for U.S. banks with regard to foreign-bank competitors. Finally, the unit-banking system as it is now structured is fraught with problems of inadequate capital and liquidity, particularly critical issues in an economic period where the comptroller of the currency has indicated that over two hundred U.S. banks are in a less-than-ideal financial position. Whether the deliberation concerns international or domestic loans makes no real difference. Because of the tremendous amount of interbank loans and deposits, the interlocking dependence that has been created between banks in the United States and banks overseas is enormous. Recent domestic failures have revealed this vulnerability; yet the possibility exists that the huge Polish, Argentine, and Mexican debts owed to American banks, totaling $14.3 billion, could severely cripple the capital base and liquidity positions of a number of U.S. institutions should they be defaulted. We believe that interstate branching and merger would permit a safer diversification of loan portfolios and deposit structures, spreading the risk. This would encourage less capital concentration and a greater degree of liquidity, thus mitigating the peril of any domino effect.

The fear that bank involvement in nonbanking commercial activities would compromise the security and integrity of U.S. banks is unwarranted in the present competitive environment. The separation of commerce and banking intrinsic to the Glass-Steagall provisions of the 1933 Banking Act belongs to another era. The disintermediation created by the restrictions of regulation Q in an interest-rate environment of upward spirals has led to a diversion of lower-cost savings deposits from U.S. banks to higher-yielding treasury bills, commercial paper, and money-market instruments. This situation has placed enormous profitability pressures on the U.S. banking industry. In order to compete with nonbanking and nondepository institutions and foreign banks in the U.S. market, U.S. banks must be allowed to offer other related types of nonbanking services and to participate in equity investment in the same manner as their competitors.

Although foreign banking organizations like U.S. nondepository institutions have been able to participate more fully in equity investment, this problem has not gone wholly unnoticed. A recent ruling by the board of governors of the federal reserve system in April 1982 gave Edge corporations the authority to offer investment management services to foreign customers and to U.S. customers seeking advice about their holdings of foreign stocks and other assets. The board noted that such offerings of investment advice and portfolio management services would eliminate restrictions that unnecessarily inhibit competition between Edge subsidiaries and foreign banks that do business in the United States. However, it is still clear that U.S. banks are denied the opportunity of taking over the operational management of U.S. producers or other businesses owned by foreign investors. Nonetheless, we believe that more such revision is yet to come.

While more-complete banking powers in the area of securities activities have been proffered by S. 1720 and the Reagan administration's version, either of which has a reasonable chance of passage, other ground-breaking legislation, the Export Trading Company Act of 1980, has also reached Congress. Supported by the Reagan administration and sponsored by Senator Adlai Stevenson of Illinois, S. 2718 received Senate approval on September 3, 1980.[1] Specifically, the act authorizes the formation of one-stop export trading companies that can offer all of the services necessary for U.S. companies to market their goods abroad. The purpose is to loosen some of the fetters of government regulation that prevent these organizational entities from consolidating and to encourage well-capitalized and experienced trading companies to compete actively in world markets for the benefit of smaller U.S. producers, which do not ordinarily engage in exporting. The most-significant part of the Export Trading Company Act is the portion that gives U.S. commercial banks the authority to participate in the equity ownership of the trading companies. Banks would be permitted to invest up to an aggregate amount of $10 million in one or more export trading companies without the prior approval of the appropriate federal agency, and, with such approval, they could participate in excess of that amount, with the trading company becoming a bank subsidiary if so desired.

S. 2718 has detractors inside Congress as well as outside, but the overwhelming evidence tends to support a substantial U.S. commercial banking role in this export plan. Proponents postulate that the enormity of success that Japanese trading companies have exhibited has, in large part, been due to their close relationship to home-country banks. It is quite common in Japan for both banking and trading company organizations to be owned by large conglomerates. Indeed, evidence has also shown that a sizable portion of non-Japanese trading companies are owned and effectively directed by European banks. For example, Hong Kong and Shanghai Banking Corporation operates through Hutchinson, Whampoa Ltd.; Midland Bank Limited through Drake America; Barclays Bank Ltd. through Toser, Kemsley; Credit Lyonnais through Essor; Société Générale through Sogexport; and Banque Nationale de Paris through Compex.

Clearly these foreign competitors have integrated their banking and commercial activities to the extent that they are able to serve their customers more comprehensively than can U.S. banks. Yet bill supporters contend, and rightly so, that U.S. banks are the ideal organizations to establish trading companies to meet the total needs of potential U.S. exporters. They can provide important trade services such as research, foreign-market knowledge and experience, expertise in documentation, and, most importantly, financing. Moreover, the money-center bank and more-aggressive regional banks possess a long-range view of global markets in sharp contrast to the often short-term profit orientations of many U.S. producers. Without doubt, the trading company and the commercial bank are a perfect match. As Anthony J. Walton, senior vice-president of Chase Manhattan NA, told a 1980 meeting of the U.S. Chamber of Congress, "striking similarities appear to exist between the basic operations of an export trading company and those of a bank—similarities that suggest transferability of management and service skills and an opportunity to mitigate risk. I do not think that it is an exaggeration to say that banks are, in fact, trading companies in their own right and their profit dynamics are approximately the same as those of trading companies."

The benefits that would accrue to all U.S. banks from such equity participation is clear. The U.S. regional bank in particular should take a long look at this possible opportunity. If, as the regional banks have indicated, they intend to rely on a marketing strategy of providing a total banking relationship to select customers with an integrated package of products, then the concept of bank participation in trading firms should be especially appealing. Through this vehicle, the U.S. regional bank would be able to offer a vertically integrated array of financial products and services finely tuned to the needs of their market segments.

Bank equity participation in trading-company activities has now become a reality. A compromise bill, S. 734, sponsored by Senator John Heinz of Pennsylvania finally passed the House of Representatives on July 27, 1982, and the Senate-House Conference Committee on October 1, 1982. President Reagan signed the bill into law on October 8, 1982. Consequently, U.S. banks will now be allowed to participate in such nonbanking activities without the fear of antitrust prosecution.

**Market Structure**

The traditional commercial banking concept of localized and protected markets is gone from the U.S. banking environment forever. Competition from nonbanking and nondepository institutions and foreign banks is increasing, severely affecting the scope of both domestic and international operations of U.S. banks. In particular, it is expected that rivalry between U.S. banks and foreign banks will continue for ever-increasing shares of the lucrative international business emanating from U.S. shores and overseas. U.S. banks, competing among themselves and with foreign competitors, are finding that the lines of market authority increasingly are blurred. Local competition has expanded to regional, regional to national, and national often to global. This competitive milieu is further muddled by the internationalization of asset and liability management. Funds may not only be loaned in either domestic or overseas markets but raised in either arena as well.

These events have led to an evolvement of markets and marketing strategy in the United States not unlike that witnessed by the U.S. manufactured-goods industry. While initially serving the increased international needs of U.S. domestic customers, many U.S. banks, particularly money centers and larger regionals, have moved in the direction of a global approach to their international banking business, offering international financial products to whomever in the world demonstrates a need and can be profitably served. For huge money-center banks, this may presage a movement to transnational ownership, a trend that has been realized in worldwide manufacturing and investment banking operations. To coincide with their present needs for global marketing and asset and liability management, money-center banks may find that the multinational form of organization is appropriate for their own profitable performance. This transnational approach, however, while suitable for very large bank operations, does not deny an international banking role for smaller regional banks. Thousands of middle-sized and smaller firms continue to need the numerous international financial products that U.S. regional banks can provide.

Growth and profitable competition in any type of market is premised, in large part, on new-product development. Such is the case for international banking competitors in the United States. The changing nature of the U.S. and worldwide economic environment will compel U.S. money-center, regional, and foreign banks to push out to their often-overlapping markets to satisfy the changing needs of their customers. Innovations in such areas as computer data bases and servicing are crucial to all competitors for efficiency of operations and reduced overhead cost. Still, it is not necessary or recommended that all competitors select similar marketing strategies because they do not possess the same capabilities.

Money-center banks are characterized by asset strength, specialized expertise and market knowledge, and worldwide networks; they can take advantage of a number of international banking opportunities that their competitors are denied. They have the best likelihood of becoming truly multinational concerns. But because their market opportunities are so vast, to attempt to satisfy all the needs of all prospective customers may not be the most-profitable approach. Thus, it becomes extremely important for money-center banks to segment their markets carefully and to concentrate on those customers that can be most profitably served. Certainly they would not argue for expanded retail services or concentrate on the export needs of the smallest of U.S. firms. What is needed is an accentuation of their specialized expertise and market knowledge in the growing areas of international cash management, international leasing, foreign consumer and real-estate financing, foreign-currency dealings, and country risk analysis. Coupled with specialized industry expertise, a computer-based network of global support, and an extensive worldwide call officer program, they should be able to serve many large private U.S. and foreign firms, other foreign and U.S. banks, and government agencies worldwide. Their unique knowledge of foreign financial markets in both the private and government sectors should enable U.S. money-center banks to monopolize the international banking needs of Eastern Bloc countries and many LDCs. Their need to maintain stable policy priorities and consistent customer-banking relationships is real. Even with recent management reorganization, money-center banks should make every effort to retain key management personnel who possess extensive banking experience and knowledge of customer markets.

Regional banks in the United States can serve a profitable role in international banking. Although some of the larger regional banks may have sufficient expertise and capital to compete with money-center banks in some market areas, the market niche in which they can excel is the middle-sized corporate market. Here they can achieve a competitive advantage by providing a personalized and total banking relationship to this customer segment. By positioning themselves in industries where they have substantial knowledge and experience, they can provide an integrated package of international and domestic financial products to serve all the needs of these customers. In this manner, they become the general practitioners of the U.S. international banking industry, referring specialized cases for which they lack capability to money-center specialist. Should U.S. regional banks be allowed to participate in export trading companies, they could further capitalize on their present market approach and become full management consultants to their international banking customers, who have a crucial need for such service.

Undoubtedly foreign-bank growth in the United States will continue, albeit at a more-moderate and sustaining rate than in the past, and many of these banks will maintain their aggressive posture toward U.S. markets and bank competitors. Nevertheless, foreign banks have some problems. Banks that genuinely desire to penetrate U.S. business markets for long-term gain and market share must deal with the issues of overly centralized home-office decision making, a lack of sufficient U.S. industry and investment knowledge, and a perceived lack of community involvement.

Many foreign banks in the United States, especially with regard to dealings of larger magnitude, do not possess sufficient flexibility in their decision making to be able to react appropriately and with sufficient speed to various opportunities that may arise. These decisions are forwarded to the parent overseas, lengthening the time frame for reaction and often subjecting the decision to individuals who are not familiar with the industry involved. For instance, in one case a Belgian bank located in the United States was required to forward to its home-country office a financial decision concerning a loan within the U.S. health-care industry. But because socialized medicine is more the norm in Europe, there was no real understanding there of the profitability of U.S. health-care opportunities, and the loan decision was negative. This lack of knowledge of U.S. industry and investment opportunities may be one of the most-serious problems that foreign banks confront. It might be expected that more participation by the foreign bank's office in the United States would remedy this dilemma; however, the management team of most foreign banks, particularly the Japanese, is comprised predominantly of home-country officers, who generally are not as familiar with American industry as U.S. managers would be.

Finally, foreign banks in the United States have been perceived as economic beings without due regard to the social and civic considerations intrinsic to the regions in which they operate. This is an area in which U.S. banks have excelled through contributions and other support to nonprofit organizations and local government. If foreign banks expect to maintain a profitable presence in the United States over the long term and expand their international banking business into the market segments of their U.S. competitors, then they must recognize that these short-term approaches are incompatible with their goals. Price cutting alone is not sufficient.

Overall the future for international banking competitors in the U.S. market is bright. If foreign banks are aggressive enough, they will continue to concentrate on asset growth and will remain substantial and real competitors to U.S. banks, especially regional banks. Should U.S. banks be allowed to compete fully in investment banking, equity ownership, real estate, and all phases of consumer financing, which we believe they should and eventually will, foreign banks would have a formidable force.

## Financial Environment

Today's interdependence of world trade and financial markets no longer permits economies to isolate themselves from the destabilizing and volatile factors of the rest of the world. The U.S. interest-rate environment greatly affects the economies of Europe, and restrictive trade practices in Europe deal havoc within the United States. This situation aggravates the already difficult task of asset and liability management that banks must perform. It is a problem of major proportions. U.S. banks have concentrated on the matching of assets to liabilities within U.S. domestic financial markets, but this is not enough. The internationalization of banking opportunities requires proficient asset and liability management on an international scale. The increasing integration of worldwide financial markets demands that U.S. banks dealing in international business pay particular attention to the issues of interest-rate and maturity-gap analysis on a global basis. In this way, funds can be raised at the lowest available world rates and loaned at the highest possible margins to buyers around the globe, regardless of their national and geographic origins. Such expertise does not fully exist at many banks, nor is it easily achieved. Extensive training and education is required. Top management must support related management-development programs for both domestic and international banking officers. Short-term seminars, for example, are available through the World Trade Center in New York City and at a number of major universities. For selected managerial personnel, lengthier programs may be feasible, requiring leaves of absence, but leading to more-extensive certification as typified by university banking schools and international business programs.

U.S. banks must also seek to improve their credit analysis of foreign borrowers. As global lending by U.S. banks increases, bank risk is compounded. The fact that foreign financial reporting systems often differ from those guided by U.S. standards results in greater problems of analysis and interpretation for creditworthiness. Greater reliance on thorough management and marketing information systems is needed for easy access to accurate and consistent foreign financial data. This is only the first step. The differences in foreign reporting systems preclude sole dependence on computer data. Banks must search for more-qualitative assessments of the creditworthiness of these foreign borrowers. Face-to-face meetings with potential borrowers, facilitated by extensive call-officer programs, and continuing personal relationships with committed loan customers are essential for maintaining profitability. U.S. banks must continue to improve their country-risk analysis. Not only is the overall financial and economic environment of a foreign country important to the payback probability of a foreign customer; the political and social risk must be considered as well. Undoubtedly the extensive use of foreign nationals in U.S. money-center banks and trends toward transnational ownership are steps in the right direction.

Most of the industrialized countries of the world are already represented by home-country banks within the United States; therefore future growth in the number of foreign banking institutions is expected to be moderate. Some increase in foreign banks from LDCs should at least sustain a somewhat lower growth rate. Nevertheless, U.S. banks should not be misled into believing that foreign-bank competition will abate. As long as foreign banks continue to remain aggressive in U.S. markets, their asset base will continue to grow, often at the expense of their U.S. competitors. As individual states search for ways to increase business activity, they will move toward repeal of state legislation prohibiting foreign branches and agencies. This will facilitate foreign-bank operation and lead to a more-competitive financial environment. It is also envisioned that foreign banks will find acquisition of U.S. banks increasingly attractive. Bargain purchases of small and medium-sized banks that have run into financial difficulty will present foreign banks with ready-made staffs and markets, exacerbating further an already mercurial financial and competitive environment for banking services.

Overall it is anticipated that worldwide interest rates and foreign-currency exchange rates will continue to be volatile. Therefore, profitable operation for international banking competitors in the United States will depend not only on successful marketing strategies but on their ability to manage their asset and liability positions on a worldwide scale.

## Conclusion

Contrary to what many believe, both U.S. money-center and regional banks possess a competitive advantage in providing international banking services. Their industry knowledge and staff resources give them superior tools with which to compete against foreign banks in the U.S. market. But such advantages will be realized only if U.S. banks capitalize on their opportunities. The economic and political environment is now ripe for such a

move. The declining importance of several of the manufacturing sectors of
the U.S. economy and a new concentration on U.S. service sectors, accompanied by a loosening of legal restrictions in the banking arena, serve to set
the stage for U.S. banks to recapture the dominant leadership role in world
banking. All that is needed are strong and effective asset and liability
management and careful targeting of appropriate customer segments to
which innovative international financial products of high quality can be
marketed.

Although foreign banks have increased their international lending
worldwide, U.S. banks still provide the bulk of capital necessary to satisfy
the funding needs of most of the rest of the world. These funds are the
primary source of international economic development. Without these
private funds from U.S. banks, many countries, particularly Third World
nations, could not import the advanced technology and capital equipment
so essential to raising their standard of living on the way to becoming self-
sustaining economies. Thus, not only do U.S. banks remain a substantive
part of the U.S. economy, but they play a vital role in the world pattern of
development.

In spite of the recent political and social turmoil in the socialist countries of the Eastern Bloc, numerous countries in Latin America, and those
in the Middle East, we are convinced that continued efforts by U.S. banks
to maintain an economically viable utilization of international capital and
commercial lending will serve as a sustaining force for international peace.
If international capital flows can be preserved and economic interdependence increased, it is highly probable that worldwide political and
military tension can be reduced. The economic well-being of individuals is a
strong motivator for peace. Of course, a tranquil and satisfying world
economy will also serve to benefit the business interests of international
bankers. Indeed, peace and prosperity do go hand in hand.

### Note

1. For further insight, see U.S. Congress, Senate, Committee on Banking, Housing, and Urban Affairs, *Export Trading Companies and Trade
Associations, Hearings*, before a subcommittee on international finance of
the Committee on Banking, Housing, and Urban Affairs, Senate, on S. 864,
S. 1499, S. 1663, and S. 1744, 96th Cong., 2d sess., 1979, pp. 1-694; U.S.
Congress, Senate, Select Committee on Small Business, *Small Business Participation in U.S. Exports, Hearings*, before the Committee, Senate, on
testimony, 96th Cong., 1st sess., 1979, pp. 1-259; and U.S. Congress, Senate,
Committee on Banking, Housing, and Urban Affairs, *Financial Institutions
and Export Trading Companies, Hearings*, before the Committee, Senate, on
S. 2718, 96th Cong., 2d sess., 1980, pp. 1-363.

# Appendix A:
# List of Interviewees

**International Bankers**

**John Akin,** senior vice-president, Seattle First National Bank, Washington

**Arthur J. Appl, Jr.,** supervising examiner, Commission of Banks & Trust Companies, Illinois

**John W. Ballantine,** vice-president, First National Bank of Chicago

**William Bush,** president, Boatmen's National Bank, St. Louis

**H.J. Buhr,** executive vice-president, Deutsche Bank in New York

**G. Russell Gant,** assistant vice-president, Wachovia Bank, Winston-Salem, North Carolina

**Ephraim Graff,** vice-president, Citibank International, Houston

**Andrew Harris,** manager, Barclays Bank in Pittsburgh

**J.L. Harvey,** economist, Federal Reserve Bank of Chicago

**Michael J. Horgan,** senior vice-president, Citibank of New York

**John B. Haseltine,** senior vice-president, First National Bank of Chicago

**John Hunkin,** general manager, Canadian Imperial Bank of Commerce, Toronto

**Akbar Husain,** senior vice-president, Mercantile Trust Co. in St. Louis

**Peter P. Jay,** vice-president, First National Bank of Fort Worth

**B. Peter Knudson,** vice-president, Manufacturers Bank in Los Angeles

**Andreas Ludewig,** vice-president, Bank America International, St. Louis

**Alfred F. Miossi,** executive vice-president, Continental Illinois National Bank, Chicago

**K. Morita,** senior vice-president, Golden State Sanwa Bank, Los Angeles

**Gregorio Obregon,** vice-president, Bankers Trust International, Miami

**Jesun Paik,** executive vice-president, Union Bank (Standard Chartered Bank), Los Angeles

**Sang K. Park,** manager, Korea Exchange Bank in Chicago

**Jose V. Pombo,** vice-president, Citibank International, Miami

**François C. Van Reepinghen,** vice-president, First Chicago Edge Corp.

**Atsuyuki Sato,** vice-president, Rainier National Bank in Seattle

**Robert F. Sebastian,** vice-president, Bank Hapoalim in Chicago

**Michael Slattery,** assistant manager, Dai-Ichi Kangyo Bank in New York

**Wayne Smith,** vice-president, Citibank International, St. Louis

**Richard W. Stranger,** vice-president, First National Bank of Chicago

**John W. Taylor III,** senior vice-president, The Northern Trust Co., Chicago

**Robert E. Vanden Bosch,** senior vice-president, Harris Trust and Savings Bank, Chicago

**Joaquin P. Viadero,** president, Northern Trust Interamerican Bank in Miami

**William Whitaker,** vice-president, First Interstate Bank of Washington

**Thomas Wilcox,** vice-president, Kredietbank in St. Louis

**International Financial Managers**

**Joseph Kraft,** assistant treasurer, Mallinckrodt Co., St. Louis

**Mark Maley,** treasurer, Fisher Controls International, St. Louis

**John Rolls,** treasurer, Monsanto Company, St. Louis

**Antonio Vila,** director of international finance, Ralston Purina Co., St. Louis

# Appendix B:
# International Banking
# Act of 1978

## Public Law 95-369
## 95th Congress

## An Act

To provide for Federal regulation of participation by foreign banks in domestic financial markets.

Sept. 17, 1978
[H.R. 10899]

*Be it enacted by the Senate and House of Representatives of the United States of America in Congress assembled,*

International Banking Act of 1978.
12 USC 3101 note.

SHORT TITLE; DEFINITIONS AND RULES OF CONSTRUCTION

SECTION 1. (a) This Act may be cited as the "International Banking Act of 1978".

12 USC 3101.

(b) For the purposes of this Act—

(1) "agency" means any office or any place of business of a foreign bank located in any State of the United States at which credit balances are maintained incidental to or arising out of the exercise of banking powers, checks are paid, or money is lent but at which deposits may not be accepted from citizens or residents of the United States;

(2) "Board" means the Board of Governors of the Federal Reserve System;

(3) "branch" means any office or any place of business of a foreign bank located in any State of the United States at which deposits are received;

(4) "Comptroller" means the Comptroller of the Currency;

(5) "Federal agency" means an agency of a foreign bank established and operating under section 4 of this Act;

(6) "Federal branch" means a branch of a foreign bank established and operating under section 4 of this Act;

(7) "foreign bank" means any company organized under the laws of a foreign country, a territory of the United States, Puerto Rico, Guam, American Samoa, or the Virgin Islands, which engages in the business of banking, or any subsidiary or affiliate, organized under such laws, of any such company. For the purposes of this Act the term "foreign bank" includes, without limitation, foreign commercial banks, foreign merchant banks and other foreign institutions that engage in banking activities usual in connection with the business of banking in the countries where such foreign institutions are organized or operating;

(8) "foreign country" means any country other than the United States, and includes any colony, dependency, or possession of any such country;

(9) "commercial lending company" means any institution, other than a bank or an organization operating under section 25 of the Federal Reserve Act, organized under the laws of any State of the United States, or the District of Columbia which maintains credit balances incidental to or arising out of the exercise of banking powers and engages in the business of making commercial loans;

(10) "State" means any State of the United States or the District of Columbia;

(11) "State agency" means an agency of a foreign bank established and operating under the laws of any State;

(12) "State branch" means a branch of a foreign bank established and operating under the laws of any State;

(13) the terms "bank", "bank holding company", "company", "control", and "subsidiary" have the same meanings assigned to those terms in the Bank Holding Company Act of 1956, and the terms "controlled" and "controlling" shall be construed consistently with the term "control" as defined in section 2 of the Bank Holding Company Act of 1956; and

12 USC 1841.

(14) "consolidated" means consolidated in accordance with generally accepted accounting principles in the United States consistently applied.

### DIRECTORS OF NATIONAL BANKS

SEC. 2. Section 5146 of the Revised Statutes (12 U.S.C. 72) is amended by striking out the period at the end of the first sentence and adding the following new provision: ", except that in the case of an association which is a subsidiary or affiliate of a foreign bank, the Comptroller of the Currency may in his discretion waive the requirement of citizenship in the case of not more than a minority of the total number of directors.".

### EDGE ACT CORPORATIONS

12 USC 611a note.
12 USC 611-632.

SEC. 3. (a) It is the purpose of this section to eliminate or modify provisions in section 25(a) of the Federal Reserve Act that (1) discriminate against foreign-owned banking institutions, (2) disadvantage or unnecessarily restrict or limit corporations organized under section 25(a) of the Federal Reserve Act in competing with foreign-owned banking institutions in the United States or abroad or (3) impede the attainment of the Congressional purposes set forth in section 25(a) of the Federal Reserve Act as amended by subsection (b) of this section. In furtherance of such purpose, the Congress believes that the Board should review and revise its rules, regulations, and interpretations issued pursuant to section 25(a) of the Federal Reserve Act to eliminate or modify any restrictions, conditions, or limitations not required by section 25(a) of the Federal Reserve Act, as amended, that (1) discriminate against foreign-owned banking institutions, (2) disadvantage or unnecessarily restrict or limit corporations organized under section 25(a) of the Federal Reserve Act in competing with foreign-owned banking institutions in the United States or abroad, or (3) impede the attainment of the Congressional purposes set forth in section 25(a) of the Federal Reserve Act as

Effective date.

amended by subsection (b) of this section. Rules and regulations pursuant to this subsection and section 25(a) of the Federal Reserve Act shall be issued not later than 150 days after the date of enactment of this section and shall be issued in final form and become effective not later than 120 days after they are first issued.

(b) Section 25(a) of the Federal Reserve Act is amended by adding after the first paragraph (12 U.S.C. 611), the following new paragraph:

12 USC 611a.

"The Congress hereby declares that it is the purpose of this section to provide for the establishment of international banking and financial corporations operating under Federal supervision with powers sufficiently broad to enable them to compete effectively with similar foreign-owned institutions in the United States and abroad; to afford to the United States exporter and importer in particular, and to United

States commerce, industry, and agriculture in general, at all times a means of financing international trade, especially United States exports; to foster the participation by regional and smaller banks throughout the United States in the provision of international banking and financing services to all segments of United States agriculture, commerce, and industry, and, in particular small business and farming concerns; to stimulate competition in the provision of international banking and financing services throughout the United States; and, in conjunction with each of the preceding purposes, to facilitate and stimulate the export of United States goods, wares, merchandise, commodities, and services to achieve a sound United States international trade position. The Board of Governors of the Federal Reserve System shall issue rules and regulations under this section consistent with and in furtherance of the purposes described in the preceding sentence, and, in accordance therewith, shall review and revise any such rules and regulations at least once every five years, the first such period commencing with the effective date of rules and regulations issued pursuant to section 3(a) of the International Banking Act of 1978, in order to ensure that such purposes are being served in light of prevailing economic conditions and banking practices.". **Regulations.**

(c) The second sentence of the fourth paragraph of section 25(a) of the Federal Reserve Act (12 U.S.C. 614) is amended by striking out ", all of whom shall be citizens of the United States" after "to elect or appoint directors".

(d) The first sentence of the sixth paragraph of section 25(a) of the Federal Reserve Act (12 U.S.C. 615(a)) is amended by striking ", but in no event having liabilities outstanding thereon at any one time exceeding ten times its capital stock and surplus"; and the first sentence of the twelfth paragraph of section 25(a) of the Federal Reserve Act (12 U.S.C. 618) is amended by inserting a period after "and in section 25 of the Federal Reserve Act as amended", and by striking the remainder of the sentence.

(e) The third sentence of the sixth paragraph of section 25(a) of the Federal Reserve Act (12 U.S.C. 615(a)) is amended by striking ", but in no event less than ten per centum of its deposits" and inserting in lieu thereof "for member banks of the Federal Reserve System".

(f) The thirteenth paragraph of section 25(a) of the Federal Reserve Act (12 U.S.C. 619) is deleted and the following paragraph is inserted in lieu thereof:

"Except as otherwise provided in this section, a majority of the shares of the capital stock of any such corporation shall at all times be held and owned by citizens of the United States, by corporations the controlling interest in which is owned by citizens of the United States, chartered under the laws of the United States or of a State of the United States, or by firms or companies, the controlling interest in which is owned by citizens of the United States. Notwithstanding any other provisions of this section, one or more foreign banks, institutions organized under the laws of foreign countries which own or control foreign banks, or banks organized under the laws of the United States, the States of the United States, or the District of Columbia, the controlling interests in which are owned by any such foreign banks or institutions, may, with the prior approval of the Board of Governors of the Federal Reserve System and upon such terms and conditions and subject to such rules and regulations as the Board of Governors of the Federal Reserve System may prescribe, own and hold 50 per centum or more of the shares of the capital stock of

Definitions.

12 USC 1841.

Report to
Congress.
12 USC 247 note.
12 USC
601–632.
12 USC 247 note.
12 USC
241–247.

12 USC
601–632.

12 USC 3102.

Regulations.

12 USC 38.

12 USC 221.

12 USC 1813.

any corporation organized under this section, and any such corporation shall be subject to the same provisions of law as any other corporation organized under this section, and the terms 'controls' and 'controlling interest' shall be construed consistently with the definition of 'control' in section 2 of the Bank Holding Company Act of 1956. For the purposes of the preceding sentence of this paragraph the term 'foreign bank' shall have the meaning assigned to it in the International Banking Act of 1978.".

(g) The Board shall report to the Congress not later than 270 days after the date of enactment of this Act its recommendations with respect to permitting corporations organized or operating under section 25 or 25(a) of the Federal Reserve Act, to become members of Federal Reserve Banks.

(h) As part of its annual report pursuant to section 10 of the Federal Reserve Act, the Board shall include its assessment of the effects of the amendments made by this Act on the capitalization and activities of corporations organized or operating under section 25 or 25(a) of the Federal Reserve Act, and on commercial banks and the banking system.

### FEDERAL BRANCHES AND AGENCIES

SEC. 4. (a) Except as provided in section 5, a foreign bank which engages directly in a banking business outside the United States may, with the approval of the Comptroller, establish one or more Federal branches or agencies in any State in which (1) it is not operating a branch or agency pursuant to State law and (2) the establishment of a branch or agency, as the case may be, by a foreign bank is not prohibited by State law.

(b) In establishing and operating a Federal branch or agency, a foreign bank shall be subject to such rules, regulations, and orders as the Comptroller considers appropriate to carry out this section, which shall include provisions for service of process and maintenance of branch and agency accounts separate from those of the parent bank. Except as otherwise specifically provided in this Act or in rules, regulations, or orders adopted by the Comptroller under this section, operations of a foreign bank at a Federal branch or agency shall be conducted with the same rights and privileges as a national bank at the same location and shall be subject to all the same duties, restrictions, penalties, liabilities, conditions, and limitations that would apply under the National Bank Act to a national bank doing business at the same location, except that (1) the requirements of section 5240 of the Revised Statutes (12 U.S.C. 481) shall be met with respect to a Federal branch or agency if it is examined at least once in each calendar year; (2) any limitation or restriction based on the capital stock and surplus of a national bank shall be deemed to refer, as applied to a Federal branch or agency, to the dollar equivalent of the capital stock and surplus of the foreign bank, and if the foreign bank has more than one Federal branch or agency the business transacted by all such branches and agencies shall be aggregated in determining compliance with the limitation; (3) a Federal branch or agency shall not be required to become a member bank, as that term is defined in section 1 of the Federal Reserve Act; and (4) a Federal agency shall not be required to become an insured bank as that term is defined in section 3(h) of the Federal Deposit Insurance Act.

(c) In acting on any application to establish a Federal branch or agency, the Comptroller shall take into account the effects of the proposal on competition in the domestic and foreign commerce of the United States, the financial and managerial resources and future prospects of the applicant foreign bank and the branch or agency, and the convenience and needs of the community to be served.

(d) Notwithstanding any other provision of this section, a foreign bank shall not receive deposits or exercise fiduciary powers at any Federal agency. A foreign bank may, however, maintain at a Federal agency for the account of others credit balances incidental to, or arising out of, the exercise of its lawful powers.

(e) No foreign bank may maintain both a Federal branch and a Federal agency in the same State.

(f) Any branch or agency operated by a foreign bank in a State pursuant to State law and any commercial lending company controlled by a foreign bank may be converted into a Federal branch or agency with the approval of the Comptroller. In the event of any conversion pursuant to this subsection, all of the liabilities of such foreign bank previously payable at the State branch or agency, or all of the liabilities of the commercial lending company, shall thereafter be payable by such foreign bank at the branch or agency established under this subsection.

(g)(1) Upon the opening of a Federal branch or agency in any State and thereafter, a foreign bank, in addition to any deposit requirements imposed under section 6 of this Act, shall keep on deposit, in accordance with such rules and regulations as the Comptroller may prescribe, with a member bank designated by such foreign bank, dollar deposits or investment securities of the type that may be held by national banks for their own accounts pursuant to paragraph "Seventh" of section 5136 of the Revised Statutes, as amended, in an amount as hereinafter set forth. Such depository bank shall be located in the State where such branch or agency is located and shall be approved by the Comptroller if it is a national bank and by the Board of Governors of the Federal Reserve System if it is a State Bank. *Regulations.* *12 USC 24.*

(2) The aggregate amount of deposited investment securities (calculated on the basis of principal amount or market value, whichever is lower) and dollar deposits for each branch or agency established and operating under this section shall be not less than the greater of (1) that amount of capital (but not surplus) which would be required of a national bank being organized at this location, or (2) 5 per centum of the total liabilities of such branch or agency, including acceptances, but excluding (A) accrued expenses, and (B) amounts due and other liabilities to offices, branches, agencies, and subsidiaries of such foreign bank. The Comptroller may require that the assets deposited pursuant to this subsection shall be maintained in such amounts as he may from time to time deem necessary or desirable, for the maintenance of a sound financial condition, the protection of depositors, and the public interest, but such additional amount shall in no event be greater than would be required to conform to generally accepted banking practices as manifested by banks in the area in which the branch or agency is located.

(3) The deposit shall be maintained with any such member bank pursuant to a deposit agreement in such form and containing such limitations and conditions as the Comptroller may prescribe. So long

as it continues business in the ordinary course such foreign bank shall, however, be permitted to collect income on the securities and funds so deposited and from time to time examine and exchange such securities.

**Conditions and requirements.**

(4) Subject to such conditions and requirements as may be prescribed by the Comptroller, each foreign bank shall hold in each State in which it has a Federal branch or agency, assets of such types and in such amount as the Comptroller may prescribe by general or specific regulation or ruling as necessary or desirable for the maintenance of a sound financial condition, the protection of depositors, creditors and the public interest. In determining compliance with any such prescribed asset requirements, the Comptroller shall give credit to (A) assets required to be maintained pursuant to paragraphs (1) and (2) of this subsection, (B) reserves required to be maintained pursuant to section 7(a) of this Act, and (C) assets pledged, and surety bonds payable, to the Federal Deposit Insurance Corporation to secure the payment of domestic deposits. The Comptroller may prescribe different asset requirements for branches or agencies in different States, in order to ensure competitive equality of Federal branches and agencies with State branches and agencies and domestic banks in those States.

(h) A foreign bank with a Federal branch or agency operating in any State may (1) with the prior approval of the Comptroller establish and operate additional branches or agencies in the State in which such branch or agency is located on the same terms and conditions and subject to the same limitations and restrictions as are applicable to the establishment of branches by a national bank if the principal office of such national bank were located at the same place as the initial branch or agency in such State of such foreign bank and (2) change the designation of its initial branch or agency to any other branch or agency subject to the same limitations and restrictions as are applicable to a change in the designation of the principal office of a national bank if such principal office were located at the same place as such initial branch or agency.

(i) Authority to operate a Federal branch or agency shall terminate when the parent foreign bank voluntarily relinquishes it or when such parent foreign bank is dissolved or its authority or existence is otherwise terminated or canceled in the country of its organization. If (1) at any time the Comptroller is of the opinion or has reasonable cause to believe that such foreign bank has violated or failed to comply with any of the provisions of this section or any of the rules, regulations, or orders of the Comptroller made pursuant to this section, or (2) a conservator is appointed for such foreign bank or a similar proceeding is initiated in the foreign bank's country of organization, the Comptroller shall have the power, after opportunity for hearing, to revoke the foreign bank's authority to operate a Federal branch or agency. The Comptroller may, in his discretion, deny such opportunity for hearing if he determines such denial to be in the public interest. The Comptroller may restore any such authority upon due proof of compliance with the provisions of this section and the rules, regulations, or orders of the Comptroller made pursuant to this section.

**Hearing.**

(j)(1) Whenever the Comptroller revokes a foreign bank's authority to operate a Federal branch or agency or whenever any creditor of any such foreign bank shall have obtained a judgment against it arising out of a transaction with a Federal branch or agency in any court of record of the United States or any State of the United States and made application, accompanied by a certificate from the clerk of the court stating that such judgment has been rendered and has remained unpaid for the space of thirty days, or whenever the Comptroller shall become satisfied that such foreign bank is insolvent, he may, after due consideration of its affairs, in any such case, appoint a receiver who shall take possession of all the property and assets of such foreign bank in the United States and exercise the same rights, privileges, powers, and authority with respect thereto as are now exercised by receivers of national banks appointed by the Comptroller.

(2) In any receivership proceeding ordered pursuant to this subsection (j), whenever there has been paid to each and every depositor and creditor of such foreign bank whose claim or claims shall have been proved or allowed, the full amount of such claims arising out of transactions had by them with any branch or agency of such foreign bank located in any State of the United States, except (A) claims that would not represent an enforceable legal obligation against such branch or agency if such branch or agency were a separate legal entity, and (B) amounts due and other liabilities to other offices or branches or agencies of, and wholly owned (except for a nominal number of directors' shares) subsidiaries of, such foreign bank, and all expenses of the receivership, the Comptroller or the Federal Deposit Insurance Corporation, where that Corporation has been appointed receiver of the foreign bank, shall turn over the remainder, if any, of the assets and proceeds of such foreign bank to the head office of such foreign bank, or to the duly appointed domiciliary liquidator or receiver of such foreign bank.

### INTERSTATE BANKING OPERATIONS

Sec. 5. (a) Except as provided by subsection (b), (1) no foreign bank may directly or indirectly establish and operate a Federal branch outside of its home State unless (A) its operation is expressly permitted by the State in which it is to be operated, and (B) the foreign bank shall enter into an agreement or undertaking with the Board to receive only such deposits at the place of operation of such Federal branch as would be permissible for a corporation organized under section 25(a) of the Federal Reserve Act under rules and regulations administered by the Board; (2) no foreign bank may directly or indirectly establish and operate a State branch outside of its home State unless (A) it is approved by the bank regulatory authority of the State in which such branch is to be operated, and (B) the foreign bank shall enter into an agreement or undertaking with the Board to receive only such deposits at the place of operation of such State branch as would be permissible for a corporation organized under section 25(a) of the Federal Reserve Act under rules and regulations administered by the Board; (3) no foreign bank may directly or indirectly establish and operate a Federal agency outside of its home State unless its operation is expressly permitted by the State in which it is to be operated; (4) no foreign bank may directly or indirectly establish and operate a State agency or commercial lending company subsidiary outside of its home State, unless its establishment and operation is approved by the bank regulatory authority of the State in which it is to be operated; and (5) no foreign bank may directly or indirectly acquire any voting shares of, interest in, or substantially all of the assets of a bank

12 USC 3103.

12 USC 611-632.

12 USC 1842.

located outside of its home State if such acquisition would be prohibited under section 3(d) of the Bank Holding Company Act of 1956 if the foreign bank were a bank holding company the operations of whose banking subsidiaries were principally conducted in the foreign bank's home State. Notwithstanding any other provisions of Federal or State law, deposits received by any Federal or State branch subject to the limitations of an agreement or undertaking imposed under this subsection shall not be subject to any requirement of mandatory insurance by the Federal Deposit Insurance Corporation.

(b) Unless its authority to do so is lawfully revoked otherwise than pursuant to this section, a foreign bank, notwithstanding any restriction or limitation imposed under subsection (a) of this section, may establish and operate, outside its home State, any State branch, State agency, or bank or commercial lending company subsidiary which commenced lawful operation or for which an application to commence business had been lawfully filed with the appropriate State or Federal authority, as the case may be, on or before July 27, 1978.

(c) For the purposes of this section, the home State of a foreign bank that has branches, agencies, subsidiary commercial lending companies, or subsidiary banks, or any combination thereof, in more than one State, is whichever of such States is so determined by election of the foreign bank, or, in default of such election, by the Board.

INSURANCE OF DEPOSITS

12 USC 3104.

12 USC 1813.

SEC. 6. (a) No foreign bank may establish or operate a Federal branch which receives deposits of less than $100,000 unless the branch is an insured branch as defined in section 3(s) of the Federal Deposit Insurance Act, or unless the Comptroller determines by order or regulation that the branch is not engaged in domestic retail deposit activities requiring deposit insurance protection, taking account of the size and nature of depositors and deposit accounts.

(b) After the date of enactment of this Act no foreign bank may establish a branch, and after one year following such date no foreign bank may operate a branch, in any State in which the deposits of a bank organized and existing under the laws of that State would be required to be insured, unless the branch is an insured branch as defined in section 3(s) of the Federal Deposit Insurance Act, or unless the branch will not thereafter accept deposits of less than $100,000, or unless the Federal Deposit Insurance Corporation determines by order or regulation that the branch is not engaged in domestic retail deposit activities requiring deposit insurance protection, taking account of the size and nature of depositors and deposit accounts.

(c)(1) The Federal Deposit Insurance Act (12 U.S.C. 1811-1832) is amended as set forth hereinafter in this subsection, in which section numbers not otherwise identified refer to sections of that Act.

(2) Section 3(h) is amended by inserting "(including a foreign bank having an insured branch)" immediately after "(h) The term 'insured bank' means any bank".

(3) Section 3(j) is amended by inserting "or of a branch of a foreign bank" immediately before the period at the end thereof.

(4) Section 3(m) is amended (A) by changing "(m) The" to read "(m)(1) Subject to the provisions of paragraph (2) of this subsection, the", and (B) by adding at the end thereof the following new paragraph:

"(2) In the case of any deposit in a branch of a foreign bank, the ther 'insured deposit' means an insured deposit as defined in paragraph (1) of this subsection which—

"(A) is payable in the United States to—

"(i) an individual who is a citizen or resident of the United States,

"(ii) a partnership, corporation, trust, or other legally cognizable entity created under the laws of the United States or any State and having its principal place of business within the United States or any State, or

"(iii) an individual, partnership, corporation, trust, or other legally cognizable entity which is determined by the Board of Directors in accordance with its regulations to have such business or financial relationships in the United States as to make the insurance of such deposit consistent with the purposes of this Act;

and

"(B) meets any other criteria prescribed by the Board of Directors by regulation as necessary or appropriate in its judgment to carry out the purposes of this Act or to facilitate the administration thereof.".

(5) Section 3(q) is amended to read as follows:                    12 USC 1813.

"(q) The term 'appropriate Federal banking agency' shall mean—

"(1) the Comptroller of the Currency in the case of a national banking association, a District bank, or a Federal branch or agency of a foreign bank;

"(2) the Board of Governors of the Federal Reserve System—

"(A) in the case of a State member insured bank (except a District bank),

"(B) in the case of any branch or agency of a foreign bank with respect to any provision of the Federal Reserve Act which is made applicable under the International Banking Act of 1978,

"(C) in the case of any foreign bank which does not operate an insured branch,

"(D) in the case of any agency or commercial lending company other than a Federal agency, and

"(E) in the case of supervisory or regulatory proceedings arising from the authority given to the Board of Governors under section 7(c)(1) of the International Banking Act of 1978, including such proceedings under the Financial Institutions Supervisory Act, and

"(3) the Federal Deposit Insurance Corporation in the case of a State nonmember insured Bank (except a District bank) or a foreign bank having an insured branch.

Under the rule set forth in this subsection, more than one agency may be an appropriate Federal banking agency with respect to any given institution. For the purposes of subsections (b) through (n) of     Insured section 8 of this Act, the term 'insured bank' shall be deemed to include     bank. any uninsured branch or agency of a foreign bank or any commercial lending company owned or controlled by a foreign bank.".

(6) Section 3 is amended by adding at the end thereof the following new subsections:

"(r) The terms 'foreign bank' and 'Federal branch' shall be construed consistently with the usage of such terms in the International Banking Act of 1978.

Insured
branch.

12 USC 1815.

Regulations.

"(s) The term 'insured branch' means a branch of a foreign bank any deposits in which are insured in accordance with the provisions of this Act.".

(7) Section 5 is amended (A) by changing "SEC. 5." to read "SEC. 5. (a)" and (B) by adding at the end thereof the following new subsections:

"(b) Subject to the provisions of this Act and to such terms and conditions as the Board of Directors may impose, any branch of a foreign bank, upon application by the bank to the Corporation, and examination by the Corporation of the branch, and approval by the Board of Directors, may become an insured branch. Before approving any such application, the Board of Directors shall give consideration to—

"(1) the financial history and condition of the bank,

"(2) the adequacy of its capital structure,

"(3) its future earnings prospects,

"(4) the general character of its management, including but not limited to the management of the branch proposed to be insured,

"(5) the convenience and needs of the community to be served by the branch,

"(6) whether or not its corporate powers, insofar as they will be exercised through the proposed insured branch, are consistent with the purposes of this Act, and

"(7) the probable adequacy and reliability of information supplied and to be supplied by the bank to the Corporation to enable it to carry out its functions under this Act.

"(c)(1) Before any branch of a foreign bank becomes an insured branch, the bank shall deliver to the Corporation or as the Corporation may direct a surety bond, a pledge of assets, or both, in such amounts and of such types as the Corporation may require or approve, for the purpose set forth in paragraph (4) of this subsection.

"(2) After any branch of a foreign bank becomes an insured branch, the bank shall maintain on deposit with the Corporation, or as the Corporation may direct, surety bonds or assets or both, in such amounts and of such types as shall be determined from time to time in accordance with such regulations as the Board of Directors may prescribe. Such regulations may impose differing requirements on the basis of any factors which in the judgment of the Board of Directors are reasonably related to the purpose set forth in paragraph (4).

"(3) The Corporation may require of any given bank larger deposits of bonds and assets than required under paragraph (2) of this subsection if, in the judgment of the Corporation, the situation of that bank or any branch thereof is or becomes such that the deposits of bonds and assets otherwise required under this section would not adequately fulfill the purpose set forth in paragraph (4). The imposition of any such additional requirements may be without notice or opportunity for hearing, but the Corporation shall afford an opportunity to any such bank to apply for a reduction or removal of any such additional requirements so imposed.

"(4) The purpose of the surety bonds and pledges of assets required under this subsection is to provide protection to the deposit insurance fund against the risks entailed in insuring the domestic deposits of a foreign bank whose activities, assets, and personnel are in large part outside the jurisdiction of the United States. In the implementation of its authority under this subsection, however, the Corporation shall endeavor to avoid imposing requirements on such banks which would

PUBLIC LAW 95–369—SEPT. 17, 1978                92 STAT. 617

unnecessarily place them at a competitive disadvantage in relation to domestically incorporated banks.

"(5) In the case of any failure or threatened failure of a foreign  Injunction. bank to comply with any requirement imposed under this subsection (c), the Corporation, in addition to all other administrative and judicial remedies, may apply to any United States district court, or United States court of any territory, within the jurisdiction of which any branch of the bank is located, for an injunction to compel such bank and any officer, employee, or agent thereof, or any other person having custody or control of any of its assets, to deliver to the Corporation such assets as may be necessary to meet such requirement, and to take any other action necessary to vest the Corporation with control of assets so delivered. If the court shall determine that there has been any such failure or threatened failure to comply with any such requirement, it shall be the duty of the court to issue such injunction. The propriety of the requirement may be litigated only as provided in chapter 7 of title 5 of the United States Code, and may not be made  5 USC 701 an issue in an action for an injunction under this paragraph.".  *et seq.*

(8) The first sentence of section 7(a)(1) is amended by inserting  12 USC 1817. "and each foreign bank having an insured branch which is not a Federal branch" immediately before "shall make to the Corporation".

(9) The first sentence of section 7(a)(3) is amended (A) by inserting "and each foreign bank having an insured branch (other than a Federal branch)" immediately before "shall make to the Corporation" and (B) by inserting ", each foreign bank having an insured branch which is a Federal branch," immediately before "and each insured district".

(10) Section 7(a) is amended by adding at the end thereof the following new paragraph:

"(7) In respect of any report required or authorized to be supplied or published pursuant to this subsection or any other provision of law, the Board of Directors or the Comptroller of the Currency, as the case may be, may differentiate between domestic banks and foreign banks to such extent as, in their judgment, may be reasonably required to avoid hardship and can be done without substantial compromise of insurance risk or supervisory and regulatory effectiveness.".

(11) Section 7(b) is amended (A) by changing "(4) A bank's assessment base" to read "(4)(A) Except as provided in subparagraph (B) of this paragraph, a bank's assessment base" and (B) by adding at the end thereof the following new subparagraph:

"(B) In determining the assessment base and assessment base  Regulations. additions and deductions of a foreign bank having an insured branch, such adjustments shall be made as the Board of Directors may by regulation prescribe in order to provide equitable treatment for domestic and foreign banks.".

(12) Section (7)(j)(1) is amended (A) by changing "(j)(1) Whenever" to read "(j)(1)(A) Except as provided in subparagraph (B) of this paragraph, whenever", and (B) by adding at the end thereof the following new subparagraph:

"(B) The Board of Directors may by regulation exempt from the  Regulations. reporting requirements of subparagraph (A) of this paragraph any transaction in the stock of a foreign bank to the extent that the making of any such report would be prohibited by the laws of the country of domicile of the foreign bank in effect at the time such bank makes its application under section 5(b) of this Act, or rendered impracticable  12 USC 1815. by the customs and usages of such country, but the Board of Directors shall weigh the existence of any such prohibition or impracticability in connection with its consideration of the factors enumerated in

12 USC 1815.   sections 5(b)(4) and 5(b)(7).".

12 USC 1817.      (13) Section 7(j)(2) is amended by changing "(2) Whenever" to read "(2)(A) Except as provided in subparagraph (B) of this paragraph, whenever" and by adding at the end thereof the following new subparagraphs:

"(B) The requirements of subparagraph (A) of this paragraph shall not apply in the case of a loan secured by the stock of a foreign bank if the lending bank is a foreign bank under the laws of whose domicile the report otherwise required by subparagraph (A) would be prohibited.

"(C) No foreign bank under the laws of whose domicile a report in compliance with subparagraph (A) of this paragraph would be prohibited in the case of a loan to acquire the stock of an insured bank which is not a foreign bank may make, acquire, or retain any such loan. Each report of condition filed under subsection (a) by any foreign bank to which this subparagraph applies shall contain either a statement of the amount of each loan made, retained, or acquired by the foreign bank in violation of this subparagraph during the period from the date it became an insured bank or the date of its last report of condition, whichever is later, to the date of the report of condition, or a statement that no such loans were made and no such loans were outstanding during such period.".

12 USC 1818.      (14) The first sentence of section 8(a) is amended by inserting ", a foreign bank having an insured branch which is a Federal branch, a foreign bank having an insured branch which is required to be insured under section 6 (a) or (b) of the International Banking Act of 1978," immediately after "(except a national member bank".

(15) Section 8 is amended by adding at the end thereof the following new subsection:

"(r)(1) Except as otherwise specifically provided in this section, the provisions of this section shall be applied to foreign banks in accordance with this subsection.

"(2) An act or practice outside the United States on the part of a foreign bank or any officer, director, employee. or agent therof may not constitute the basis for any action by any officer or agency of the United States under this section, unless—

"(A) such officer or agency alleges a belief that such act or practice has been, is, or is likely to be a cause of or carried on in connection with or in furtherance of an act or practice within any one or more States which, in and of itself, would constitute an appropriate basis for action by a Federal officer or agency under this section; or

"(B) the alleged act or practice is one which, if proven, would, in the judgment of the Board of Directors, adversely affect the insurance risk assumed by the Corporation.

"(3) In any case in which any action or proceeding is brought pursuant to an allegation under paragraph (2) of this subsection for the suspension or removal of any officer, director, or other person associated with a foreign bank, and such person fails to appear promptly as a party to such action or proceeding and to comply with any effective order or judgment therein, any failure by the foreign bank to secure his removal from any office he holds in such bank and from any further participation in its affairs shall, in and of itself, constitute grounds for termination of the insurance of the deposits in any branch of the bank.

"(4) Where the venue of any judicial or administrative proceeding under this section is to be determined by reference to the location of the home office of a bank, the venue of such a proceeding with respect to a foreign bank having one or more branches or agencies in not more than one judicial district or other relevant jurisdiction shall be within such jurisdiction. Where such a bank has branches or agencies in more than one such jurisdiction, the venue shall be in the jurisdiction within which the branch or branches or agency or agencies involved in the proceeding are located, and if there is more than one such jurisdiction, the venue shall be proper in any such jurisdiction in which the proceeding is brought or to which it may appropriately be transferred.

"(5) Any service required or authorized to be made on a foreign bank may be made on any branch or agency located within any State, but if such service is in connection with an action or proceeding involving one or more branches or one or more agencies located in any State, service shall be made on at least one branch or agency so involved.".

(16) (A) The first sentence of section 10(b) is amended (i) by inserting "any insured State branch of a foreign bank, any State branch of a foreign bank making application to become an insured bank," immediately after "(except a District bank)", and (ii) by inserting "or branch" before the comma after "any closed insured bank".            12 USC 1820.

(B) The second sentence of section 10(b) is amended by inserting ", insured Federal branch of a foreign bank," between the words "national bank" and "or District bank".

(C) The third sentence of section 10(b) is amended by inserting ", and in the case of a foreign bank, a binding commitment by such bank to permit such examination to the extent determined by the Board of Directors to be necessary to carry out the purposes of this Act shall be required as a condition to the insurance of any deposits" immediately before the period at the end thereof.

(17) Section 11(c) is amended by inserting ", insured Federal branch of a foreign bank," immediately before "or insured District bank,".            12 USC 1821.

(18) The first sentence of section 11(e) is amended by inserting "or any insured branch (other than a Federal branch) of a foreign bank" immediately before "shall have been closed".

(19) The second sentence of section 11(e) is amended by changing "such insured State bank," to read "such insured State bank or insured branch of a foreign bank,".

(20) Section 11(f) is amended by inserting "or insured branch of a foreign bank" immediately before "shall have been closed".

(21) The first sentence of section 11(g) is amended by inserting ", insured branch of a foreign bank," immediately before "or District bank,".

(22) The third sentence of section 11(g) is amended by changing "In the case of any closed insured bank," to read "In the case of any closed insured bank or closed insured branch of a foreign bank,".

(23) Section 12(a) is amended by inserting ", branch of a foreign bank," immediately after "a closed national bank".            12 USC 1822.

(24) Section 13 is amended by adding at the end thereof the following new subsection:            12 USC 1823.

"(g) The powers conferred on the Board of Directors and the Corporation by this section to take action to reopen a closed insured bank or to avert the closing of an insured bank may be used with

respect to an insured branch of a foreign bank if, in the judgment of
the Board of Directors, the public interest in avoiding the closing
of such branch substantially outweighs any additional risk of loss
to the insurance fund which the exercise of such powers would entail.".

12 USC 1828.

(25) Section 18(c) is amended by adding at the end thereof the
following new paragraph:
"(11) The provisions of this subsection do not apply to any merger
transaction involving a foreign bank if no party to the transaction
is principally engaged in business in the United States.".

(26) Section 18(d) is amended by inserting the following new
sentence immediately after the first sentence thereof: "No foreign
bank may move any insured branch from one location to another
without such consent.".

(27) The first sentence of section 18(g) is amended by inserting
"and in insured branches of foreign banks" immediately after "in
insured nonmember banks".

(28) Section 18(j) is amended by adding at the end thereof the
following new sentence: "The provisions of this subsection shall not
apply to any foreign bank having an insured branch with respect to
dealings between such bank and any affiliate thereof.".

12 USC 1829b.

(29) Section 21 is amended by adding at the end thereof the
following new subsection:
"(i) The provisions of this section shall not apply to any foreign
bank except with respect to the transactions and records of any
insured branch of such a bank.".

12 USC 1831b.

(30) The first sentence of section 25(a) is amended by inserting
"insured branch of a foreign bank," immediately after "No insured
bank,".

### AUTHORITY OF FEDERAL RESERVE SYSTEM

12 USC 3105.

SEC. 7. (a)(1)(A) Except as provided in paragraph (2) of this
subsection, subsections (a), (b), (c), (d), (f), (g), (i), (j), (k), and
the second sentence of subsection (e) of section 19 of the Federal
12 USC
374, 463.
Reserve Act shall apply to every Federal branch and Federal agency of
a foreign bank in the same manner and to the same extent as if the
Federal branch or Federal agency were a member bank as that term is
12 USC
221, 226.
defined in section 1 of the Federal Reserve Act; but the Board either
by general or specific regulation or ruling may waive the minimum
12 USC 142,
371a, 371b,
and maximum reserve ratios prescribed under section 19 of the Federal
374, 374a,
Reserve Act and may prescribe any ratio, not more than 22 per centum,
461, 462b,
for any obligation of any such Federal branch or Federal agency that
463-466.
the Board may deem reasonable and appropriate, taking into consideration the character of business conducted by such institutions and
the need to maintain vigorous and fair competition between and among
such institutions and member banks. The Board may impose reserve
requirements on Federal branches and Federal agencies in such grad-
uated manner as it deems reasonable and appropriate.

(B) After consultation and in cooperation with the State bank
supervisory authorities, the Board may make applicable to any State
branch or State agency any requirement made applicable to, or which
the Board has authority to impose upon, any Federal branch or agency
under subparagraph (A) of this paragraph.

(2) A branch or agency shall be subject to this subsection only if
(A) its parent foreign bank has total worldwide consolidated bank
assets in excess of $1,000,000,000; (B) its parent foreign bank is con-
trolled by a foreign company which owns or controls foreign banks

PUBLIC LAW 95-369—SEPT. 17, 1978                    92 STAT. 621

that in the aggregate have total worldwide consolidated bank assets in excess of $1,000,000,000; or (C) its parent foreign bank is controlled by a group of foreign companies that own or control foreign banks that in the aggregate have total worldwide consolidated bank assets in excess of $1,000,000,000.

(b) Section 13 of the Federal Reserve Act is amended by adding at the end thereof the following new paragraph:

12 USC 247d.
12 USC 82,
342-347,
347c, 372.

"Subject to such restrictions, limitations, and regulations as may be imposed by the Board of Governors of the Federal Reserve System, each Federal Reserve bank may receive deposits from, discount paper endorsed by, and make advances to any branch or agency of a foreign bank in the same manner and to the same extent that it may exercise such powers with respect to a member bank if such branch or agency is maintaining reserves with such Reserve bank pursuant to section 7 of the International Banking Act of 1978. In exercising any such powers with respect to any such branch or agency, each Federal Reserve bank shall give due regard to account balances being maintained by such branch or agency with such Reserve bank and the proportion of the assets of such branch or agency being held as reserves under section 7 of the International Banking Act of 1978. For the purposes of this paragraph, the terms 'branch', 'agency', and 'foreign bank' shall have the same meanings assigned to them in section 1 of the International Banking Act of 1978.".

Definitions.

(c)(1) The Board may make examinations of each branch or agency of a foreign bank, and of each commercial lending company or bank controlled by one or more foreign banks or by one or more foreign companies that control a foreign bank, the cost of which shall be assessed against and paid by such foreign bank or company, as the case may be. The Board shall, insofar as possible, use the reports of examinations made by the Comptroller, the Federal Deposit Insurance Corporation, or the appropriate State bank supervisory authority for the purposes of this subsection.

12 USC 3105.

(2) Each branch or agency of a foreign bank, other than a Federal branch or agency, shall be subject to paragraph 20 and the provision requiring the reports of condition contained in paragraph 6 of section 9 of the Federal Reserve Act (12 U.S.C. 335 and 324) to the same extent and in the same manner as if the branch or agency were a State member bank. In addition to any requirements imposed under section 4 of this Act, each Federal branch and agency shall be subject to subparagraph (a) of section 11 of the Federal Reserve Act (12 U.S.C. 248(a)) and to paragraph 5 of section 21 of the Federal Reserve Act (12 U.S.C. 483) to the same extent and in the same manner as if it were a member bank.

(d) On or before two years after enactment of this Act, the Board after consultation with the appropriate State bank supervisory authorities shall report to the Committee on Banking, Finance and Urban Affairs of the United States House of Representatives and the Committee on Banking, Housing, and Urban Affairs of the United States Senate its recommendations with respect to the implementation of this Act, including any recommended requirements such as limitations on loans to affiliates or capital adequacy requirements which should be imposed on foreign banks to carry out the purposes of this Act. Not later than one hundred and eighty days after the enactment of this Act, the Board shall report to such Committees the steps which have been taken to consult and cooperate with State bank supervisory authorities as required by subsection (a)(1)(B).

Report to congressional committees.

### NONBANKING ACTIVITIES

12 USC 3106.

Sec. 8. (a) Except as otherwise provided in this section (1) any foreign bank that maintains a branch or agency in a State, (2) any foreign bank or foreign company controlling a foreign bank that controls a commercial lending company organized under State law, and (3) any company of which any foreign bank or company referred to in (1) and (2) is a subsidiary shall be subject to the provisions of the Bank Holding Company Act of 1956, and to sections 105 and 106 of the Bank Holding Company Act Amendments of 1970 in the same manner and to the same extent that bank holding companies are subject thereto, except that any such foreign bank or company shall not by reason of this subsection be deemed a bank holding company for purposes of section 3 of the Bank Holding Company Act of 1956.

12 USC 1841
note.
12 USC 1850,
1971-1978.

12 USC 1842.

(b) Until December 31, 1985, a foreign bank or other company to which subsection (a) applies on the date of enactment of this Act may retain direct or indirect ownership or control of any voting shares of any nonbanking company in the United States that it owned, controlled, or held with power to vote on the date of enactment of this Act or engage in any nonbanking activities in the United States in which it was engaged on such date.

(c) After December 31, 1985, a foreign bank or other company to which subsection (a) applies on the date of enactment of this Act may continue to engage in nonbanking activities in the United States in which directly or through an affiliate it was lawfully engaged on July 26, 1978 (or on a date subsequent to July 26, 1978, in the case of activities carried on as the result of the direct or indirect acquisition, pursuant to a binding written contract entered into on or before July 26, 1978, of another company engaged in such activities at the time of acquisition), and may engage directly or through an affiliate in non-banking activities in the United States which are covered by an application to engage in such activities which was filed on or before July 26, 1978; except that the Board by order, after opportunity for hearing, may terminate the authority conferred by this subsection (c) on any such foreign bank or company to engage directly or through an affiliate in any activity otherwise permitted by this subsection (c) if it determines having due regard to the purposes of this Act and the Bank Holding Company Act of 1956, that such action is necessary to prevent undue concentration of resources, decreased or unfair competition, conflicts of interest, or unsound banking practices in the United States. Notwithstanding subsection (a) of this section, a foreign bank or company referred to in this subsection (c) may retain ownership or control of any voting shares (or, where necessary to prevent dilution of its voting interest, acquire additional voting shares) of any domestically-controlled affiliate covered in 1978 which engages in the business of underwriting, distributing, or otherwise buying or selling stocks, bonds, and other securities in the United States. Except in the case of affiliates described in the preceding sentence, nothing in this subsection (c) shall be construed to authorize any foreign bank or company referred to in this subsection (c), or any affiliate thereof, to engage in activities authorized by this subsection (c) through the acquisition, pursuant to a contract entered into after July 26, 1978, of any interest in or the assets of a going concern engaged in such activities. Any foreign bank or company that is authorized to engage in any activity pursuant to this subsection (c) but, as a result of action of the Board, is required to terminate such activity may retain the ownership of con-

12 USC 1841
note.

trol of shares in any company carrying on such activity for a period of two years from the date on which its authority was so terminated by the Board. As used in this subsection, the term "affiliate" shall mean any company more than 5 per centum of whose voting shares is directly or indirectly owned or controlled or held with power to vote by the specified foreign bank or company, and the term "domestically-controlled affiliate covered in 1978" shall mean any affiliate the majority of whose voting shares is owned by a company or group of companies organized under the laws of the United States or any State thereof, if it has been under continuous domestic majority-controlling ownership since July 26, 1978, and if a foreign bank or group of foreign banks does not own or control, directly or indirectly, 25 per centum or more of its voting shares.

*Definitions.*

(d) Nothing in this section shall be construed to define a branch or agency of a foreign bank or a commercial lending company controlled by a foreign bank or foreign company that controls a foreign bank as a "bank" for the purposes of any provisions of the Bank Holding Company Act of 1956, or section 105 of the Bank Holding Company Act Amendments of 1970, except that any such branch, agency or commercial lending company subsidiary shall be deemed a "bank" or "banking subsidiary", as the case may be, for the purposes of applying the prohibitions of section 106 of the Bank Holding Company Act Amendments of 1970 and the exemptions provided in sections 4(c)(1), 4(c)(2), 4(c)(3), and 4(c)(4) of the Bank Holding Company Act of 1956 (12 U.S.C. 1843(c)(1), (2), (3), and (4)) to any foreign bank or other company to which subsection (a) applies.

12 USC 1841 note. 12 USC 1850.

12 USC 1971–1978.

(e) Section 2(h) of the Bank Holding Company Act of 1956 is amended (1) by striking out "(h) The" and inserting in lieu thereof "(h)(1) Except as provided by paragraph (2), the", (2) by striking out the proviso, and (3) by inserting at the end thereof the following:

12 USC 1841.

"(2) The prohibitions of section 4 of this Act shall not apply to shares of any company organized under the laws of a foreign country (or to shares held by such company in any company engaged in the same general line of business as the investor company or in a business related to the business of the investor company) that is principally engaged in business outside the United States if such shares are held or acquired by a bank holding company organized under the laws of a foreign country that is principally engaged in the banking business outside the United States, except that (1) such exempt foreign company (A) may engage in or hold shares of a company engaged in the business of underwriting, selling or distributing securities in the United States only to the extent that a bank holding company may do so under this Act and under regulations or orders issued by the Board under this Act, and (B) may engage in the United States in any banking or financial operations or types of activities permitted under section 4(c)(8) or in any order or regulation issued by the Board under such section only with the Board's prior approval under that section, and (2) no domestic office or subsidiary of a bank holding company or subsidiary thereof holding shares of such company may extend credit to a domestic office or subsidiary of such exempt company on terms more favorable than those afforded similar borrowers in the United States.".

12 USC 1843.

STUDY OF FOREIGN TREATMENT OF UNITED STATES BANKS

SEC. 9. The Secretary of the Treasury, in conjunction with the Secretary of State, the Board, the Comptroller, and the Federal Deposit

12 USC 601 note.

Insurance Corporation shall within 90 days after enactment of this bill commence a study of the extent to which banks organized under the laws of the United States or any State thereof are denied, whether by law or practice, national treatment in conducting banking operations in foreign countries, and the effects, if any, of such discrimination on United States exports to those countries. On or before one year after enactment of this section, the Secretary of the Treasury shall be required to report his findings, conclusions, and recommendations from such study to the Congress and describe the efforts undertaken by the United States to eliminate any foreign laws or practices that discriminate against banks organized under the laws of the United States or any State thereof, or that serve as a barrier to the financing of United States exports to any foreign country.

*Report to Congress.*

### REPRESENTATIVE OFFICES

*Rules.*
*12 USC 3107.*

SEC. 10. (a) Any foreign bank that maintains an office other than a branch or agency in any State shall register with the Secretary of the Treasury in accordance with rules prescribed by him, within one hundred and eighty days after the date of enactment of this Act or the date on which the office is established, whichever is later.

(b) This Act does not authorize the establishment of any such office in any State in contravention of State law.

### CEASE-AND-DESIST ORDERS

SEC. 11. Subsection (b) of section 8 of the Federal Deposit Insurance Act (12 U.S.C. 1818(b)) is amended by adding at the end thereof the following new paragraph:

"(4) This subsection and subsections (c), (d), (h), (i), (k), (l), (m), and (n) of this section shall apply to any foreign bank or company to which subsection (a) of section 8 of the International Banking Act of 1978 applies and to any subsidiary (other than a bank) of any such foreign bank or company in the same manner as they apply to a bank holding company and any subsidiary thereof (other than a bank) under subparagraph (3) of this subsection. For the purposes of this subparagraph, the term 'subsidiary' shall have the meaning assigned to it in section 2 of the Bank Holding Company Act of 1956.".

*"Subsidiary."*

*12 USC 1841.*

### AMENDMENT TO THE BANKING ACT OF 1933

SEC. 12. Section 21 of the Banking Act of 1933 (12 U.S.C. 378) is amended by striking clause (B) of paragraph (2) of subsection (a) thereof and inserting in lieu thereof the following: "(B) shall be permitted by the United States, any State, territory, or district to engage in such business and shall be subjected by the laws of the United States, or such State, territory, or district to examination and regulations or,".

### REGULATION AND ENFORCEMENT

*12 USC 3108.*

SEC. 13. (a) The Comptroller, the Board, and the Federal Deposit Insurance Corporation, are authorized and empowered to issue such rules, regulations, and orders as each of them may deem necessary in order to perform their respective duties and functions under this Act and to administer and carry out the provisions and purposes of this Act and prevent evasions thereof.

PUBLIC LAW 95-369—SEPT. 17, 1978                 92 STAT. 625

(b) In addition to any powers, remedies, or sanctions otherwise provided by law, compliance with the requirements imposed under this Act or any amendment made by this Act may be enforced under section 8 of the Federal Deposit Insurance Act by any appropriate Federal banking agency as defined in that Act.

12 USC 1818.

(c) In the case of any provision of the Federal Reserve Act to which a foreign bank or branch thereof is subject under this Act, and which is made applicable to nonmember insured banks by the Federal Deposit Insurance Act, whether by cross-reference to the Federal Reserve Act or by a provision in substantially the same terms in the Federal Deposit Insurance Act, the administration, interpretation, and enforcement of such provision, insofar as it relates to any foreign bank or branch thereof as to which the Board is an appropriate Federal banking agency, are vested in the Board, but where the making of any report to the Board or a Federal Reserve bank is required under any such provision, the Federal Deposit Insurance Corporation may require that a duplicate of any such report be sent directly to it. This subsection shall not be construed to impair any power of the Federal Deposit Insurance Corporation to make regular or special examinations or to require special reports.

12 USC 226.

12 USC 1811 note.

REPORT ON MC FADDEN ACT

SEC. 14. (a) The President, in consultation with the Attorney General, the Secretary of the Treasury, the Board, the Comptroller, and the Federal Deposit Insurance Corporation, shall transmit a report to the Congress containing his recommendations concerning the applicability of the McFadden Act to the present financial, banking, and economic environment, including an analysis of the effects of any proposed amendment to such Act on the structure of the banking industry and on the financial and economic environment in general.

12 USC 36 note.

44 Stat. 1224.

(b) The report required by subsection (a) shall be transmitted to the Congress not later than one year after the date of enactment of this Act.

Transmittal to Congress, effective date.

Approved September 17, 1978.

LEGISLATIVE HISTORY:

HOUSE REPORT No. 95-910 (Comm. on Banking, Finance and Urban Affairs).
SENATE REPORT No. 95-1073 (Comm. on Banking, Housing, and Urban Affairs).
CONGRESSIONAL RECORD, Vol. 124 (1978):
    Apr. 6, considered and passed House.
    Aug. 15, considered and passed Senate, amended.
    Aug. 17, House concurred in Senate amendment.

# Appendix C:
# Location of Foreign Banking Institutions in the United States, June 1981

**Table C-1**

| Family | Massachusetts | New York | Pennsylvania | Pennsylvania | Washington, D.C. | Florida | Georgia | Illinois | Texas | California | Hawaii | Oregon | Washington | Total |
|---|---|---|---|---|---|---|---|---|---|---|---|---|---|---|
| **Belgium** | | | | | | | | | | | | | | |
| Kredietbank | | B | | | | | | | | | | | | 1 |
| **Denmark** | | | | | | | | | | | | | | |
| Privatbanken | | B | | | | | | | | | | | | 1 |
| **France** | | | | | | | | | | | | | | |
| Banque Nationale de Paris | | B  I | | | | | | B | | AAS | | | | 6 |
| Banque Francaise du Commerce Exterieur | | B | | | | | | | | | | | | 1 |
| Banque de Paris et des Pays Bas | | B | | | | | | | | A | | | | 2 |
| Banque de L'Union Europeene | | B | | | | | | | | | | | | 1 |
| Banques de Arabes and Françcais | | S | | | | | | | | | | | | 1 |
| Compagnie Financiere de Suez | | BB | | | | | | B | | | | | | 3 |
| Crédit Agricole | | | | | | | | B | | | | | | 1 |
| Crédit Commerciale de France | | B | | | | | | B | | | | | | 2 |
| Crédit Lyonnais | | B | | | | | | B | | AA | | | | 4 |
| Société Générale | | B | | | | | | | | A | | | | 2 |
| **Germany** | | | | | | | | | | | | | | |
| Bayerische Hypotheken und Weschel Bank | | B | | | | | | | | | | | | 1 |
| Berliner Handels und Frankfurter Bank | | B | | | | | | | | | | | | 1 |
| Bank Fuer Gemeinwirtschaft | | B | | | | | | | | | | | | 1 |
| Commerzbank | | B | | | | | A | B | | | | | | 3 |
| Deutsche Bank | | B | | | | | | | | | | | | 1 |
| Deutsche Genossenschafts Bank | | B | | | | | | | | A | | | | 2 |
| Dresdner Bank | | B | | | | | | B | | A | | | | 3 |
| Hessische Landesbank-Girozentrale | | B | | | | | | | | | | | | 1 |
| Union Bank of Bavaria | | B | | | | | A | B | | A | | | | 4 |
| Westdeutsche Landesbank Girozentrale | | B | | | | | | | | | | | | 1 |
| **Greece** | | | | | | | | | | | | | | |
| National Bank of Greece | B | S | | | | | | B | | | | | | 3 |
| **Ireland** | | | | | | | | | | | | | | |
| Allied Irish Banks | | B | | | | | | B | | | | | | 2 |
| Bank of Ireland | | B | | | | | | | | | | | | 1 |
| **Italy** | | | | | | | | | | | | | | |
| Banca Commerciale Italiana | | B | | | | | | B | | A | | | | 3 |
| Banca Nationale del Lavoro | | B | | | | | | | | A | | | | 2 |
| Banco di Napoli | | B | | | | | | | | | | | | 1 |
| Banco di Roma | | B | | | | | B | S | | A | | | | 4 |
| Banco di Sicilia | | B | | | | | | | | | | | | 1 |
| Banca di Nationale dell Agricoltura | | B | | | | | | | | | | | | 1 |
| Credito Italiano | | B | | | | | | | | A | | | | 2 |
| Instituto Bancario | | A | | | | | | | | | | | | 1 |

| Bank | 1 | 2 | 3 | 4 | 5 | 6 | 7 | Freq |
|---|---|---|---|---|---|---|---|---|
| **Netherlands** | | | | | | | | |
| Algemene Bank Nederland | B | | B | A | B | S | AA | 7 |
| Nederlandsche Midcenstandsbank | B | | | | | | | 1 |
| **Portugal** | | | | | | | | |
| Banco Totta & Acores | A | | | | | | | 1 |
| Banco Portugues Do Atlantico | A | | | | | | | 1 |
| **Spain** | | | | | | | | |
| Banca Catalana | B | | | | | | | 1 |
| Banco Atlantico | A | | | | | | | 1 |
| Banco Central | B | S | | | | | | 2 |
| Banco de Bilbao | B | | | A | | | | 2 |
| Banco de Santander | B | S | | A | | | | 2 |
| Banco de Vizcaya | B | | | A | | | | 3 |
| Banco Exterior de Espana | | | | A | | A | | 2 |
| Banco Urquijo | A | | | | | | | 1 |
| Banco Hispano Americano | B | | | | | | | 1 |
| Banco Zaragozano | | | | S | | | | 1 |
| **Sweden** | | | | | | | | |
| Svenska Handelsbanken | I | | | | | | | 1 |
| **Switzerland** | | | | | | | | |
| Baer American Banking Corp. | I | | | | | | | 1 |
| Swiss Bank Corp. | B | | | A | B | | | 4 |
| Credit Suisse | B | | | A | | | | 2 |
| Union Bank of Switzland | B | | | A | B | | | 3 |
| **United Kingdom** | | | | | | | | |
| Barclays Group | B | S | B | A | B | A | S | 10 |
| Grindlays Bank | A | | B | A | | | | 1 |
| Lloyds Group | B | | B | A | | S | | 6 |
| Midland Bank Group | A | | | | B | A | | 1 |
| National Westminster Bank | B | S | | | | A | | 4 |
| Royal Bank of Scotland | B | | | | | A | | 2 |
| Schroder Group | S | I | | | | | | 2 |
| Standard-Chartered Group | B | | | A | B | A | S | 6 |
| **Yugoslavia** | | | | | | | | |
| Yugoslavia Banka-United Bank | A | | | | | | | 1 |
| **Other Western Europe** | | | | | | | | |
| American Scandinavia Group | I | | | | | | | 1 |
| European-American Group | S | I | | | C | | | 3 |
| **Canada** | | | | | | | | |
| Bank of British Columbia | | | | | | A | A | 1 |
| Bank of Montreal | A | S | B | | | A | S | 4 |
| Bank of Nova Scotia | A | S | | A | | A | S | 7 |
| Canadian Commercial & Industrial Bank | | | | | | A | A | 1 |
| Canadian Imperial Bank of Commerce | A | | | B(4) | | A | S | 10 |
| National Bank of Canada | A | | | | | A | A | 1 |
| Royal Bank of Canada | A | S | | | | A | S | 5 |
| Toronto Dominion Bank | A | S | | | | A | S | 5 |

Schroder Group[a]

*Table C-1 (continued)*

| Family | Massa-chusetts | New York | Penn-syl-vania | Penn-syl-vania | Washing-ton, D.C. | Florida | Georgia | Illinois | Texas | Cali-fornia | Hawaii | Oregon | Wash-ington | Total |
|---|---|---|---|---|---|---|---|---|---|---|---|---|---|---|
| **Puerto Rico** | | | | | | | | | | | | | | |
| Banco de Ponce | | B | | | | | | | | B | | | | 2 |
| Banco de Popular | | B | | | | | | | | | | | | 1 |
| Banco de Santander | | B | | | | | | | | | | | | 1 |
| **(Latin America)** | | | | | | | | | | | | | | |
| **Argentina** | | | | | | | | | | | | | | |
| Argentine Banking Group | | I | | | | | | | | | | | | 1 |
| Banco de Intercambia | | B | | | | | | | | | | | | 1 |
| Banco de La Nacion | | B | | | | A | | B | | A | | | | 4 |
| Banco Rio de La Plata | | A | | | | | | | | | | | | 1 |
| Banco Province Buenos Aires | | A | | | | A | | | | A | | | | 3 |
| **Brazil** | | | | | | | | | | | | | | |
| Banco de Credito Nacional | | B | | | | | | | | | | | | 1 |
| Banco do Brasil | | B | | | | A | | | | AA | | | | 4 |
| Banco Economico | | B | | | | | | | | | | | | 1 |
| Banco Itau São Paulo | | A | | | | | | | | | | | | 1 |
| Banco Nacional | | A | | | | | | | | | | | | 1 |
| Banco Real | | B | | | | A | | | | A | | | | 3 |
| Commercial Industrial Banco de São Paulo | | A | | | | | | | | | | | | 1 |
| Estado de São Paulo | | A | | | | A | | | | AA | | | | 4 |
| Mercantile Banco de São Paulo | | A | | | | | | | | | | | | 1 |
| Union Banco de Brasileros | | A | | | | | | | | | | | | 1 |
| **Colombia** | | | | | | | | | | | | | | |
| Banco de Bogotá | | A  S | | | | A | | | | | | | | 3 |
| **Mexico** | | | | | | | | | | | | | | |
| Banco de Commercio | | A | | | | | | | | A | | | | 2 |
| Banco Nacional de Mexico | | A | | | | | | | | A | | | | 3 |
| Banca Serfin | | A | | | | | | | | S | | | | 2 |
| Commercio Mexico | | A | | | | | | | | A | | | | 2 |
| **Venezuela** | | | | | | | | | | | | | | |
| Banco de Venezuela | | A | | | | | | | | | | | | 1 |
| Banco Industrial de Venezuela | | A | | | | | | | | | | | | 1 |
| Banco Union | | A  S | | | | | | | | | | | | 2 |
| **(Asia)** | | | | | | | | | | | | | | |
| **Bahrain** | | | | | | | | | | | | | | |
| Gulf International Bank, B.S.C. | | B | | | | | | | | | | | | 1 |
| National Bank of Abu Dhabi | | | | | B | | | | | | | | | 1 |

| Bank | 1 | 2 | 3 | 4 | 5 | Rank |
|---|---|---|---|---|---|---|
| **Hong Kong** | | | | | | |
| Chekaing First Bank | | | | A | | 1 |
| Dah Sing Bank | B | S | | A | | 1 |
| Hong Kong and Shanghai Bank | | | B | AA | B | 7 |
| Liu Chong Hing Bank | | | | A | | 1 |
| Overseas Trust Cc. | | | | B | | 1 |
| Shanghai Commerce Bank | | | | A | | 1 |
| **India** | | | | | | |
| Bank of India | B | | B | A | | 2 |
| State Bank of India | B | | | A | | 3 |
| Bank of Baroda | B | | | | | 1 |
| **Iran** | | | | | | |
| Bank Melli Iran | A | | | A | | 2 |
| Bank Saderat Iran | A | | | A | | 2 |
| Bank Sanaye Iran | A | | | | | 1 |
| Bank Sepah | A | | | | | 1 |
| **Israel** | | | | | | |
| Bank Hapoalim | B | | B | A | | 6 |
| Bank Leumi Le-Israel | A | S | B | A | | 6 |
| Israel Discount Bank | B | S | | A | | 3 |
| United Mizrahi Bank | A | S | | | | 2 |
| **Japan** | | | | | | |
| Bank of Tokyo | A | S | | C | B | 9 |
| Bank of Yokohama | B | | | A | | 1 |
| Chuo Trust & Banking Co. | A | S | | A | | 1 |
| Dai-Ichi Kangyo Bank | B | | | A | A | 3 |
| Daiwa Bank | A | S | | A | | 4 |
| Fuji Bank | B | | | A | | 3 |
| Hokkaido Takushoku Bank | A | S | | A | B | 3 |
| Industrial Bank of Japan | B | | | A | S | 3 |
| Kyowa Bank | B | | | A | | 3 |
| Long Term Credit Bank | B | | | A | S | 2 |
| Mitsubishi Bank | B | | | A | | 4 |
| Mitsubishi Trust & Banking Co. | B | | | A | S | 2 |
| Mitsui Bank | B | | | A | | 4 |
| Mitsui Trust & Barking Co. | B | | | A | S | 1 |
| Nippon Credit Bank | B | | | A | B | 2 |
| Saitama Bank | B | | | A | | 2 |
| Sanwa Bank | B | | | A | | 4 |
| Sumitomo Bank | B | | | A | S | 5 |
| Sumitomo Trust & Banking Co. | B | | | A | S | 2 |
| Taiyo Kobe Bank | B | | | A | B | 3 |
| Tokai Bank | B | | | A | | 4 |
| Toyo Trust & Banking Co., Ltd. | B | | | A | S | 2 |
| Yasuda Trust & Banking Co. | B | | | A | B | 2 |

## Table C-1 (continued)

| Family | Massachusetts | New York | Pennsylvania | Pennsylvania | Washington, D.C. | Florida | Georgia | Illinois | Texas | California | Hawaii | Oregon | Washington | Total |
|---|---|---|---|---|---|---|---|---|---|---|---|---|---|---|
| **South Korea** | | | | | | | | | | | | | | |
| Bank of Seoul Trust Co. Korea | | A | | | | | | | | A | | | | 2 |
| Cho-Heung Bank | | A | | | | | | | | A | | | | 2 |
| Commercial Bank of Korea | | A | | | | | | | | A | | | | 2 |
| Hanil Bank | | A | | | | | | | | A | | | | 2 |
| Korea Exchange Bank | | B | | | | | | B | | A  S | | | | 4 |
| Korea First Bank | | A | | | | | | B | | A | | | | 3 |
| **Malaysia** | | | | | | | | | | | | | | |
| Bank Bumiptra | | B | | | | | | | | A | | | | 2 |
| **Pakistan** | | | | | | | | | | | | | | |
| Habib Bank | | B | | | | | | | | | | | | 1 |
| National Bank of Pakistan | | B | | | B | | | B | | | | | | 3 |
| United Bank | | B | | | | | | | | | | | | 1 |
| **Philippines** | | | | | | | | | | | | | | |
| Metropolitan Bank & Trust Co. | | A | | | | | | | | A  S | | | | 3 |
| Philippine Commerce & Industrial Bank | | A | | | | | | | | A | | | | 2 |
| Philippine National Bank | | B | | | | | | | | A | A | | | 3 |
| **Singapore** | | | | | | | | | | | | | | |
| Development Bank of Singapore | | A | | | | | | | | | | | | 1 |
| Overseas Unio Bank | | A | | | | | | | | | | | | 1 |
| United Overseas Bank | | A | | | | | | | | A | | | | 2 |
| **China (Republic of Taiwan)** | | | | | | | | | | | | | | |
| International Commerce Bank of China | | A | | | | | | B | | | | | | 2 |
| **Thailand** | | | | | | | | | | | | | | |
| Bangkok Bank | | A | | | | | | | | AA | | | | 3 |
| Bangkok Metropolitan Bank | | A | | | | | | | | | | | | 1 |
| Siam Commercial Bank | | A | | | | | | | | | | | | 1 |
| Thai Farmers Bank | | B | | | | | | | | A | | | | 2 |
| **Australia-New Zealand** | | | | | | | | | | | | | | |
| Australia-New Zealand Bank | | B | | | | | | | | A | | | | 2 |
| Bank of New South Wales | | B | | | | | | | | A | | | | 2 |
| Bank of New Zealand | | A | | | | | | | | A | | | | 2 |
| Commonwealth Bank of Australia | | A | | | | | | | | | | | | 1 |
| Commerce Bank of Australia | | B | | | | | | | | | | | | 1 |
| Commerce Bank of Sydney | | B | | | | | | | | | | | | 1 |
| National Bank of Australasia | | B | | | | | | | | A | | | | 2 |

| | | | | | | | | | | | | | | Total |
|---|---|---|---|---|---|---|---|---|---|---|---|---|---|---|
| **Total** | | | | | | | | | | | | | | |
| A | 0 | 57 | 0 | 0 | 0 | 17 | 9 | — | — | 92 | 2 | 0 | 0 | 177 |
| B | 4 | 92 | 2 | 3 | 2 | 0 | 0 | 32 | — | 2 | 0 | 8 | 8 | 154 |
| S | 0 | 23 | 0 | 0 | 0 | 1 | 0 | 3 | 0 | 17 | 0 | 0 | 0 | 44 |
| C | 0 | 0 | 0 | 0 | 0 | 0 | 0 | 1 | 1 | 0 | 0 | 0 | 0 | 2 |
| I | — | 7 | — | — | — | — | — | — | — | — | — | — | — | 7 |
| **All Reporters** | 4 | 179 | 2 | 3 | 2 | 18 | 9 | 36 | 1 | 111 | 2 | 8 | 8 | 384 |

Total Families = 167

Total families with at least one agency or one branch in U.S. = 160.

Source: Federal Reserve Board, Washington, D.C., 1981.

Notes: The table does not include offices located in territories or possessions of the United States.

A = agencies  B = branches
S = subsidiary commercial banks
C = agreement corporations
I = New York investment companies
Agreement corporations

# Appendix D:
# Sample G-11 Call
# Report for Foreign
# Banks

# FEDERAL RESERVE statistical release

G.11(412)

FEBRUARY 11, 1980

THE...
RELEASE

MONTHLY REPORT OF CONDITION FOR
U.S. AGENCIES, BRANCHES AND DOMESTIC
BANKING SUBSIDIARIES OF FOREIGN BANKS
AS OF REPORT DATE IN DECEMBER 1979

TOTALS* FOR:
ALL REPORTING INSTITUTIONS

    AGENCIES, BRANCHES, NEW YORK INVESTMENT COMPANIES,
    AND AGREEMENT CORPORATIONS

    SUBSIDIARY COMMERCIAL BANKS**

*INSTITUTIONS LOCATED IN TERRITORIES OR POSSESSIONS OF
THE UNITED STATES ARE NOT INCLUDED.

**SUBSIDIARY COMMERCIAL BANKS ACQUIRED BY FOREIGN
BANKS IN 1979 ARE NOT INCLUDED.

INTERNATIONAL BANKING SECTION
BOARD OF GOVERNORS OF THE
        FEDERAL RESERVE SYSTEM
WASHINGTON D.C.    20551

PAGE 1

A S S E T S

MONTHLY REPORT OF CONDITION FOR
U.S. AGENCIES, BRANCHES AND DOMESTIC
BANKING SUBSIDIARIES OF FOREIGN BANKS

1. CASH, CASH ITEMS IN PROCESS OF COLLECTION, BALANCES WITH FEDERAL RESERVE, AND DUE FROM OTHER THAN DIRECTLY RELATED COMMERCIAL BANKS
   A. CURRENCY AND COIN
      (1) U.S.
      (2) OTHER
   B. CASH ITEMS IN PROCESS OF COLLECTION
   C. BALANCES WITH FEDERAL RESERVE
   D. DUE FROM OTHER THAN DIRECTLY RELATED COMMERCIAL BANKS
      (1) DEPOSITS OR CREDIT BALANCES DUE FROM COMMERCIAL BANKS IN THE U.S.
         (A) DEMAND
         (B) TIME
      (2) DEPOSITS DUE FROM BANKS IN FOREIGN COUNTRIES
   TOTAL CASH ASSETS

2. BONDS, STOCKS AND OTHER SECURITIES
   A. U.S. TREASURY SECURITIES
   B. OBLIGATIONS OF U.S. GOVERNMENT AGENCIES AND CORPORATIONS
   C. OBLIGATIONS OF STATES AND POLITICAL SUBDIVISIONS OF THE U.S.
   D. OTHER BONDS, STOCKS AND SECURITIES
      (1) OF PARTIES IN THE U.S.
      (2) OF PARTIES IN FOREIGN COUNTRIES
   TOTAL BONDS, STOCKS AND OTHER SECURITIES

3. LOANS OTHER THAN TO DIRECTLY RELATED INSTITUTIONS, GROSS
   A. TO COMMERCIAL BANKS IN THE U.S.
      (1) MATURING IN ONE DAY AND SETTLED IN IMMEDIATELY AVAILABLE FUNDS
      (2) ALL OTHER
   B. TO OTHER FINANCIAL INSTITUTIONS IN THE U.S.
   C. TO BANKS IN FOREIGN COUNTRIES
   D. TO BROKERS AND DEALERS FOR PURCHASING OR CARRYING SECURITIES
      (1) BROKERS AND DEALERS IN THE U.S.
      (2) BROKERS AND DEALERS IN FOREIGN COUNTRIES
   E. TO OTHER PARTIES FOR PURCHASING OR CARRYING SECURITIES
      (1) PARTIES IN THE U.S.
      (2) PARTIES IN FOREIGN COUNTRIES
   F. TO FOREIGN GOVERNMENTS, CENTRAL BANKS AND INTERNATIONAL MONETARY INSTITUTIONS
   G. COMMERCIAL AND INDUSTRIAL LOANS
      (1) TO PARTIES IN THE U.S.
          ( OF WHICH, OWN ACCEPTANCES PURCHASED OR DISCOUNTED )
      (2) TO PARTIES IN FOREIGN COUNTRIES
          ( OF WHICH, OWN ACCEPTANCES PURCHASED OR DISCOUNTED )
   H. ALL OTHER LOANS
      (1) TO PARTIES IN THE U.S.
      (2) TO PARTIES IN FOREIGN COUNTRIES
   TOTAL LOANS TO OTHER THAN DIRECTLY RELATED INSTITUTIONS

Entry columns:

1.
A. (1)
   (2)
B.
C.
D. (1)
   (A)
   (B)
   (2)
   **

2.
A.
B.
C.
D. (1)
   (2)
   **

3.
A. (1)
   (2)
B.
C.
D. (1)
   (2)
E. (1)
   (2)
F.
G. (1)   ( )
   (2)   ( )
H. (1)
   (2)
   **

PAGE 2

MONTHLY REPORT OF CONDITION FOR
U.S. AGENCIES, BRANCHES AND DOMESTIC
BANKING SUBSIDIARIES OF FOREIGN BANKS

A S S E T S

4. CUSTOMERS' LIABILITIES ON ACCEPTANCES OUTSTANDING
   A. PARTIES IN U.S.
      ( OF WHICH, LIABILITIES OF DIRECTLY RELATED U.S. INSTITUTIONS )
   B. PARTIES IN FOREIGN COUNTRIES
      ( OF WHICH, LIABILITIES OF DIRECTLY RELATED FOREIGN INSTITUTIONS )
   TOTAL CUSTOMERS' LIABILITIES ON ACCEPTANCES OUTSTANDING

5. CUSTOMERS' LIABILITIES ON DEFERRED PAYMENT LETTERS OF CREDIT
   A. PARTIES IN THE U.S.
      ( OF WHICH, LIABILITIES OF DIRECTLY RELATED U.S. INSTITUTIONS )
   B. PARTIES IN FOREIGN COUNTRIES
      ( OF WHICH, LIABILITIES OF DIRECTLY RELATED FOREIGN INSTITUTIONS )
   TOTAL CUSTOMERS' LIABILITIES ON DEFERRED PAYMENT LETTERS OF CREDIT

6. DUE FROM DIRECTLY RELATED INSTITUTIONS
   A. HEAD OFFICE OR PARENT(S)
      ( OF WHICH, OWN ACCEPTANCES PURCHASED OR DISCOUNTED )
   B. BRANCHES AND AGENCIES
      (1) IN THE U.S.
      (2) IN FOREIGN COUNTRIES
          ( OF WHICH, OWN ACCEPTANCES PURCHASED OR DISCOUNTED )
   C. WHOLLY OWNED SUBSIDIARIES
      (1) COMMERCIAL BANKS IN THE U.S.
      (2) IN FOREIGN COUNTRIES
          ( OF WHICH, OWN ACCEPTANCES PURCHASED OR DISCOUNTED )
      (3) OTHER INSTITUTIONS
          (A) IN THE U.S.
          (B) IN FOREIGN COUNTRIES
              ( OF WHICH, OWN ACCEPTANCES PURCHASED OR DISCOUNTED )
   TOTAL DUE FROM DIRECTLY RELATED INSTITUTIONS
   ( OF WHICH, DUE FROM RELATED BANKING INSTITUTIONS IN THE U.S. )
   ( OF WHICH, DUE FROM ALL RELATED INSTITUTIONS IN FOREIGN COUNTRIES )

7. OTHER ASSETS

8. TOTAL ASSETS

PAGE 3

MONTHLY REPORT OF CONDITION FOR
U.S. AGENCIES, BRANCHES AND DOMESTIC
BANKING SUBSIDIARIES OF FOREIGN BANKS

# L I A B I L I T I E S

9. DEMAND DEPOSITS OR CREDIT BALANCES DUE FROM OTHER THAN DIRECTLY RELATED INSTITUTIONS
   - A. DUE TO INDIVIDUALS, PARTNERSHIPS AND CORPORATIONS
     - (1) IN THE U.S.
     - (2) IN FOREIGN COUNTRIES
   - B. DUE TO THE U.S. GOVERNMENT
   - C. DUE TO STATES AND POLITICAL SUBDIVISIONS OF THE U.S.
   - D. DUE TO FOREIGN GOVERNMENTS, CENTRAL BANKS AND MONETARY INSTITUTIONS
   - E. DUE TO COMMERCIAL BANKS IN THE U.S.
   - F. DUE TO BANKS IN FOREIGN COUNTRIES
   - G. CERTIFIED AND OFFICERS CHECKS, TRAVELERS CHECKS, LETTERS OF CREDIT, ETC.
   - TOTAL DEMAND DEPOSITS AND CREDIT BALANCES **

10. TIME AND SAVINGS DEPOSITS DUE OR ISSUED TO OTHER THAN DIRECTLY RELATED INSTITUTIONS
    - A. SAVINGS DEPOSITS
      - (1) DUE TO PARTIES IN THE U.S.
      - (2) DUE TO PARTIES IN FOREIGN COUNTRIES
    - B. TIME DEPOSITS
      - (1) DUE OR ISSUED TO INDIVIDUALS, PARTNERSHIPS AND CORPORATIONS
        - (A) IN THE U.S.
        - (B) IN FOREIGN COUNTRIES
      - (2) DUE OR ISSUED TO THE U.S. GOVERNMENT
      - (3) DUE OR ISSUED TO STATES AND POLITICAL SUBDIVISIONS OF THE U.S.
      - (4) DUE OR ISSUED TO FOREIGN GOVERNMENTS, CENTRAL BANKS AND INTERNATIONAL MONETARY INSTITUTIONS
      - (5) DUE OR ISSUED TO COMMERCIAL BANKS IN THE U.S.
      - (6) DUE OR ISSUED TO BANKS IN FOREIGN COUNTRIES
    - TOTAL TIME AND SAVINGS DEPOSITS **

11. BORROWING FROM OTHER THAN DIRECTLY RELATED INSTITUTIONS
    - A. FROM COMMERCIAL BANKS IN THE U.S.
      - (1) MATURING IN ONE DAY AND SETTLED IN IMMEDIATELY AVAILABLE FUNDS
      - (2) ALL OTHER
    - B. FROM OTHER PARTIES IN THE U.S.
    - C. FROM PARTIES IN FOREIGN COUNTRIES
    - TOTAL BORROWING FROM OTHER THAN DIRECTLY RELATED INSTITUTIONS **

12. LIABILITIES ON ACCEPTANCES OUTSTANDING

13. LIABILITIES ON DEFERRED PAYMENT LETTERS OF CREDIT OUTSTANDING

14. OTHER LIABILITIES TO OTHER THAN DIRECTLY RELATED INSTITUTIONS

PAGE 4

MONTHLY REPORT OF CONDITION FOR
U.S. AGENCIES, BRANCHES AND DOMESTIC
BANKING SUBSIDIARIES OF FOREIGN BANKS

L I A B I L I T I E S

15.  DUE TO DIRECTLY RELATED INSTITUTIONS      15.
    A.  HEAD OFFICE OR PARENT(S)      A.
    B.  BRANCHES AND AGENCIES      B.
        (1)  IN THE U.S.      (1)
        (2)  IN FOREIGN COUNTRIES      (2)
    C.  WHOLLY OWNED SUBSIDIARIES      C.
        (1)  COMMERCIAL BANKS IN THE U.S.      (1)
        (2)  BANKS IN FOREIGN COUNTRIES      (2)
        (3)  OTHER INSTITUTIONS      (3)
            (A)  IN THE U.S.      (A)
            (B)  IN FOREIGN COUNTRIES      (B)

TOTAL DUE TO DIRECTLY RELATED INSTITUTIONS      **
( OF WHICH, DUE TO RELATED BANKING INSTITUTIONS IN THE U.S. )      (**)
( OF WHICH, DUE TO ALL RELATED INSTITUTIONS IN FOREIGN COUNTRIES )      (**)

16.  RESERVES FOR BAD DEBT LOSSES AND OTHER RESERVES ON LOANS AND SECURITIES      16.

17.  RESERVES FOR CONTINGENCIES      17.

18.  CAPITAL ACCOUNTS      18. _____
    TOTAL RESERVES AND CAPITAL      **

19.  TOTAL LIABILITIES, RESERVES AND CAPITAL ACCOUNTS      19.

TOTAL CLAIMS ON FOREIGNERS      FGN CL
TOTAL LIABILITIES TO FOREIGNERS      FGN LIAB
NET FOREIGN POSITION      NET

NUMBER OF INSTITUTIONS REPORTING      REPORTERS

# Appendix E:
# Sample Report of Assets and Liabilities of U.S. Branches and Agencies of Foreign Banks

Board of Governors of the Federal Reserve System
Federal Deposit Insurance Corporation
Office of the Comptroller of the Currency

FFIEC 002
Approved by the Federal Financial Institutions
Examination Council – November 1979

This report is required by law [12 U.S.C. §3105
(b)(2); 12 U.S.C. §1817(a)(1) and (3); and 12 U.S.C.
§3102(b)].

lose of business on _____, 19 ____

Please read carefully "Instructions for the Preparation of Report of Assets and Liabilities of U.S. Branches and Agencies of Foreign Banks."

Please indicate legal status: ☐ Branch  ☐ Agency

Legal Title of Branch or Agency

Street Address

City　　　　　　　　County

State　　　　　　　　Zip Code

Legal Title of Foreign Bank Parent

City　　　　　　　　Country

Person to be contacted concerning this report

Telephone Number (including area code and extension)

NOTE:
This report must be signed by an authorized officer and attested by the senior executive officer.

I, _____
Name of Officer Authorized to Sign Report

Title of Officer Authorized to Sign Report

of the branch or agency specified do hereby declare that this Report of Assets and Liabilities (including the supporting schedules) has been prepared in conformance with the instructions issued by the Federal Financial Institutions Examination Council and is true to the best of my knowledge and belief.

Signature of Officer Authorized to Sign Report

SAMPLE

I, _____
Name of Senior Executive Officer

Title of Senior Executive Officer

attest the correctness of this Report of Assets and Liabilities (including the supporting schedules) and declare that it has been examined by us, and to the best of our knowledge and belief, has been prepared in conformance with the instructions issued by the Federal Financial Institutions Examination Council and is true and correct.

Signature of Senior Executive Officer

Return original and 3 copies to the Federal Reserve Bank in whose district the branch or agency is located.

Board of Governors of the Federal Reserve System
Federal Deposit Insurance Corporation
Office of the Comptroller of the Currency

FFIEC 002
Page 2

## Report of Assets and Liabilities of _____

Legal Title of Branch or Agency

at close of business on _____, 19____

| | Dollar Amount in Thousands | Bil | Mil | Thou | |
|---|---|---|---|---|---|

**ASSETS**

| | | | |
|---|---|---|---|
| 1. Cash and due from depository institutions (From Schedule C, Item 8)............................ | | | 1. |
| 2. U.S. Treasury securities ........................................................... | | | 2. |
| 3. Obligations of other U.S. Government agencies and corporations ........................... | | | 3. |
| 4. Obligations of states and political subdivisions in the United States....................... | | | 4. |
| 5. Other bonds, notes, debentures, and corporate stock .................................... | | | 5. |
| 6. Federal funds sold and securities purchased under agreements to resell (From Schedule N, Item 3)........ | | | 6. |
| 7. Loans, Total (excluding unearned income) (From Schedule A, Item 9) ....................... | | | 7. |
| 8. Lease financing receivables ........................................................ | | | 8. |
| 9. Customers' liability to this branch or agency on acceptances outstanding: | | | |
|    a. U.S. addressees (domicile)...................................................... | | | 9.a. |
|    b. Non-U.S. addressees (domicile) .................................................. | | | 9.b. |
| 10. Other assets (claims on non-related parties) (From Schedule G, Item 3)...................... | | | 10. |
| 11. Net due from head office and other related institutions in the U.S. and in foreign countries (From Schedule M, Part 1, Item 4)................................................. | | | 11. |
| 12. TOTAL ASSETS (Sum of Items 1 thru 11) ............................................ | | | 12. |

**LIABILITIES**

| | | | |
|---|---|---|---|
| 13. Total deposits and credit balances (From Schedule F, Item 7) ........................... | | | 13. |
| 14. Federal funds purchased and securities sold under agreements to repurchase (From Schedule O, Item 3) .... | | | 14. |
| 15. Other liabilities for borrowed money (From Schedule L, Column A, Item 3) .................. | | | 15. |
| 16 Branch or agency liability on acceptances executed and outstanding ......................... | | | 16. |
| 17. Other liabilities to non-related parties (From Schedule H, Item 3)........................ | | | 17. |
| *8. Net due to head office and other related institutions in the U.S. and in foreign countries (From Schedule M, Part 1, Item 4)................................................. | | | 18. |
| 19. TOTAL LIABILITIES (Sum of Items 13 thru 18) ...................................... | | | 19. |

**MEMORANDA**

| | | | |
|---|---|---|---|
| 1. Amounts outstanding as of report date: | | | Memo |
|   a. (1) Standby letters of credit, total........................................... | | | 1.a.(1) |
|       (a) To U.S. addressees (domicile) ......................................... | | | 1.a.(1)(a) |
|       (b) To non-U.S. addressees (domicile) ...................................... | | | 1.a.(1)(b) |
|     (2) Amount of standby letters of credit in Memo Item 1.a.(1) conveyed to others through participations . | | | 1.a.(2) |
|   b. Time certificates of deposit in denominations of $100,000 or more ......................... | | | 1.b. |
|   c. Other time deposits in amounts of $100,000 or more........................................ | | | 1.c. |
|   d. Commercial letters of credit .................................................... | | | 1.d. |
|   e. Amount of acceptances reported in Item 16 that have been reaccepted by another bank in the U.S. ...... | | | 1.e. |
|   f. Statutory or regulatory asset pledge requirement....................................... | | | 1.f. |
|     Check the appropriate box (es) below: | | | |
|       ☐ Asset maintenance    ☐ Security or cash deposit | | | |
|       ☐ Asset pledge    ☐ Other | | | |
| 2. Average for 30 calendar days (or calendar month) ending with report date: | | | |
|   a. Cash and due from depository institutions (Corresponds to Asset Item 1 above) ................. | | | 2.a. |
|   b. Federal funds sold and securities purchased under agreements to resell (Corresponds to Asset Item 6 above)............................................................. | | | 2.b. |
|   c. Total loans (Corresponds to Asset Item 7 above)........................................ | | | 2.c. |
|   d. Time certificates of deposit in denominations of $100,000 or more (Corresponds to Memorandum Item 1.b. above) ............................................................ | | | 2.d. |
|   e. Total deposits and credit balances (Corresponds to Liability Item 13 above)..................... | | | 2.e. |
|   f. Federal funds purchased and securities sold under agreements to repurchase (Corresponds to Liability Item 14 above)............................................................. | | | 2.f. |
|   g. Other liabilities for borrowed money (Corresponds to Liability Item 15 above).................. | | | 2.g. |
|   h. Total assets (Corresponds to Asset Item 12 above)....................................... | | | 2.h. |

FFIEC 002
Page 3

Legal Title of Branch or Agency

## Schedule A—Loans

| | Dollar Amount in Thousands | Bil | Mil | Thou | |
|---|---|---|---|---|---|
| 1. Real estate loans (including only loans secured primarily by real estate). | | | | | 1. |
| Loans to financial institutions: | | | | | |
| a. To commercial banks in the U.S.: | | | | | |
| (1) U.S. branches and agencies of other foreign banks | | | | | 2.a.(1) |
| (2) Other commercial banks in the U.S. | | | | | 2.a.(2) |
| b. To banks in foreign countries: | | | | | |
| (1) Foreign branches of U.S. banks | | | | | 2.b.(1) |
| (2) Other banks in foreign countries. | | | | | 2.b.(2) |
| c. To other financial institutions | | | | | 2.c. |
| 3. Loans for purchasing or carrying securities. | | | | | 3. |
| 4. Commercial and industrial loans (except those secured primarily by real estate): | | | | | |
| a. To U.S. addressees (domicile) | | | | | 4.a. |
| b. To non-U.S. addressees (domicile) | | | | | 4.b. |
| 5. Loans to individuals for household, family, and other personal expenditures. | | | | | 5. |
| 6. Loans to foreign governments and official institutions | | | | | 6. |
| 7. All other loans | | | | | 7. |
| 8. Less: unearned income on loans. | | | | | 8. |
| 9. TOTAL LOANS (excluding unearned income) (Must equal Asset Item 7). | | | | | 9. |

### MEMORANDA

| | | Bil | Mil | Thou | |
|---|---|---|---|---|---|
| 1. Holdings of commercial paper included in Schedule A | | | | | Memo 1. |
| 2. Holdings of acceptances included in Item 4 of Schedule A. | | | | | 2. |
| 3. Loans to banks in foreign countries—average for 30 calendar days, or calendar month, ending with the report date (Corresponds to sum of Items 2.b.(1) and 2.b.(2) of Schedule A). | | | | | 3. |
| 4. Commercial and industrial loans with remaining maturity of one year or less: | | | | | |
| a. With predetermined interest rates. | | | | | 4.a. |
| b. With floating interest rates | | | | | 4.b. |
| 5. Commercial and industrial loans with remaining maturity of more than one year: | | | | | |
| a. With predetermined interest rates. | | | | | 5.a. |
| b. With floating interest rates | | | | | 5.b. |

## Schedule C—Cash and Due from Depository Institutions

| | Dollar Amount in Thousands | Bil | Mil | Thou | |
|---|---|---|---|---|---|
| 1. Cash items in process of collection and unposted debits | | | | | 1. |
| 2. Demand balances with commercial banks in the U.S. | | | | | 2. |
| 3. Time and savings balances with commercial banks in the U.S. | | | | | 3. |
| 4. Balances with other depository institutions in the U.S. | | | | | 4. |
| 5. Balances with banks in foreign countries: | | | | | |
| a. Foreign branches of U.S. banks | | | | | 5.a. |
| b. Other banks in foreign countries. | | | | | 5.b. |
| 6. Balances with central banks: | | | | | |
| a. Federal Reserve Banks | | | | | 6.a. |
| b. Other central banks. | | | | | 6.b. |
| 7. Currency and coin (U.S. and foreign) | | | | | 7. |
| 8. TOTAL (Must equal Asset Item 1) | | | | | 8. |

FFIEC 002
Page 4

Legal Title of Branch or Agency

## Schedule F—Deposit Liabilities and Credit Balances

| Dollar Amount in Thousands | A. Demand | | | B. Savings | | | C. Time | | | D. Credit Balances | | | |
|---|---|---|---|---|---|---|---|---|---|---|---|---|---|
| | Bil | Mil | Thou | Bil | Mil | Thou | Bil | Mil | Thou | Bil | Mil | Thou | |
| 1. Deposits and credit balances of individuals, partnerships, and corporations: | | | | | | | | | | | | | |
| a. U.S. addressees (domicile)................. | | | | | | | | | | | | | 1.a. |
| b. Non-U.S. addressees (domicile) ............. | | | | | | | | | | | | | 1.b. |
| 2. Deposits and credit balances of United States Government and of states and political subdivisions in the U.S. .................................. | | | | | | | | | | | | | 2. |
| 3. Deposits and credit balances of foreign governments and official institutions................... | | | | | | | | | | | | | 3. |
| 4. Deposits and credit balances of commercial banks in the United States: | | | | | | | | | | | | | |
| a. U.S. branches and agencies of other foreign banks ... | | | | | | | | | | | | | 4.a. |
| b. Other commercial banks in the U.S. ........... | | | | | | | | | | | | | 4.b. |
| 5. Deposits and credit balances of banks in foreign countries: | | | | | | | | | | | | | |
| a. Foreign branches of U.S. banks .............. | | | | | | | | | | | | | 5.a. |
| b. Other banks in foreign countries ............. | | | | | | | | | | | | | 5.b. |
| 6. Certified and officers' checks, travelers' checks, and letters of credit sold for cash ................. | | | | | | | | | | | | | 6. |
| 7. TOTAL DEPOSITS AND CREDIT BALANCES (Sum of Columns A, B, C, & D must equal Liability Item 13) .................... | | | | | | | | | | | | | 7. |
| MEMORANDA | | | | | | | | | | | | | Memo |
| 1. Savings deposits authorized for automatic transfer and NOW accounts included in Item 1, Column B above.... | | | | | | | | | | | | | 1. |
| 2. Money market time deposits in denominations of $10,000 but less than $100,000 with original maturities of 26 weeks included in Item 7, Column C above ..................................... | | | | | | | | | | | | | 2. |
| 3. Time certificates of deposit in denominations of $100,000 or more with remaining maturity of more than 12 months included in Item 7, Column C above ... | | | | | | | | | | | | | 3. |

FFIEC 002
Page 5

_____
Legal Title of Branch or Agency

## Schedule G—Other Assets

|  | Dollar Amount in Thousands | Bil | Mil | Thou |  |
|---|---|---|---|---|---|
| 1. Income earned or accrued on loans but not collected . . . . . . . . . . . . . . . . . . . . . . . . . . . . . . . . . . . . |  |  |  |  | 1. |
| 2. All other (List items over 10% of Item 3 below, unless less than $100,000) . . . . . . . . . . . . . . . . . . |  |  |  |  | 2. |
| _____ |  |  |  |  |  |
| _____ |  |  |  |  |  |
| _____ |  |  |  |  |  |
| 3. TOTAL (Must equal Asset Item 10) . . . . . . . . . . . . . . . . . . . . . . . . . . . . . . . . . . . . . . . . . . . . . . |  |  |  |  | 3. |

## Schedule H—Other Liabilities

|  | Dollar Amount in Thousands | Bil | Mil | Thou |  |
|---|---|---|---|---|---|
| 1. Expenses accrued and unpaid. . . . . . . . . . . . . . . . . . . . . . . . . . . . . . . . . . . . . . . . . . . . . . . . . . . |  |  |  |  | 1. |
| 2. All other (List items over 10% of Item 3 below, unless less than $100,000) . . . . . . . . . . . . . . . . . . |  |  |  |  | 2. |
| _____ |  |  |  |  |  |
| _____ |  |  |  |  |  |
| _____ |  |  |  |  |  |
| 3. TOTAL (Must equal Liability Item 17) . . . . . . . . . . . . . . . . . . . . . . . . . . . . . . . . . . . . . . . . . . . . |  |  |  |  | 3. |

## Schedule L—Other Liabilities for Borrowed Money

|  | A. Total | | | B. To U.S. Addressees | | | C. To Non-U.S. Addressees | | |  |
|---|---|---|---|---|---|---|---|---|---|---|
| Dollar Amount in Thousands | Bil | Mil | Thou | Bil | Mil | Thou | Bil | Mil | Thou |  |
| 1. Owed to banks . . . . . . . . . . . . . . . . . . . . . . . . . . . . . |  |  |  |  |  |  |  |  |  | 1. |
| 2. Owed to others. . . . . . . . . . . . . . . . . . . . . . . . . . . . . |  |  |  |  |  |  |  |  |  | 2. |
| 3. TOTAL (Column A must equal Liability Item 15). . . . . . . . . . . . . . . . |  |  |  |  |  |  |  |  |  | 3. |

MEMORANDUM

| | | | | | | | | | | |
|---|---|---|---|---|---|---|---|---|---|---|
| 1. Immediately available funds with a maturity greater than one day included in other liabilities for borrowed money . . . . . . . . . . . . . . . . . |  |  |  |  |  |  |  |  |  | Memo 1. |

FFIEC 002
Page 6

Legal Title of Branch or Agency

## Schedule M—Due to/Due from Head Office and Other Related Institutions in the U.S. and in Foreign Countries

The Federal Financial Institutions Examination Council regards the individual respondent information provided by each reporting institution on this schedule as confidential. If it should be determined subsequently that any information collected on this schedule must be released, respondents will be notified.

| | A. Gross due to | | | B. Gross due from | | | |
|---|---|---|---|---|---|---|---|
| Dollar Amount in Thousands | Bil | Mil | Thou | Bil | Mil | Thou | |
| **PART 1.** Transactions with related institutions reflected in net due to/net due from items (Items 11 and 18) on the face of the report. | | | | | | | Part 1. |
| Amounts outstanding as of report date: | | | | | | | |
| 1. Related institutions domiciled in the United States | | | | | | | |
| a. Related branches and agencies in the U.S. | | | | | | | |
| (1) In same state as the reporting office | | | | | | | 1.a.(1) |
| (2) In other states. | | | | | | | 1.a.(2) |
| b. U.S. offices of related N.Y. investment companies. | | | | | | | 1.b. |
| c. U.S. offices of related Edge Act and Agreement corporations. | | | | | | | 1.c. |
| d. U.S. offices of related U.S. banks | | | | | | | 1.d. |
| 2. Related institutions domiciled outside the United States | | | | | | | |
| a. Head office and its non-U.S. branches and agencies | | | | | | | 2.a. |
| b. Other non-U.S. related companies and offices, excluding nonbanking subsidiaries domiciled outside the U.S. | | | | | | | 2.b. |
| 3. TOTAL | | | | | | | 3. |
| 4. Net due to/due from related institutions (Item 3, Column A minus Column B. The *absolute* value of the result must equal Liability Item 18 if Column A minus Column B is positive, or Asset Item 11 if Column A minus Column B is negative.) | | | | | | | 4. |
| **MEMORANDA** | | | | | | | Memo |
| 1. Amount of Item 3 for wholly-owned subsidiaries in Items 1.b, 1.c, 1.d, and 2.b above | | | | | | | 1. |
| Average of daily amounts for the preceding 30 calendar days (or calendar month) ending with report date: | | | | | | | |
| 2. Related offices in the U.S. (Corresponds to the sum of Items 1.a through 1.d above) | | | | | | | 2. |
| 3. Related offices in foreign countries and in Puerto Rico and U.S. territories and possessions (Corresponds to the sum of Items 2.a and 2.b above) | | | | | | | 3. |
| **PART 2.** Transactions with related institutions *not* reflected in net due to/net due from items (Items 11 and 18) on the face of the report. | | | | | | | Part 2. |
| Amounts outstanding as of report date: | | | | | | | |
| 1. Nonbanking related subsidiaries in the U.S. | | | | | | | 1. |
| 2. Nonbanking related subsidiaries in foreign countries and in Puerto Rico and U.S. territories and possessions. | | | | | | | 2. |
| **MEMORANDUM** | | | | | | | Memo |
| 1. Amount of Items 1 and 2 above for wholly-owned subsidiaries. | | | | | | | 1. |

Legal Title of Branch or Agency

## Schedule N—Federal Funds Sold and Securities Purchased Under Agreements to Resell

| Dollar Amount in Thousands | Bil | Mil | Thou | |
|---|---|---|---|---|
| 1. Loans of immediately available funds with one-day maturity or continuing contract: | | | | |
| a. Securities purchased under agreements to resell. | | | | 1.a. |
| b. Other | | | | 1.b. |
| 2. Other securities purchased under agreements to resell. | | | | 2. |
| 3. Federal funds sold and securities purchased under agreements to resell—Total (Sum of Items 1.a, 1.b, and 2; also equals sum of Items 3.a, 3.b, and 3.c below) (Must equal Asset Item 6) | | | | 3. |
| a. With commercial banks in the U.S. | | | | 3.a. |
| b. With brokers and dealers in securities | | | | 3.b. |
| c. With others | | | | 3.c. |

## Schedule O— Federal Funds Purchased and Securities Sold Under Agreements to Repurchase

| Dollar Amount in Thousands | Bil | Mil | Thou | |
|---|---|---|---|---|
| 1. Borrowings of immediately available funds with one-day maturity or continuing contract: | | | | |
| a. Securities sold under agreements to repurchase. | | | | 1.a. |
| b. Other | | | | 1.b. |
| 2. Other securities sold under agreements to repurchase. | | | | 2. |
| 3. Federal funds purchased and securities sold under agreements to repurchase—Total (Sum of Items 1.a, 1.b, and 2 above; also equals sum of Items 3.a through 3.f below) (Must equal Liability Item 14). | | | | 3. |
| a. With commercial banks in the U.S. | | | | 3.a. |
| b. With savings and loan associations and mutual savings banks | | | | 3.b. |
| c. With nonfinancial businesses in the U.S.. | | | | 3.c. |
| d. With state and local governments in the U.S.. | | | | 3.d. |
| e. With U.S. Government agencies and corporations, banks in foreign countries, and foreign official institutions. | | | | 3.e. |
| f. With others | | | | 3.f. |

# Appendix F:
# Market-Survey
# Questionnaire

This survey consists of a total of ten brief questions regarding your organization and the financial products (services) you provide for the conduct of international business.

Questions 1 through 8 are aimed at eliciting your opinion as to the importance you attach to each of several factors or statements (per relevant question) regarding the international financial services you offer. To the right of each factor or statement is a rating scale from 1 to 5. You are asked to circle the appropriate number indicating the degree of importance you attach to each factor or statement corresponding to each question. For example:

*Degree of Importance*

| Least Important | Somewhat Important | Important | Very Important | Most Important |
|---|---|---|---|---|
| 1 | 2 | 3 | 4 | 5 |

If you circle 1, it would mean that you believe a factor or statement to be the *least important* in regard to the question being asked; however, if you circle 3, it would mean that you believe it to be *important,* and if you circle 5, it would mean that the factor or statement is *most important* to the particular question.

Questions 9 through 11 simply require that you either circle the alphabetical letter that corresponds to your choice, fill in a figure, or state your opinion briefly.

1. How important was each of the following factors in initially establishing or motivating your organization to provide international banking services?

| | | *Degree of Importance* | | | | |
|---|---|---|---|---|---|---|
| | | *Least* | | | | *Most* |
| a. | Higher profitability | 1 | 2 | 3 | 4 | 5 |
| b. | New business opportunities | 1 | 2 | 3 | 4 | 5 |
| c. | Legal advantages | 1 | 2 | 3 | 4 | 5 |
| d. | Geographical proximity to customers | 1 | 2 | 3 | 4 | 5 |
| e. | Serving existing customers | 1 | 2 | 3 | 4 | 5 |
| f. | Other (please specify) | 1 | 2 | 3 | 4 | 5 |
| | _____ | 1 | 2 | 3 | 4 | 5 |
| | _____ | 1 | 2 | 3 | 4 | 5 |

2. How important is each of the following international financial products (services) to the primary functioning of your business?

| | | Degree of Importance | | | | |
|---|---|:---:|:---:|:---:|:---:|:---:|
| | | *Least* | | | | *Most* |
| a. | Foreign loans (medium and longterm) | 1 | 2 | 3 | 4 | 5 |
| b. | Export-import financing (for example, letters of credit, bankers' acceptance) | 1 | 2 | 3 | 4 | 5 |
| c. | Funds transfer | 1 | 2 | 3 | 4 | 5 |
| d. | Foreign exchange dealings | 1 | 2 | 3 | 4 | 5 |
| e. | Noncommercial banking services (for example, equity participation, investment banking) | 1 | 2 | 3 | 4 | 5 |
| f. | Other (please specify) | 1 | 2 | 3 | 4 | 5 |
| | _____ | 1 | 2 | 3 | 4 | 5 |
| | _____ | 1 | 2 | 3 | 4 | 5 |

3. How important is each of the following factors in the marketing of your international financial products (services)?

| | | Degree of Importance | | | | |
|---|---|:---:|:---:|:---:|:---:|:---:|
| | | *Least* | | | | *Most* |
| a. | Product (service) packaging (total integrated services) | 1 | 2 | 3 | 4 | 5 |
| b. | Customer need satisfaction | 1 | 2 | 3 | 4 | 5 |
| c. | Market segmentation | 1 | 2 | 3 | 4 | 5 |
| d. | Promotion of product (service) | 1 | 2 | 3 | 4 | 5 |
| e. | Product (service) pricing | 1 | 2 | 3 | 4 | 5 |
| f. | Proximity to customer | 1 | 2 | 3 | 4 | 5 |
| g. | Other (please specify) | 1 | 2 | 3 | 4 | 5 |
| | _____ | 1 | 2 | 3 | 4 | 5 |
| | _____ | 1 | 2 | 3 | 4 | 5 |

4. How important is each of the following factors in determining the price of your international financial products (services)?

| | | Degree of Importance | | | | |
|---|---|:---:|:---:|:---:|:---:|:---:|
| | | *Least* | | | | *Most* |
| a. | Capital requirements (for example, competitive differentials | 1 | 2 | 3 | 4 | 5 |
| b. | Cost of raising funds | 1 | 2 | 3 | 4 | 5 |
| c. | Short-run profit objectives | 1 | 2 | 3 | 4 | 5 |
| d. | Long-run profit objectives | 1 | 2 | 3 | 4 | 5 |
| e. | Customer risk | 1 | 2 | 3 | 4 | 5 |
| f. | Other (please specify) | 1 | 2 | 3 | 4 | 5 |
| | _____ | 1 | 2 | 3 | 4 | 5 |
| | _____ | 1 | 2 | 3 | 4 | 5 |

5. How important is each of the following types of customers in providing your organization a source of business?

|  |  | Least |  |  |  | Most |
|---|---|---|---|---|---|---|
| a. | Government agencies | 1 | 2 | 3 | 4 | 5 |
| b. | Commercial banks | 1 | 2 | 3 | 4 | 5 |
| c. | Other financial institutions | 1 | 2 | 3 | 4 | 5 |
| d. | Large private businesses | 1 | 2 | 3 | 4 | 5 |
| e. | Small or medium-sized private businesses | 1 | 2 | 3 | 4 | 5 |
| f. | Other (please specify) | 1 | 2 | 3 | 4 | 5 |
|  | _____ | 1 | 2 | 3 | 4 | 5 |
|  | _____ | 1 | 2 | 3 | 4 | 5 |

*Degree of Importance*

6. How important is each of the following factors in providing your organization a market advantage over your competitors?

*Degree of Importance*

|  |  | Least |  |  |  | Most |
|---|---|---|---|---|---|---|
| a. | Availability of large amount of funds | 1 | 2 | 3 | 4 | 5 |
| b. | Personalized services | 1 | 2 | 3 | 4 | 5 |
| c. | Specialized expertise | 1 | 2 | 3 | 4 | 5 |
| d. | Lower financing cost | 1 | 2 | 3 | 4 | 5 |
| e. | Knowledge of customer business needs (operations and markets) | 1 | 2 | 3 | 4 | 5 |
| f. | Aggressive marketing of financial products (services) | 1 | 2 | 3 | 4 | 5 |
| g. | Other (please specify) | 1 | 2 | 3 | 4 | 5 |
|  | _____ | 1 | 2 | 3 | 4 | 5 |
|  | _____ | 1 | 2 | 3 | 4 | 5 |

7. How important do you believe each of the following pieces of legislation has been (or will be) in expanding your international banking business?

*Degree of Importance*

|  |  | Least |  |  |  | Most |
|---|---|---|---|---|---|---|
| a. | International Banking Act of 1978 | 1 | 2 | 3 | 4 | 5 |
| b. | Edge Act (and related amendments and regulations) | 1 | 2 | 3 | 4 | 5 |
| c. | Depository Institutions Deregulation and Monetary Control Act of 1980 (Omnibus Banking Act) | 1 | 2 | 3 | 4 | 5 |
| d. | Restrictions of U.S. capital outflows of the 1960s | 1 | 2 | 3 | 4 | 5 |
| e. | Establishment of floating exchange rates in March 1973 | 1 | 2 | 3 | 4 | 5 |
| f. | Other (please specify) | 1 | 2 | 3 | 4 | 5 |
|  | _____ | 1 | 2 | 3 | 4 | 5 |
|  | _____ | 1 | 2 | 3 | 4 | 5 |

8. How important will the emphasis of each of the following market (customer) segments be to your organization in the decade of 1980s?

| | | Degree of Importance | | | | |
|---|---|---|---|---|---|---|
| | | Least | | | | Most |
| a. | Local or regional customers | 1 | 2 | 3 | 4 | 5 |
| b. | National-interstate customers (in continental United States) | 1 | 2 | 3 | 4 | 5 |
| c. | Foreign customers (advanced countries outside continental United States) | 1 | 2 | 3 | 4 | 5 |
| d. | Foreign customers (developing countries outside continental United States) | 1 | 2 | 3 | 4 | 5 |
| e. | Other (please specify) | 1 | 2 | 3 | 4 | 5 |
| | _____ | 1 | 2 | 3 | 4 | 5 |
| | _____ | 1 | 2 | 3 | 4 | 5 |

9. Which of the following classifications describes your type of organization? (Please circle the alphabetical letter that corresponds to your choice.)

| | | Degree of Importance | | | | |
|---|---|---|---|---|---|---|
| | | Least | | | | Most |
| a. | U.S. commercial bank (money-center bank) | 1 | 2 | 3 | 4 | 5 |
| b. | U.S. commercial bank (regional bank) | 1 | 2 | 3 | 4 | 5 |
| c. | Edge Act corporation | 1 | 2 | 3 | 4 | 5 |
| d. | Foreign-bank subsidiary | 1 | 2 | 3 | 4 | 5 |
| e. | Foreign-bank branch | 1 | 2 | 3 | 4 | 5 |
| f. | Other (please specify) | 1 | 2 | 3 | 4 | 5 |
| | _____ | 1 | 2 | 3 | 4 | 5 |
| | _____ | 1 | 2 | 3 | 4 | 5 |

10. Please specify the approximate dollar size of your organization in regard to:

    a. Total assets _____

    b. Total equity capital _____

11. Do you feel that approval of the interstate banking proposal (Carter proposal) will increase your organization's international banking business? Please explain your position briefly.

_____

_____

_____

# Bibliography

## Documentary Sources and Special Reports

Board of Governors of the Federal Reserve System. "Corporations doing Foreign Banking or Other Foreign Financing under the Federal Reserve Act, Regulation K." *Federal Reserve Bulletin*. Washington, D.C.: Board of Governors of the Federal Reserve System, December 1956.

_____ . "Corporations Engaged in Foreign Banking and Financing under the Feder Reserve Act, Regulation K, 12 CFR Part 211." *Federal Reserve Bulletin*. Washington, D.C.: Board of Governors of the Federal Reserve System, September 1963.

_____ . *Foreign Takeovers of United States Banks*. Staff Report. Washington, D.C.: Federal Reserve Board, 1980.

_____ . "International Bank Operations, Regulation K, 12 CFR Part 211." *Federal Reserve Bulletin*. Washington, D.C.: Board of Governors of the Federal Reserve System, June 1979.

California. *State Financial Code*. January 1, 1981.

Controller General of the United States. *Considerable Increase in Foreign Banking in the United States since 1972*. Washington, D.C.: Office of the Controller General of the United States, August 1, 1979.

Financial Accounting Standards Board. *Statement of Financial Accounting Standards, No. 8*. Stamford, Conn.: Financial Accounting Standards Board, December 1975.

_____ . *Statement of Financial Accounting Standards*, No. 52. Stamford, Conn.: Financial Accounting Standards Board, December 1981.

Houpt, James V. "Performance and Characteristics of Edge Corporations." Staff Studies. Washington, D.C.: Federal Reserve Board, January 1981.

Illinois. *Foreign Banking Office Act, Annotated Statutes*. August 17, 1973, P.A. 78-346.

Longbrake, M. Quinn, and Walter, J. "Foreign Acquisitions of U.S. Banks: Facts and Patterns." Staff Papers. Washington, D.C.: U.S. Controller of the Currency, June 1980.

Mastrapasqua, Frank, "The Foreign Branch Operations of American Banks and United States Monetary Control: A Quantitative Analysis." Ph.D. dissertation, New York University, 1970.

Odjagor, Marianne. "Foreign Ownership Policies of United States Multinational Banks." Ph.D. dissertation, Harvard University, 1978.

Stuhldreher, Thomas J. "The Federal Regulation of Foreign Banking in the United States—An Analysis of Attitudes and Implications." Ph.D. dissertation, Kent State University, 1979.

U.S. Congress. House. *An Act to Amend Certain Sections of the Act Entitled "Federal Reserve Act," Approved December 23, 1913.* P.L. 270, 64th Cong., 1916, H.R. 13391.

————. *An Act to Provide for the Consolidation of National Banking Associations.* P.L. 639, 69th Cong., 2d sess., 1927, H.R. 2.

————. *Bank Holding Company Act of 1956.* P.L. 511, 84th Cong., 2d sess., 1956, H.R. 6227.

————. *Bank Holding Company Act Amendments of 1970.* P.L. 91-607, 91st Cong., 2d sess., 1970, H.R. 6778.

————. *Banking Act of 1933.* P.L. 66, 73rd Cong., 1st sess., 1933, H.R. 5661.

————. *A Bill to Enhance the Competitiveness of Thrift Institutions, to Protect Depositors and Creditors of Such Institutions, and for Other Purposes.* H.R. 4724, 97th Cong., 1st sess., 1981.

————. *Depository Institutions Deregulation and Monetary Control Act of 1980.* P.L. 96-221, 96th Cong., 2d sess., 1980, H.R. 4986.

————. *Federal Reserve Act.* P.L. 43, 63rd Cong., 1913, H.R. 7837.

————. Committe on Government Operations. *Foreign Bank Holding Companies. Hearings before a Subcommittee of the House Committee on Government Operations on Commerce, Consumer, and Monetary Affairs.* 96th Cong., 2d sess, May 15, June 25, 1980.

————. *International Banking Act of 1978.* A House Report to Accompany H.R. 10899, 1978.

————. *To Amend the Bank Holding Company Act of 1956.* P.L. 89-485, 89th Cong., 2d sess., 1966, H.R. 7371.

U.S. Congress. Senate. *An Act to Amend the Act Approved December 23, 1913, Known as the Federal Reserve Act.* P.L. 106, 66th Cong., 2d sess., 1919, S. 2472.

————. *Amending the International Banking of 1978.* Senate Report to Accompany S. 1646. Washington, D.C.: Government Printing Office, 1979.

————. *Bank Holding Company Act Amendments of 1970.*

————. Committee on Banking, Housing, and Urban Affairs. *Edge Corporation Branching, Foreign Bank Takeovers, and International Banking Facilities. Hearings before the Senate Committee on Banking, Housing, and Urban Affairs.* 96th Cong., 1st sess, July 16, 20, 1979.

————. Committee on Banking, Housing, and Urban Affairs. *Export Trading Companies and Trade Associations, Hearings before a Subcommittee on International Finance of the Committee on Banking, Housing, and Urban Affairs.* Senate, on S. 864, S. 1499, S. 1663, and S. 1744, 96th Cong., 2d sess., 1979.

————. Committee on Banking, Housing, and Urban Affairs. *Foreign Bank Act of 1975. Hearings before a Subcommittee on Banking, Housing, and Urban Affairs on Financial Institutions.* 94th Cong., 2d Sess., on S. 958, 1976.

_____ . Committee on Banking, Housing, and Urban Affairs. *Financial Institutions and Export Trading Companies, Hearings Before the Committee.* Senate, on S.2718, 86th Cong., 2d sess., 1980.

_____ . Committee on Banking, Housing, and Urban Affairs. *Financial Institutions Restructuring Act of 1981, Hearings.* Statement of Donald T. Regan, Secretary, Department of Treasury, before the Committee, Senate, on S. 1720, 97th Cong., 1st sess., 1981.

_____ . Committee on Banking, Housing, and Urban Affairs. *International Banking Act of 1978. Hearings before a Subcommittee of the Committee on Banking, Housing, and Urban Affairs on Financial Institutions.* 95th Cong., 2d sess., on H.R. 10899, June 21, 1978.

_____ . *International Banking Act of 1978, A Report of the Committee on Banking, Housing, and Urban Affairs.* 1978.

_____ . *International Banking Act of 1978.* A Senate Report to Accompany H.R. 10899, 1978.

U.S. Department of Treasury. *Report to Congress on Foreign Government Treatment of U.S. Commercial Banking Organizations.* Washington, D.C.: Government Printing Office, 1979.

U.S. General Accounting Office. *Considerable Increase in Foreign Banking in the United States since 1972.* A Report by the Comptroller General of the United States. Washington, D.C.: Government Printing Office, 1979.

World Bank. *Debt Service Tables.* Washington, D.C., 1981.

Zwick, Z. *Foreign Banking in the U.S.* Joint Economic Committee of the U.S. Congress, 1966.

**Books**

Alexander, Ralph S. *Marketing Definitions: A Glossary of Marketing Terms.* Chicago: American Marketing Association, 1960.

Angelini, A.; Eng, M.; and Lees, R. *International Lending Risks and the Eurodollars.* New York: John Wiley, 1979.

Auburn, H.W. *Comparative Banking.* London: Waterlow and Sons Limited, 1963.

Baughn, W.H., and Walker, C.E. *The Bankers' Handbook.* New York: Dow-Jones, Irwin, 1978.

Brayant, Edward C. *Statistical Analysis.* New York: McGraw-Hill, 1960.

Compton, Eric N. *Inside Commercial Banking.* New York: John Wiley, 1980.

Crosse, Howard, and Hempel, George H. *Management Policies for Commercial Banks.* 3d ed. Englewood cliffs, N.J.: Prentice-Hall, 1980.

Davis, Steven. *The Management Function in International Banking.* New York: John Wiley, 1979.

Donaldson, T.H. *Lending in International Commercial Banking.* Somerset, N.J.: Halsted, 1979.

Dornbush, R., and Frankel, J. *International Economic Policy*. Baltimore, Md.: Johns Hopkins University Press, 1979.

Dougall, Herbert E., and Gaumnitz, Jack E. *Capital Markets and Institutions*. 3d ed. Foundations in Science. Englewood cliffs, N.J.: Prentice-Hall, 1975.

Dufey, Gunter, and Giddy, Ian. *The International Money Market*. Englewood Cliffs, N.J.: Prentice-Hall, 1978.

Dunkman, William E. *Money Credit and Banking*. New York: Random House, 1970.

Foulke, Ray A. *Practical Financial Statement Analysis*. New York: McGraw-Hill, 1950.

Freeman, O. *The Multinational Co.: Instrument for World Growth*. New York: Praeger, 1981.

Garcia, F.L. *How to Analyze a Bank Statement*. Boston: Bankers Publishing Co., 1974.

Gies, Thomas, and Apilardo, Vincent P., eds. *Banking Markets and Financial Institutions*. Homewood, Ill.: Richard D. Irwin, 1971.

Grone, Howard D., and Hempel, George H. *Management Policies for Commercial Banks*. Englewood Cliffs, N.J.: Prentice-Hall, 1973.

Grossack, Irvin M. *The International Economy and the National Interest*. Bloomington: Indiana University Press, 1980.

Gup, Benton E. *Financial Intermediaries: An Introduction*. Boston: Houghton Mifflin, 1980.

Homer, Sidney. *A History of Interest Rates*. New Brunswick, N.J.: Rutgers University Press, 1977.

Hornbostel, Peter. *International Banking Operations in the United States, An Update*. New York: Practicing Law Institute, 1979.

Howard, D.S., and Hoffman, G.M. *Evolving Concepts of Bank Capital Management*. New York: Citicorp, 1980.

Huch, S.W.; Cornier, W.H., and Bounds, W.G., Jr. *Reading Statistics and Research*. New York: Harper and Row, 1974.

Hudson, R.L. *Money and Exchange Dealing in International Banking*. Somerset, N.J.: Wiley, 1979.

Jessup, Paul F. *Modern Bank Management*. St. Paul, Minn.: West Publishing Co., 1980.

_____ , ed. *Innovations in Bank Management—Selected Readings*. Hinsdale, Ill.: Dryden Press, 1969.

Khoury, S. *Dynamics of International Banking*. New York: Praeger, 1980.

Klise, Eugene S. *Money and Banking*. Cincinnati: Southwestern Publishing Co., 1972.

Kotler, Philip. *Marketing Management: Analysis, Planning and Control*. Englewood Cliffs, N.J.: Prentice-Hall, 1980.

_____ . *Principles of Marketing*. Englewood Cliffs, N.J.: Prentice-Hall, 1980.

Lee, Francis A. *Foreign Banking and Investments in the United States: Issues and Alternatives*. New York: John Wiley, 1976.

Lees, Francis A., and Eng, Maximo. *International Financial Markets Development of the Present System and Future Prospects*. New York: Praeger, 1975.

Levich, Richard. *Exchange Risk and Exposure*. Lexington, Mass.: Lexington Books, D.C. Heath and Company, 1980.

Prindl, A.R. *Foreign Exchange Risk*. New York: John Wiley, 1976.

Pringle, Robin. *Banking in Britain*. London: Charles Knight and Co., Ltd., 1973.

Reed, Edward W. *Commercial Bank Management*. New York: Harper and Row, 1963.

Reed, Edward W.; Gill, Edward K.; and Smith, Richard K. *Commercial Banking*. 2d ed. N.J.: Prentice-Hall, 1980.

Rilter, L. "The Flow of Funds Accounts: A Framework for Financial Analysis." In M. Polakoff, ed., *Financial Institutions and Markets*. Boston: Houghton Mifflin, 1970.

Robinson, Roland T. *The Management of Bank Funds*. 2d ed. New York: McGraw-Hill, 1962.

Rugman, Alan. *International Diversification and the Multinational Enterprise*. Lexington, Mass.: Lexington Books, D.C. Heath and Company, 1979.

Scotten, Donald W., and Zallocco, Ronald L. *Readings in Market Segmentation*. Chicago: American Marketing Association, 1980.

Spero, Joan E. *The Failure of the Franklin National Bank*. New York: Columbia University Press, 1979.

*United States Multinational Banking*. New York: Salomon Brothers & Co., 1976.

Woodworth, Walter. *The Money Market and Monetary Management*. New York: Harper & Row, 1972.

**Articles**

Abrams, R.K. "Regional Banks and International Banking." *Economic Review* (November 1980):3-14.

Anderson, Gerald. "Current Developments in the Regulation of International Banking." *Economic Review*, Federal Reserve Bank of Cleveland (January 1980):1-15.

"Annual Financing Report." *Euromoney* (March 1981): supp. pp. 2-40.

Arista, J.D. "Foreign Bank Invasion." *Bankers Magazine* (Autumn 1977): 43-48.

Arpan, J., and Ricks, D. "Foreign Direct Investments for the U.S. and Some Attendant Research Problems." *Journal of International Business Studies* (Spring 1974):1-7.

Asher, Joe. "Tough Bill, Soft Bill, Foreign Banks Are Here to Stay." *Banking* 68 (November 1976):76-84.

Ashley, David. "Will the Eurodollar Market Go Back Home?" *Banker* (February 1981):93-97.

"Assets and Liabilities of U.S. Branches and Agencies of Foreign Banks, June 30, 1980." *Federal Reserve Bulletin* 67 (March 1981):A68-A71.

Barry, Leonard L. "Era of Competition." *American Banker*, July 13, 1977.

Battey, Phil. "Fed Tightens Restrictions on Outside Businesses Run by Foreign Banks in U.S." *American Banker*, November 14, 1980, p. 11.

Bellanger, S. "Foreign Challenge to U.S. Banks." *Banker* 128 (October 1978):37-40.

———. "Foreign Banks in New York—Optimism Gives Way to Realism in the 1980s." *Banker* 130 (February 1980):87-95.

Borch, Fred J. "The Marketing as a Way of Business Life." In *The Marketing Concept: Its Meaning to Management*, pp. 3-5. Marketing Series No. 99, New York, American Management Association, 1957.

Brennan, Peter. "Japan Runs a Powerhouse Economy." *ABA Banking Journal* 71 (July 1979):34, 36, 38.

Brewer, Elijah; T. Gittings; A. Gonczy; R. Merris; L. Mote; D. Nichols; and A. Reicheit. "The Depository Institutions Deregulation and Monetary Control Act of 1980." *Economic Perspectives* 4 (September-October 1980):5.

Brimmer, Andrew. "Multinational Banks and the Management of Monetary Policy in the United States." *Journal of Finance* (March 1973).

Brimmer, A.F., and Frederick, D.R. "Growth of American International Banking: Implications for Public Policy." *Journal of Finance* (May 1975).

Burke, William M. "The Rise of the West." *Banker* 126 (October 1976): 1155-1159.

Burr, Rosemary. "The Changing World of Foreign Banks." *Banker* 28 (April 1978):45, 47.

Carlozzi, Nicholas. "Regulating the Eurocurrency Market." *FRB of Philadelphia* (March-April 1981):15-23.

Carlson, Eugene. *Wall Street Journal*, December 15, 1981, p. 31.

Cates, D.C. "Foreign Banks Are Cracking the Facade of U.S. Banking." *Fortune*, August 28, 1978, pp. 94-96.

Choffray, J.M., and Lilien, G.L. "A New Approach to Industrial Market Segmentation." *Sloan Management Review* (Spring 1978):17-29.

Citicorp. *Citicorp Annual Report and 10-K*. New York: Citicorp, 1980.

"Competing in America." *Economist*, March 4, 1978, pp. 51-52.

"The Country Risk League Table." *Euromoney* (October 1980):26-40.

Crawford, C.T. "Fallacy of the Fungible." *Euromoney* (November 1979): 130.

"The Crocker Bid Stirs New Fears of Invasion." *Business Week*, July 28, 1980, pp. 45-48.

Dabboud, I. "Helping OPEC Carry the Burden of Surpluses." *Euromoney* (December 1980):145.

Darista, Jane. "The Foreign Bank Invasion." *Bankers Magazine* 160 (Autumn 1977):43-48.

Davis, Robert R. "Private Credit to Developing Countries." *Bankers Magazine* (May-June 1978):61-66.

Dean, J., and Giddy, I. *Averting International Banking Crises*. Monograph Series. New York: Graduate School of Business Administration, New York University, 1981.

Deane, M. "International Banking Act: Fair to All?" *Economist*, March 31, 1979.

"Deutsch Bank Is Its Own Rival." *Business Week*, May 7, 1979, p. 46.

Dillon, L.W. "Cracking the U.S. Commercial Paper Market." *Institutional Investor* (June 1979):20.

Dixon, George H. "Consumer Will Benefit from Financial-Institutions Bill." *Treasury Papers* 2 (August 1975):14-15.

"Drive to Keep Foreign Banks at Bay." *Business Week*, March 19, 1979, pp. 31-32.

Edwards, Franklin R., and Zwick, Jack. "Activities and Regulatory Issues— Foreign Banks in the United States." *Columbia Journal of World Business* 1 (Spring 1975):58-73.

Edwards, R.D. "International Banking Growth Sparks Capital Concern United States." *Banker*, October 10, 1977, pp. 29-31.

"The Establishment of International Banking Facilities." *International Letter*, June 19, 1981, pp. 1-2.

Everett, R.; George, A.; and Slumberg, A. "Appraising Currency Strength and Weakness." *Journal of International Business Studies* (Fall 1980): 80-91.

Field, P. "Foreign Banks in New York: Biting into the Big Apple." *Euromoney* (June 1978):48-88.

Fisher, Gerald C. "The Structure of the Commercial Banking System, 1960-1985." *Journal of Commercial Bank Lending* (September 1979):60.

"Foreign Banks Bid for U.S. Capital." *Business Week*, April 27, 1981, p. 113.

"Foreign Banks; Chillier Wind." *Economist*, July 1, 1978, p. 39.

"Foreign Banks Get New Florida Entree." *American Banker*, February 5, 1982, p. 2.

"Foreign Banks in America: Don't Monkey with Mickey." *Economist*, March 10, 1979, pp. 111-112.

Frankel, A.B. "The Lender of Last Resort Facility in the Context of Multinational Banking." *Columbia Journal of World Business* (Winter 1975), pp. 120-128.

Ganoe, C.S. "Banking across Boarders: Reciprocity and Equality." *Burroughs Clearing House* (February 1974):18-19.

Garcia, A. "Foreign Banks in the U.S.—California: Too Much of a Good Thing." *Institutional Investor* 10 (September 1976):89-91.

Gardner, Stephen S. "More Control over Operations of Foreign Banks." *Treasury Papers* 1 (February 1976):18-19.

Gaynor, Ronan L. "Trends in U.S. Regulation of Foreign Banks." *Banker* (February 1981):99-104.

Ghalib, S. "U.S. Gets the Oil Money Back." *Euromoney* (April 1980):119.

Giddy, I., and Dufey, G. "The Random Behavior of Flexible Exchange Rates." *Journal of International Business Studies* (Spring 1975):1-32.

Gilbert, Gary G. "Foreign Banking in the United States-The Congressional Debate." *Magazine of Bank Admnistration* 52 (October 1976):40-42A.

Goldberg, Lawrence G. "The Determinants of Foreign Banking Activity in the United States." *Journal of Banking and Finance* 5 (March 1981):17-32.

Goldberg, L.G., and Saunders, A. "The Causes of U.S. Bank Expansion Overseas, The Case of Great Britain." *Journal of Money, Credit and Banking,* (November 1980).

———. "The Growth of Organization Forms of Foreign Banks in the U.S." Working Paper No. 221. New York: Salomon Brothers Center, New York University, August 1980.

Goodman, L.S. "Can Risks in LDC Lending Be Diversified?" *Business Economics* (March 1982:12-15.

Greenwald, C.S. "Let's Put a Hold on Foreign Take-Overs of Our Banks." *Bankers Magazine* (November 1977):49-54.

Gulkowitz, Abraham. "Foreign Banking in the U.S.—End of the Honeymoon." *Banker* (June 1979):41-43.

Harrison, Horace H. "The Importance of Bank Operations." *Bankers Monthly,* December 15, 1974, pp. 11-13.

Harrison, Michael A. "Reciprocity in International Banking." *Bankers Magazine* 160 (Winter 1977):31-34.

Hempel, George A. "Basic Ingredient of Commercial Banks Investment Policies." *Bankers Magazine* 155 (Autumn 1972):50-59.

Hendershot, P. "The Structure of International Interest Rates." *Journal of Finance* (September 1967):455-465.

Hendrickson, Mark. "Will Congress Finally Crack Down on Foreign Banks?" *Institutional Investors* 11 (September 1977):137-139.

"Here Come Foreign Banks Again." *Business Week,* June 26, 1978, pp. 78-82.

Hershman, A. "Foreign Banks: The Sophisticated Way to Save." *Duns* 102 (December 1973):72-74.

Houpt, J.V. "Foreign Ownership and the Performance of U.S. Banks." *Federal Reserve Bulletin* 66 (July 1980):543-544.

Hutton, H.R. "The Regulation of Foreign Banks—A European Point of View." *Columbia Journal of World Business* 10 (Winter 1975):109-114.

"International Banking Facilities Approved." *International Finance,* June 22, 1981, pp. 4-5.

International Economic Indicators. Federal Reserve Bank of St. Louis. February 1982; and various issues of *International Financial Statistics,* IMF, Washington, D.C., 1972-1982.

*International Newsletter,* Federal Reserve Bank of Chicago, April 9, 1982, pp. 1-2.

Jessup, P.F., and Bochnak, M. "Market Pricing Comes to Banking." *Bankers Magazine* (Spring 1976):97-102.

Keith, Robert J. "The Marketing Revolution." *Journal of Marketing* (January 1960):35-38.

Key, S.J., and Brundy, J.M. "Implementation of the International Banking Act." *Federal Reserve Bulletin* (October 1979):785-796.

Klopstock, Fred H. "Foreign Banks in the U.S—Scope and Growth of Operations." *Federal Reserve Bank of New York Quarterly Review* 55 (June 1973):140-154.

Kohlagen, S. "The Performance of the Foreign Exchange Markets." *Journal of International Business Studies* (Fall 1975):33-39.

Kraar, L. "What the Hong Kong Amateur Is Doing in New York." *Fortune,* August 13, 1979, pp. 159-160.

Kung, S.W. "Asset-Liability Management for Smaller Banks." *Bankers Magazine* (January-February 1981):78-81.

Kwack, S. "The Structure of International Interest Rates." *Journal of Finance,* (September 1971):897-900.

"Large Canadian Banks Rile Many U.S. Rivals." *Wall Street Journal,* July 10, 1981.

"The Launch of the Euromoney Index." *Euromoney* (October 1980):15-25.

Lees, Francis A. "Which Route for Foreign Bank Regulation." *Bankers Magazine* 157 (Autumn 1974):53-57.

McKitterick, John B. "What Is the Marketing Management Concept." In *The Frontiers of Marketing Thought and Action.* Chicago: American Marketing Association, 1957, pp. 71-82.

Marshall, Robert H. "Competition in Banking." *Bankers Magazine* 156 (Winter 1973):81-86.

Matthews, Gordon. "Court Backs Comptroller's Powers over Foreign Banks." *American Banker,* October 9, 1981, p. 2.

Mitchell, George W. "How the Fed Sees Multinational Bank Regulation." *Banker* 124 (June 1974):757-760.

Morgan, D. "Fiscal Policy in Oil Exporting Countries, 1972-78." *Finance and Development* 16 (December 1979):14-17.

Much, M. "Foreign Banks Activities in U.S. Still Grows." *Industry Week,* August 21, 1978, pp. 94-96.

Munder, Barbara. "New York—The First Stop—and Still the Most Popular." *Institutional Investor* 10 (September 1976):78-85.

Nambiar, P.G. "Competitive Equality Can Be Achieved by Easing Regulations on U.S. Banks." *American Banker,* March 20, 1981, p. 15.

Nickel, H. "Right Road for OPEC's Billions." *Fortune,* November 17, 1980, pp. 38-43.

Nowzad, B. "Debt in Developing Countries: Some Issues for the 1980's." *Finance and Development* (March 1982):13-15.

O'Brien, M. "United States Sets Up the Boundaries for Foreign Banks." *Banker* (December 1978):15-19.

Ogilvie, N.R. "Foreign Banks in the U.S. and Geographic Restrictions on Banking." *Journal of Bank Research* 11 (Summer 1980):72-79.

Osborn, N. "Will Foreign Take-Overs of U.S. Banks Be Stopped?" *Institutional Investor* 13 (September 1979):157-168.

Palmer, Joy, and Acmyn, James. "Foreign Banking in North America." *Banker* 124 (April 1974):341-347.

Patterson, E.C. "Marketplace, An Alternative to More Bank Regulation." *Credit and Finance Management* (September 1978):14-15.

Payne, C. Meyrick. "Profitability Management: Banking's Next Generation." *Bankers Magazine* 160 (Spring 1977):51-57.

Perkins, J.H. "Regulation of Foreign Banking in the United States." *Columbia Journal of World Business* (Winter 1975):115-119.

Pinsky, Neil. "Edge Act and Agreement Corporations: Mediums for International Banking." *Economic Perspectives* (September-October 1978):25-26.

Platten, D.C. "The Muttering of Nationalism Threatens America's Real Interests." *Euromoney* (October 1976):66-69.

Pope, N.W. "Put Marketing in Its Place." *American Banker,* August 11, 1976.

Porzecanski, A.C. "The International Financial Role of U.S. Commercial Banks: Past and Future." *Journal of Banking and Finance* (May 1981):5-16.

"Recent Growth in Activities of U.S. Offices of Foreign Banks." *Federal Reserve Bulletin* (October 1976):815-823.

Ricks, D., and Arpan, J.S. "Foreign Banks in the United States." *Business Horizons* (February 1976):84-87.

Rose, Peter. "Foreign Banking in the United States." *Canadian Banker* 83 (May-June 1976):58-62A.

Russ, D. "The Asian Invasion." *Bankers Magazine* 164 (January-February 1981):48-52.

Saunders, A. "Regulation of United States Banks in Britain." *Bankers Magazine* 162 (July-August 1981):72-75.

Schwind, R.L. "Banks and Environment." *Banking* 63 (September 1970):33, 80.

Severiens, Jacobus. "Foreign Bank Regulation in the USA—the Options Open to Foreign Banks." *Banker* 125 (January 1975):53-57.

Severiens, J.T. "More Controls over Foreign Branching Here." *Burroughs Clearing House* 59 (December 1974):22-23, 47.

Shull, Bernard, and Morvitz, Paul M. "Branch Banking and the Structure of Competition." *National Banking Review* 1 (March 1974):301-341.

Siebert, M. "Foreign Banks in America: The Lady Outfoxed." *Economist* 7 (1979):119-120.

Solomon, Julie. "Banks Can Do Euromart Business in U.S. after 'Free Trade' Zone Starts Thursday." *Wall Street Journal,* November 30, 1981, p. 4.

"Statement of Policy on Supervision of U.S. Branches and Agencies of Foreign Banks." *Federal Reserve Bulletin* 65 (August 1979):634-635.

Stuhldreher, T.J., and Baker, J.C. "Bankers' Attitudes toward U.S. Foreign Bank Regulation." *Banker* 131 (January 1981):29-31, 33.

Swoboda, Alexander K. "Multinational Banking, the Eurodollar Market and Economic Policy." *Journal of World Trade Law* (March-April 1971).

Terzakis, J.J. "How to Regulate Foreign Banks." *Banking* (July 1976):72.

Thackray, J. "Why the Congressional Crackdown Isn't All It's Cracked Up to Be." *International Investor* (September 1978):149-160.

Thompson, I.B. "International Banking Act; For Regional Banks a New Challenge and Opportunity." *A.B.A. Banking Journal* (January 1980):45-56.

Timpson, Richard L. "Bank Asset-Liability Structure: Present and Future." *Journal of Commercial Bank Lending* 57 (December 1974):15-21.

U.S. Department of Commerce, *Survey of Current Business* (August 1981).

Vernon, Raymond. "International Investment and International Trade in the Product Cycle." *Quarterly Journal of Economics* (May 1966):190-207.

Volcker, P.A. "Treatment of Foreign Banks in the United States: Dilemmas and Opportunities." *Federal Reserve Bank of New York* (Summer 1979):1-5.

Von Furstenberg, G.M. "Incentives for International Currency Diversification." *IMF Staff Papers* (September 1981):477-494.

Walter, I. "Country Risk, Portfolio Management and Regulation in International Bank Lending." *Journal of Banking and Finance* (March 1981).

Walter, Judith. "Foreign Acquisitions of U.S. Banks." Staff Papers. U.S. Controller of the Currency, Washington, D.C., June 1980.

Watson, Justin. "A Regulatory View of Capital Adequacy." *Journal of Bank Research* (Autumn 1975):170-172.

Weiss, Steven. "National Policies on Foreign Acquisitions of Banks." *Bankers Magazine* (January-February 1981):25-27.

Welles, Chris. "Bankers, Bankers Everywhere—But How Much Business Are They Getting?" *Institutional Investors* 11 (September 1977):115-124, 130.

Welsh, G.M. "Case for Federal Regulation of Foreign Bank Operations in the United States." *Columbia Journal of World Business* (Winter 1975):98-108.

Whittle, Jack W. "You Have to Pay the Fiddler," *American Banker,* January 19, 1977.

Williams, W.C. "International Capital Markets." Occasional Paper 7. IMF, Washington, D.C.: IMF, 1981.

Woolridge, J.R., and Wiegel, K.D. "Foreign Banking Growth in the United States." *Bankers Magazine* (January-February 1981):30-38.

*World Financial Markets.* New York: Morgan Guaranty Trust Co., March 1981.

# Index

# About the Authors

**Stephen W. Miller** is professor of marketing and international business and chairman of the Department of Marketing in the School of Business and Administration at St. Louis University. He previously taught at Kent State University and Clarkson College of Technology in New York. Professor Miller has served as a consultant to both service- and product-oriented organizations and is the author of numerous international business articles, appearing in such journals as *Management International Review, Columbia Journal of World Business, Journal of Contemporary Business*, and the *Journal of International Marketing*.

**Seung H. Kim** is professor of finance and director of the International Business Program in the School of Business and Administration at St. Louis University. Previously he taught at New York University and worked in the International Banking Department of Manufacturer's Hanover Trust Company in New York City. Professor Kim is the author of a book and numerous articles, which have appeared in such journals as *Columbia Journal of World Business, California Management Review, International Journal of Accounting*, and *Journal of Contemporary Business*.

Professors Kim and Miller have collaborated over the last several years as authors of several articles and scholarly paper presentations. Their individual expertise in international finance and marketing has enabled them to join in well-conceived research efforts regarding the more broadly based issues of international business.

## DATE DUE

| DATE DUE | | | |
|---|---|---|---|
| DEC 2 3 1987 | | | |
| DEC 2 2 1988 | | | |
| AUG 1 7 1998 | | | |
| AUG 1 7 1998 | | | |
| | | | |
| | | | |
| | | | |
| | | | |
| | | | |
| | | | |
| | | | |
| | | | |
| | | | |
| | | | |
| | | | |
| | | | |
| GAYLORD | | | PRINTED IN U.S.A. |